POLITICIANS AND POACHERS

THE POLITICAL ECONOMY OF WILDLIFE POLICY IN AFRICA

Although wildlife fascinates citizens of industrialized countries, little is known about the politics of wildlife policy in Africa. In this innovative book, Clark Gibson challenges the rhetoric of television documentaries and conservation organizations to explore the politics behind the creation and change of wildlife policy in Africa. This book examines what Gibson views as a central puzzle in the debate: Why do African governments create policies that apparently fail to protect wildlife?

Moving beyond explanations of bureaucratic inefficiency and corrupt dictatorships, Gibson argues that biologically disastrous policies are retained because they meet the distributive goals of politicians and bureaucrats. Using evidence from Zambia, Kenya, and Zimbabwe, Gibson shows how institutions encourage politicians and bureaucrats to construct wildlife policies that further their own interests. Different configurations of electoral laws, legislatures, party structures, interest groups, and traditional authorities in each country shape the choices of policymakers – many of which are not consonant with conservation. This book will appeal to students of institutions, comparative politics, natural resource policy making, African politics, and wildlife conservation.

Clark C. Gibson is an assistant professor of political science and research associate at the Center for the Study of Institutions, Population, and Environmental Change at Indiana University. Drawing on fieldwork in more than a dozen countries, he focuses primarily on the politics of development in nonindustrialized countries.

D0772149

POLITICAL ECONOMY OF INSTITUTIONS AND DECISIONS

Series Editors

Randall Calvert, University of Rochester, New York
Thráinn Eggertsson, Max Planck Institute, Germany, and University of Iceland

Founding Editors

James E. Alt, Harvard University
Douglass C. North, Washington University of St. Louis

Other books in the series

Continued on first page following Index

POLITICIANS AND POACHERS

The Political Economy
of Wildlife Policy in Africa

CLARK C. GIBSON

CAMBRIDGE
UNIVERSITY PRESS

PUBLISHED BY THE PRESS SYNDICATE OF THE UNIVERSITY OF CAMBRIDGE
The Pitt Building, Trumpington Street, Cambridge, United Kingdom

CAMBRIDGE UNIVERSITY PRESS
The Edinburgh Building, Cambridge CB2 2RU, UK   http: //www.cup.cam.ac.uk
40 West 20th Street, New York, NY 10011-4211, USA   http: //www.cup.org
10 Stamford Road, Oakleigh, Melbourne 3166, Australia

First published 1999

Typeface Sabon 10/12 pt.   *System* DeskTopPro_{/UX}®   [BV]

*A catalog record for this book is available from
the British Library.*

Library of Congress Cataloging-in-Publication Data
Gibson, Clark C., 1961–
Politicians and poachers : the political economy of wildlife
policy in Africa / Clark C. Gibson.
p.   cm. – (Political economy of institutions and decisions)
Includes bibliographical references (p.   ) and index.
ISBN 0-521-62385-5 (hardback)
1. Wildlife conservation – Government policy – Africa.   2. Wildlife
conservation – Economic aspects – Africa.   I. Title.   II. Series.
QH77.A35G525   1999
333.95'416'096 – dc21   98-39627
                                                                            CIP

ISBN 0 521 62385 5 hardback
ISBN 0 521 66378 4 paperback

Transferred to digital printing 2002

To my parents

Contents

Series editors' preface

The Cambridge series on the Political Economy of Institutions and Decisions is built around attempts to answer two central questions: How do institutions evolve in response to individual incentives, strategies, and choices, and how do institutions affect the performance of political and economic systems? The scope of the series is comparative and historical rather than international or specifically American, and the focus is positive rather than normative.

In an illuminating work deeply rooted in the institutionalism, Clark Gibson analyzes the politics of wildlife policy in several African countries. The history of these policies is disappointing. Nationalist governments failed to keep their pre-independence promises to eliminate colonial wildlife laws. Bureaucracies created policies frustrating some conservation goals, while other policies designed to create animal-conserving incentives failed to stop illegal hunting. The reasons are complex. A constant theme is that individuals and groups sought to create policies advantageous to themselves. Their strategies reflected incentives created by current institutions. As institutions changed, so did strategies and policies, but not in ways necessarily conducive to conservation.

The analysis is an important follow-on to Elinor Ostrom's pathbreaking work on the problems of managing a common-pool resource against free-riding incentives to poach. It is a very institutional analysis of that problem as well, doing a convincing job of analyzing decisions at the local level, where most of the important ones were actually taken. It is an exciting empirical application of rational choice theory that gives imaginative and compelling explanations while offering general lessons about the political economy of conservation policy.

Acknowledgments

All significant journeys require work, luck, and the help of others for their success. The journey I took while writing this book was no different. I hope that my work and good fortune will be demonstrated in the book's chapters. This section, however, is devoted to acknowledging a fraction of the numerous individuals who assisted me during the project. Some made available crucial data or funds; others lent supportive ears. Some provided important comments about my study; others encouraged necessary diversions away from work. All of them offered support that I value deeply.

Funding from the Institute for the Study of World Politics, the Duke University Program in International Political Economy, the Workshop in Political Theory and Policy Analysis at Indiana University, and the Joint Committee on African Studies of the Social Science Research Council and the American Council of Learned Societies allowed me to test both my mettle and my theories in the field. I thank them wholeheartedly for providing key financial assistance at the beginning of my academic career.

Funding alone, however, does not guarantee successful fieldwork – it also depends heavily on the assistance of individuals. I was fortunate to have been helped by scores of people while in Africa. Ilse Mwanza of the University of Zambia's Institute for African Studies in Lusaka served as a sage guide to research in her country. Faculty from the University of Zambia, especially Samuel Chipungu, M. Chidumayo, and Mwelwa Musambachime, offered me helpful, orienting advice at the beginning of my project. Many officers of the Zambian National Park and Wildlife Service, including Director Akim Mwenya, Deputy Director Gilson Kaweche, Chief Prosecutor Crispin Siachibuye, and Edwin Matokwani, wildlife ranger, took time out of their busy schedules to share their insights about wildlife management. Richard Bell, Phil Berry, Dale Lewis, Fidelis Lungu, Edwin Matokwani, and Julia Nagata, among many others, of-

Acknowledgments

fered their informed opinions about the politics of wildlife policy. I spent countless hours in the office of Mike Faddy rehashing the history of African wildlife management; I am grateful for his keen memory and ever-present coffee. Chiefs Sandwe, Chitungulu, Mwanya, Chikwa, and Malama patiently answered my many questions and made me feel welcome in their areas. Jimmy Sabi determinedly tracked down data in libraries and government offices in the face of significant obstacles. Andrew and Rosemary Baldry adopted me as a family member (and Andrew's lessons in Land Rover repair proved to be invaluable when the inevitable breakdown occurred). Marshall Murphree from the Center of Applied Social Science at the University of Zimbabwe shared some of his vast experience in the fields of development and wildlife in Africa with me. The residents of Luwisha House in Lusaka – Father Titland, Father Cremins, Father Kelly, Brother Mike, and all the seminarians and staff members – will never know how important their company and community were to me. The former Zambian president, Kenneth Kaunda, graciously allowed me to discuss African wildlife policy with him. There are many others in Africa who provided me aid; I can only repay their kindness in spirit.

Of course the data I collected in the field still had to be crafted into a worthwhile study. I hope the excellent training I received from John Aldrich, Sheridan Johns, Herbert Kitschelt, Peter Lange, Meg McKean, George Tsebelis, and others in the Department of Political Science at Duke University is apparent in this book. I am especially thankful to Robert Bates, whose standards, advice, and insight have made me a better scholar.

I may not have ever finished writing this book without the encouragement and assistance of Elinor and Vincent Ostrom and their colleagues at the Workshop in Political Theory and Policy Analysis at Indiana University. The Workshop gave me financial and intellectual support during a crucial period. My colleagues in the Department of Political Science at Indiana University have also provided consistently strong support for this project. I am thankful for their intellectual challenges.

As the manuscript began to take shape, I benefited from the talents of able research and editorial assistants. Patty Dalecki, Sara Colburn, Beth Grabowski, Paula Jerrells, and Sarah Seybold each provided me with work that enabled the project to move forward when my own energy flagged.

Numerous people read and commented on parts of this manuscript. James Alt, Robert Bates, William Bernhard, York Bradshaw, Thrainn Eggertsson, Catherine Elkins, Mike Faddy, Norman Furniss, Gary Gereffi, Gregory Gibson, Harald Gibson, Paul Gibson, Robert Healy, Douglas Imig, Sheridan Johns, Fabrice Lehoucq, Burt Monroe, Charles Myers,

Acknowledgments

Stuart Marks, Michael McGinnis, Margaret McKean, Elinor Ostrom, Vincent Ostrom, Suzanne Patti, Robert Rohrschneider, Patrick Sellers, George Tsebelis, and John Williams each offered helpful insights that have improved this book. Kathryn Firmin-Sellers has probably read my work only a handful of times fewer than I have; her comments have been invariably significant and supportive. Arun Agrawal has given me years of consistent encouragement and challenging advice. He is the best colleague (and friend) someone could ever have in this business. With so much talent among my early readers, clearly any mistakes that remain in the book are mine alone.

My family listened with great tolerance to my complaints and joys about the journey of book writing. I thank each of my siblings and parents for their patience and understanding.

Finally, I thank Suzanne Elizabeth Bernadette Patti, my best friend, upon whom I have leaned so many, many times. We take this journey together. *Twa enda pamo.*

I

Politics, Institutions, and Animals:
Explaining the Content, Continuity,
and Change of African Wildlife Policy

It cannot be too strongly emphasized that in a country where vast rural areas carry small populations, the wild life in one shape or another is a main economic force just as much as the soil or the water supply.

T. G. C. Vaughan-Jones, Director of Game and
Tsetse Control, Northern Rhodesia, 1948[1]

INTRODUCTION

Africa's wildlife fascinates citizens of industrialized countries. They watch scores of television documentaries about the continent's animals. They spend large sums of money to go on safaris in Africa. They remove ivory and spotted furs from their wardrobes to help conserve African wildlife. They include Africa's fauna in curricula to teach their children the value of protecting these species. And they contribute millions of dollars to international conservation organizations who claim that – but for lack of funding – Africa's magnificent animals could be saved from destruction.

Given this intense interest in Africa's wildlife, it is surprising that we know so little about its importance to the individuals and governments of Africa itself. Although hundreds of studies have addressed the biological and ecological aspects of African fauna, relatively little research has examined the many and important roles wildlife plays in the political economy of African countries. We know little about the relationship between Africans and wildlife, about how different people and groups in Africa possess varying ideas about what constitutes good wildlife policy, about how African governments construct or change their wildlife policies, or about how political and economic institutions can shape these policies over time. Consequently, the average contributor to a conservation organization has little knowledge about the multiple and complex dimensions of wildlife's significance in Africa.

Explaining African Wildlife Policy

And yet wildlife is and has been important to millions of Africans. Before European domination, Africans distributed wildlife to solidify economic and political networks. As outside contacts with Europe widened, so did the distribution of wildlife. The ivory trade was enmeshed with the slave trade. Game meat subsidized the activities of European explorers, missionaries, and colonial administrators. Today, African farmers in rural areas still compete with wild animals for land and crops. Urban dwellers purchase game meat on shadow markets. Safari and tourism business owners lobby governments for measures to ensure high-quality animals for their industries. Rural dwellers hunt animals to augment their diet, income, and prestige. Before, during, and since the arrival of Europeans, wildlife has enhanced wealth, threatened lives, destroyed crops, provided patronage resources, cemented relationships, and inspired social protest in Africa.

Wildlife's significance makes it a political commodity. Like other political commodities, such as the power to tax and discretion over the locating infrastructure, politicians can use wildlife to discriminate between allies and enemies. At the national level, politicians construct wildlife policies that must contend with the pressures caused by constituents and friends seeking greater access to wildlife resources, and international organizations intent on limiting such access. At the bureaucratic level, officials deploy thousands of enforcement officers and spend millions of dollars to enforce conservation policies. And at the local level, rural residents challenge these policies as they struggle to gain rights to wildlife resources. Because the wildlife policies of African governments attempt to be quite comprehensive – affecting how individuals interact with wildlife, who owns wild animals, who hunts, when they hunt, what weapons and equipment they use, which species they kill, how they exchange wildlife products, which parts of wild animals they must surrender to the government, and which they may import or export – the conflict over wildlife policy reflects basic questions about access to public authority, about whose preferences over wildlife institutions will dictate policy, and, consequently, about who will gain and who will lose.

African wildlife policies change over time. As individuals and groups pressure the governments to modify policy, alterations in the boundaries of a country's protected areas, the types of species protected by law, the punishments for violating such laws, hunting license fees, and wildlife departments' enforcement levels and budgets occur. As these aspects of policies change, they produce different outcomes. Some policies increase the protection of certain species. Others promote the destruction of particular animals. Some generate revenues for governments. Others impose significant costs. Some enrich individuals. Others strip away income and food from the already impoverished.

Explaining African Wildlife Policy

But what explains the origin and change of African wildlife policies? In Zambia, Kenya, and Zimbabwe, a number of empirical puzzles confronts those studying wildlife policy. For example, the same politicians who had decried the punitive and exclusionary nature of colonial wildlife policy passed laws to strengthen and broaden it after their country's independence. But although this response was general across the three countries, they differed greatly in their reactions to a wave of poaching that swept across Africa in the 1970s and 1980s. More apparent anomalies face those who think that African politics is the purview only of strong individual leaders: Zambia's Kenneth Kaunda was an ardent conservationist, and yet his one-party parliament failed at times to pass his preferred wildlife legislation – despite the fact that he wielded the strong centralized powers of a one-party president. Kenya's president Daniel arap Moi and his allies, on the other hand, had far less affection for wildlife conservation, but they eventually created costly policies to ensure adequate wildlife populations. Zimbabwe's Robert Mugabe and his government, instead of allowing a flourishing trade in illegal wildlife products, as happened in Zambia and Kenya, enforced their wildlife laws and kept their wildlife estate relatively protected. And in all three countries, efforts to create community-level wildlife programs had different origins and outcomes.

This book explores these and other puzzles that surround the politics of wildlife policy in Africa. It does so by examining the content, continuity, and change of wildlife policy in Zambia in the postcolonial period. It then compares the Zambian case with selected cases from Kenya and Zimbabwe. Four empirical questions frame this study. First, why did the first independent governments of Zambia, Kenya, and Zimbabwe keep colonial wildlife laws intact, despite prior promises by nationalists to reverse such exclusionary measures? Second, why did these powerful African presidents respond in different ways to the rise of poaching? Third, why did the administrators of these countries' wildlife programs in the 1980s create bureaucratic structures that frustrated certain conservation goals? And fourth, why did these same programs, designed to offer incentives to conserve animals, fail to stop illegal hunting?

This book argues that because wildlife is an important economic and political resource in each of these three countries, individuals and groups have sought to structure policy to secure its benefits for themselves. These actors operate in an arena composed of numerous institutions that affect their strategies and choices.[2] The outcome of their efforts is wildlife policies that do not necessarily protect animals; in fact, many policies generated poor conservation results in Zambia, Kenya, and Zimbabwe. Rather, wildlife policies and their outcomes reflect attempts by individuals and groups to gain private advantage.

3

Explaining African Wildlife Policy

WILDLIFE AND AFRICA

It is impossible to deny the importance of wildlife to former and present-day Africa. Almost all African societies hunted as part of their subsistence strategies; even those that did not normally eat game would consume it during times of famine or use it for other social practices.[3] Animal products were part of tribute systems within and between different African communities.[4] These products, especially ivory, were central to the centuries of trade that tied Africa to the rest of the world before European expansion.[5] Later, ivory became closely connected to the slave trade.[6] Ivory and meat subsidized early European explorers, fed colonial troops, and accounted for a significant portion of the household budget of early settlers and colonial administrators.[7]

Wildlife also affected – and continues to influence – the decisions and activities of African and European farmers. Subsistence and commercial farmers contend with animals that damage their crops during and after growing seasons.[8] Larger animals such as buffalo, hippopotamus, and elephant can ruin fields over the course of a few hours, although, on average, the constant onslaught of smaller animals such as birds, rodents, baboons, and wild pigs accounts for an even higher percentage of crop loss.[9] Carnivores like lion, leopard, crocodile, hyena, and wild dog threaten domesticated stock owned by African and European alike. Certain species, acting as hosts to the trypanosomiasis-carrying tsetse fly, totally preclude the raising of certain domesticated animals in parts of Africa.[10]

In addition to the costs and benefits it imposes on activities related to food production, wildlife impinges on a wide variety of individuals' daily decisions throughout Africa. Dangerous animals threaten travel by day and by night, over land and water, affecting transportation routes and methods. Different species still cause various injuries and transmit diseases, affecting choices ranging from where Africans and Europeans build their homes, to when and where they hold social or religious events.[11] The presence of wildlife even influences the routes that children walk to school.

Wildlife has become an increasingly important part of the relationships among many African countries and industrialized countries, international nongovernmental organizations (NGOs), and international businesses. Revenue from wildlife tourism is an important source of foreign exchange in many African countries. More bi- and multilateral aid flows to wildlife conservation programs in Africa and more conservation-oriented NGOs work in Africa than ever before. Residents of industrialized countries ascribe growing importance to the fate of animals in Africa.[12]

Explaining African Wildlife Policy

Because of wildlife's multiple roles and values, wildlife policies have been at the center of numerous disputes between individuals and groups in Africa. European governments created policies to control the ivory trade. Colonial administrators crafted legislation to prevent Africans and certain Europeans from hunting and from owning firearms. European farmers pushed for regulations to eliminate those wildlife species that harbored disease as well as those animals that killed their stock. Certain Africans lobbied their government representatives to prevent the creation of natural parks and game reserves. Other Africans struggled to gain influence over the lucrative safari hunting trade. Still others sought outright ownership of the wild animals found on their traditional lands. In each of these cases, individuals and groups competed for favorable policy, and losers opposed policies through both legal and illegal activities. The benefits and costs associated with wildlife policies have influenced African independence movements, legislative debates, government elections, and international agreements.

AFRICAN WILDLIFE AND THE SOCIAL SCIENCES

Given its important and widespread roles, and the fact that most citizens of industrialized countries still view Africa through the lens of its animals, it is somewhat surprising that until quite recently, social scientists have generally ignored African wildlife as a topic of research. Although mentioned briefly by most of the early anthropologists, wildlife and its use did not fit well the concepts of either the modernization theorists or their dependency critics.[13] Subsistence hunting remained a shadowy, secondary activity set apart from the development of modern agricultural and industrial sectors of an emerging Africa. Indeed, some thought that subsistence hunting allowed both white and black citizens to escape the modern economy completely and lead "indolent" lives.[14] One result of these views was that the study of African wildlife remained the purview of natural scientists.[15]

Several events helped to shift attention to the nonbiological aspects of African wildlife. The environmental movement of the 1960s and 1970s, the increase of poaching (especially of elephant and rhinoceros) in some parts of Africa in the 1970s and 1980s, and the concomitant dramatic impact on public interest in wild species (evidenced by the fantastic growth of donations received by wildlife-related organizations), all stimulated new research in the area. One stream of research emerging from this new orientation has scholars, policy analysts, and conservation practitioners reconsidering the assumptions that undergirded conventional approaches to wildlife management.[16] Such studies feature the important "human dimensions" of wildlife policy and investigate the incentives that policies generate for the individuals who experience the externalities of living with wildlife.[17] Much of the focus of this work addresses how policy could be changed to make local communities work with, rather than against, wildlife conservation; *stakeholder* became a new word to policymakers and analysts concerned with wildlife.

Work in the human dimensions vein often views policy change as the process in which policymakers realize the importance of a new conservation policy (learning from either international or domestic entities) and then construct and implement it. That is, because there is a realization that humans living with wildlife should participate in gain and participate in conservation activities, such policies will follow. Poor policy outcomes are attributed to the weaknesses that attenuate much policy making in Africa, such as administrative incapacity,[18] lack of scientific knowledge,[19] use of Western conservation concepts in non-Western settings,[20] or government meddling resulting from an appetite for power or revenue.[21] This work generally claims that with greater political will, better information, better equipment, better staff, and more money, policymakers and their agents would create wildlife policy to improve conservation outcomes.[22]

This approach, however, lacks a persuasive account of the politics of wildlife policy. For example, although the human dimensions literature often prescribes changes through alteration to national laws, the institutions through which laws are created and the political consequences of such changes are not generally part of the analysis. Consequently, the potentially critical influence of the wider political institutional environment on policymakers' decisions is largely absent from the analysis. A more fundamental oversight of this work is its assumption that wildlife policy is created to promote conservation; in fact, much of the work implicitly or explicitly holds wildlife conservation to be a valued public good. Such a view inclines researchers to explain poor conservation outcomes in terms of phenomena that may augment or interfere with the implementation of this preferred goal.[23] Such an assumption, however, is untenable. As with most important political issues, a wide variety of actors display divergent preferences over wildlife conservation policy: Politicians, conservationists, professional hunters, rural dwellers, chiefs, tourist lodge owners, consultants, wildlife scouts, and other government personnel disagree about the appropriate distribution of property rights to land, wild animals, and their related markets. The importance of these other, nonconservation goals is dramatically illustrated by the hunters in many countries who choose to challenge conservation policies by illegally shooting wild animals – and sometimes wildlife department staff.[24]

If wildlife conservation policy is characterized by conflict, preference divergence, distribution, and political institutions, then employing distinctly political frameworks may be a more fruitful way to explain the continuity and change of African wildlife policy. Three approaches to African politics seem useful for such a study: "strongman" theories, the state/society framework, and the new institutionalism.

Strongman theories seek to explain patterns of African politics by focusing on the concentration of public authority in individual leaders. In the absence of stable political institutions, almost all African countries had civil or military authoritarian leaders within a decade of independence.[25] This personalization of power and authority led to phenomena observed throughout the continent: patronage politics, clientelism, bureaucratism, nepotism, mismanagement, corruption, and intolerance to dissent.[26] A major tenet of scholars using strongman theories is that formal institutions do not constrain personal rulers. Rather, informal patronage networks characterized by ethnicity, kinship, and client relationships exert the few limits on rulers' decisions.

The descriptions of ruler behavior forwarded by strongman approaches fit some of the actions of the leaders of Zambia, Kenya, and Zimbabwe regarding wildlife policy. For example, Zambia's President Kaunda intervened in the selection of wildlife officers, used national parks to entertain powerful friends and international visitors, and directed the military to undertake antipoaching activities. President Moi of Kenya intervened to create a new wildlife bureaucracy and to appoint its new director. Zimbabwe's President Mugabe's distrust of wildlife conservation helps to explain the tepid support his government gives the wildlife department.

Still, important aspects of African wildlife policy are not well explained by a strongman approach. For example, why was Kaunda able to get his policy accepted by parliament during the First Republic, but not during the Second? Why did Zimbabwean parliamentarians, known for their rubber stamping of Mugabe's government policy, kill a government-introduced policy regarding conservation? The critical variable in these cases was an alteration in the formal institutions of government and party, not a change in the informal networks of strongmen.

The choices of bureaucrats also tend to be lost with a strongman approach. Why did the administrators of some community-oriented wildlife programs in these countries seek out presidential support (Zambia and Kenya) whereas other administrators sought to avoid it (Zambia and Zimbabwe)? If personal rulers were the only source of public authority, we would expect all administrators to desire the backing. Although the presidents of Zambia, Kenya, and Zimbabwe enjoyed the greatest share of their country's public authority during the postindependence period, they were by no means the only important political actors. Multiple domestic and international actors both constrained their choices over policy and affected wildlife policy independently. These examples suggest that we need to look beyond simple strongman theories of African politics and investigate the influence that formal institutions have on individual decision makers and the continuity and change of African wildlife policy.

Unlike strongmen theories, the "state/society" approach does explicitly include other members of society in its treatments of African politics. Scholars using the framework move away from the preoccupation with rulers that characterizes strongman theories to incorporate the roles of social groups in socioeconomic patterns.[27] Rather than a view of the state as the sole engine of social development, a central focus of this literature is the variety of strategies that members of society employ to "disengage" from a largely predatory African state.[28]

The strategy of disengagement is a particularly persistent theme in the history of African wildlife conservation. Africans have been trying to circumvent laws protecting animals for a century. The state/society's underlying theme of state predation also resonates in the case of wildlife policy: Wildlife agencies of the central government continually sought to secure greater revenue and public authority to manage wildlife resources, at the expense of citizens. Because wildlife policy touches the lives of so many Africans, any study of that policy must take seriously the state/society approach's call to include the local, nongovernmental voice.

The state/society framework's broad generalizations about state decline and societal disengagement are less helpful, however, in the attempt to explain more precisely the continuity and change of African wildlife policy. First, the use of aggregations such as state and society does little to unpack the critical intra- and intergroup conflicts that characterize the creation and change of African wildlife policy in the periods to be studied here. Government officials often held contradictory positions on wildlife policy; nor did nonstate social groups interested in wildlife policy hold unified views as to what constituted the "best" policy. Nor do the central concepts of the state/society approach offer testable hypotheses: Asserting that tension exists between members of the central government and society does little to explain where and why that tension exists, how it changes over time, and what effects those changes. Finally, making predictions about individual behavior is difficult with the state/society distinction alone.[29] Who will disengage from the state? Individuals in and out of African governments hunted wildlife for similar reasons in the 1970s. Some parliamentarians championed local concerns and fought against their president's conservation policy, even though presidents were fellow members of "the state." And certain nongovernment groups and individuals in African society prefer more, rather than less, government intervention in wildlife conservation. These examples show

8

that a simple state/society distinction might have a difficult time explaining outcomes. Whereas that approach contributes greatly to the study of African politics by pushing researchers to include phenomena other than the formal institutions of politics, it lacks the microfoundations necessary to develop better theories of African politics.

Recent work by environmental historians and anthropologists has begun to augment our understanding of the microfoundations of wildlife politics in Africa by including both the importance of the competition between different groups interested in wildlife and some of the institutions that influence outcomes. These scholars have produced fascinating accounts of the relationship between the unfolding of European colonialism and the evolution of conservation ideas, the origin and history of specific natural reserves, and the origin and effects of conservation policies.[30] This emerging stream of studies buttresses the view that wildlife is a significant political commodity in Africa.

This book seeks to build on and extend the recent work of the environmental historians, with three important distinctions. First, unlike most research, which examines only the colonial or precolonial era, my focus is on the independence period of Africa. Few analyses have probed the politics of African conservation after 1960, and yet many of the political controversies that swirled around colonial conservation efforts have not only endured, but intensified in an era of economic distress and political uncertainty.[31] If we are to understand the trajectory of wildlife policy in Africa, we must include serious and in-depth studies of how Africans have taken the colonial conservation legacy and reshaped it. Second, realizing that wildlife policy links national politicians, bureaucrats, and individuals at the grass roots, I examine the politics of policy at each of these levels. As we will see, each level fundamentally affects the others; a systematic exploration of all three is necessary to understand the political dynamics of wildlife policy. Finally, because this study features the interaction between individuals and institutions, I use the theories and methods of the new institutionalism to investigate the politics of wildlife policy.

THEORETICAL LOCUS OF THE BOOK

New institutionalists provide tools useful to the study of African wildlife policy by placing individuals, their preferences, and institutions at the center of analysis.[32] They begin with the assumption that individuals are rational, self-interested actors who attempt to secure the outcome they most prefer. Yet, as these actors search for gains in a highly uncertain world, their strategic interactions may generate suboptimal outcomes for society as a whole. Thus, rational individuals can take actions that lead to irrational social outcomes. Classic examples of this situation include the "tragedy of the commons"[33] and the "prisoner's dilemma."[34]

New institutionalists assert that institutions help prevent such suboptimal outcomes by reducing actors' uncertainty. First, institutions provide information about the likely actions of others. This information allows rational individuals to create agreements so as to produce an outcome in which everyone gains. Second, institutions also may limit the choices of rational individuals or structure the sequence of their interactions so as to promote a greater likelihood of an optimal or stable collective outcome.[35]

Much of this work, which borrows key insights from economists' exploration of firms, views institutions as remedies to specific economic problems, that is, institutions emerge when individuals with incomplete information cannot overcome transaction costs – the costs of negotiating, monitoring, or enforcing a contractual relationship.[36] Institutions allow actors to overcome these transaction costs by reducing their incomplete and asymmetric information. Thus, transaction costs became central to explanations of institutional creation and efficiency.[37] Principal–agent theory, an especially productive refinement of the transaction costs approach, explores how principals seek to overcome the divergent preferences of their agent by constructing institutional mechanisms to monitor and control agent behavior.[38]

Taken together, these insights regarding the importance of institutions to coordinated action, the relationship between actors' divergent interests and institutional arrangements, and the influence of institutions on patterns of costs and benefits allow scholars to understand better the particular configuration of institutions.[39]

These foci address precisely those variables that appear central to explaining the content and change of wildlife policy in Africa. By focusing on the choices of individuals, the new institutionalism aids the investigation of actors' divergent preferences and choices regarding wildlife policy. By explicitly including the effects of institutions, this approach allows a more complete explanation of the effects of the formal and informal institutions that influence individual choices. And by offering theory about hierarchy, the new institutionalism provides tools to explore the many critical principal–agent relationships central to African wildlife policy, such as those between presidents and parliamentarians, presidents and party members, and wildlife department officers and scouts.

But although the insights of new institutionalists offer this study tools appropriate to the study of African wildlife policy, the work that considers institutions merely as remedies to social dilemmas can remain at odds with theoretical efforts to link institutions with rational individuals.

As does the literature on wildlife policy, many new institutionalists explain the emergence and change of institutions by virtue of the collective good they produce, such as social stability, the optimal allocation of resources, the minimization of transaction costs, or some other social goal.

But such approaches fail to identify how the collective good motivates individuals to create institutions in the first place. Explanations relying on collective goods such as social efficiency, Pareto optimality, or stability are at odds with theoretical efforts to link institutions with rational individuals. Because individuals may not benefit from the collective goods that institutions provide, they have no incentive to help in their construction or maintenance.[40] Neither do explanations based on collective goods adequately address the free-rider problem that is endemic to institutional creation; that is, even a unanimous demand for an institution does not ensure its supply, because rational individuals prefer that others spend their resources constructing it so that they can free ride on its benefits.[41]

To move beyond the institution-as-remedy view, this study aligns itself with the subset of new institutionalism that has placed the distributive nature of institutions at the center of its analyses. In part, the new institutionalism's failure to feature the distributive nature of institutions stems from its conceptualization of institutions as the result of voluntary exchanges between relatively equal actors who are seeking mutually welfare-enhancing outcomes.[42] But experience tells us that individuals' resource endowments vary, and that they construct institutions that can be extractive and redistributive.[43] Assuming individuals are rational, their participation in disadvantageous institutions may imply force. These features of institutions – extraction, redistribution, and force – lie at the heart of politics.[44]

A few scholars have begun to inject politics into institutional analysis while retaining their commitment to the assumption of individual rationality.[45] Their work differs in important ways from the earlier efforts by giving prominence to unequal and strategic actors, the structuring influence of extant institutional environments, the possibility of inefficient institutional change, and, of central interest to this study, the distributive outcomes generated by institutions. The rest of this section traces the implications of these scholars' work for our understanding of who creates institutions, of how individuals are linked to an institution's distributive outcomes, and of how institutions change.

A more political view of institutions features individuals who possess different resource endowments and who seek to construct institutions to augment their private well-being, not society's.[46] Individuals use institutions as investments, aspiring to protect their streams of benefits from uncertainty.[47] Further, individuals with the resources to build institutions are likely to choose structures that reinforce their bargaining and coercive power.[48]

An institution's builders are not necessarily the most powerful individuals in society. Coalitions of weaker groups could agree to institutions that exclude or punish the interests of groups who, individually, may actually command more resources, as when the interests of Zambian parliamentarians coincided with those of rural dwellers to thwart the interests of President Kaunda, and when members of Zimbabwe's parliament defeated a government-sponsored conservation bill. Such coalitions – and thus their preferred institutional arrangements – could cycle, as individuals and groups search for the coalition partners necessary to overcome a disadvantageous institutional arrangement.[49] Thus, side payments to coalition partners, such as access to valuable wild animals, may spread an institution's benefits more widely throughout society.[50]

The distributive effect of institutions goes beyond mere side payments. Institution builders may intentionally expand or limit the choices of others, raising their costs or benefits.[51] Institutions may also produce unintended positive or negative externalities.[52] Quite likely, institutions produce an amalgam of positive and negative effects on various social groups.[53]

Given individuals who seek advantageous outcomes, a political view of the origins of institutions has a profound effect on how we conceptualize institutional change. Change will not necessarily evolve toward the more socially efficient institutions advanced by the institution-as-remedy view, but will reflect the competition among salient actors.[54] Given rational individuals seeking private advantage, institutions change under three conditions: (1) when individuals see a net advantage from making alterations, (2) when they possess the resources necessary to do so, and (3) when the extant institutions provide an opportunity for the change.[55]

A variety of factors affect the value of institutions to individuals over time. Changes in nature or technology might alter the costs and benefits of an institution, as when the introduction of firearms reduced the costs of killing large numbers of animals in Africa. Alternatively, the beneficiaries of an institution may begin to value different types of returns, such as when parliamentarians begin to receive credit for wildlife programs that bring funds into their constituencies who had long despised any conservation regulation. Even if an individual or group would prize a different institution, however, the costs of changing an institution may exceed its expected benefits.[56] For this reason, institutions can be "sticky" and display continuity over time.

Individuals and groups can always imagine an institutional arrangement more advantageous to them, such as the local African farmer who would like the legal authority to own the wild animals he kills, but a political view of institutional change also requires actors to possess the resources to make such modifications, defeating those who may prefer a different arrangement. The original builders of an institution may lose the resources necessary to maintain the institution, or, alternatively, the builders' rivals may gain the resources required to alter or eliminate a disadvantageous institutional arrangement. In some instances, the institution itself may alter the resources of salient actors to precipitate its own retrenchment or reorganization. In all these cases, the shifting relative endowment of resources possessed by salient actors is central to explanations of the institutional change.

Extant institutions also greatly influence the choices of individuals seeking to change institutions by attaching costs and benefits to strategies and outcomes. Among the most important institutional arrangements are those that can exercise public authority, that is, the right to make and enforce law. Because governments possess a monopoly of public authority, individuals and groups often aspire to obtain the backing of the state for an institution, seeking to use political power to protect themselves from the uncertainty generated by other social aggregation devices, such as markets.[57] Terry Moe offers a simple but enlightening example of how the distributive effects of political institutions eclipse their collective benefits:

When two poor people and one rich person make up a polity governed by majority rule, the rich person is in trouble. He is not in trouble because majority rule is unstable. Nor is he in trouble because the three of them will have difficulty realizing gains from trade. He is in trouble because they will use public authority to take away some of his money. Public authority gives them the right to make themselves better off at his expense. Their decisions are legitimate and binding. They win and he loses.[58]

Of course, political institutions generate sets of rules and incentives more complex than simple majority voting. The incentives generated by nondemocratic institutions may be equally or more powerful in certain cases. Government agencies, political parties, electoral laws, and national constitutions all furnish rules that may be pivotal to institutional analysis. For example, given African presidents control over crucial political powers during the period covered by this study, we can expect that they will be at the center of many of the conflicts over wildlife policy in Africa. It is not enough that we label certain politicians as strongmen; rather, what is important is to explore factors such as the institutions under which such strongmen operate, and the institutions that the strongmen create for others.

In sum, it is clear that accounting for institutional creation and change demands attention to more than collective goods. Individuals seek to structure institutions that benefit them. The path along which institutions change relates directly to these individuals' choices, and thus scholars who seek to explain institutional creation and change on the basis of rational choice assumptions must bring politics to the center of their analyses.

This study seeks to pick up the gauntlet thrown down by Douglass North, among others, who perceive difficulties in attempts to explain comprehensively the distributive effects of institutions while hewing to rational choice assumptions.[59] It strives to account for the changes of African wildlife policy by trying to "understand not only the distribution of power within the institution but also the consequences, intended and unintended of individual decisions in the context of strategic interactions."[60] It considers the wide variety of actors salient to wildlife policy. And it places an especially strong focus on the effects that political institutions have on the distribution of wildlife's benefits. As a result, it underscores the importance of politics in an area long considered apolitical. By employing the tools of the new institutionalism and focusing on politics, this study seeks to provide explanations for the content and change of African wildlife policy.

RESEARCH DESIGN

This study examines wildlife policy in Africa within the framework of the new institutionalism while attempting to retain the assumption of individual rationality. The central hypothesis is that individuals seek to construct wildlife policy to advantage themselves. They do so under the constraints imposed by the extant institutional environment and their resource endowment. As a result, policies will reflect more the political competition between these individuals and less an efficient response to a social dilemma.

To test this general hypothesis, as well as other, more specific hypotheses, the book examines in depth the case of Zambia. To develop further the theoretical and substantive findings that emerge from the Zambian case, it compares Zambia's experiences with the politics of wildlife policy in Kenya and Zimbabwe. Although the cases of Kenya and Zimbabwe are not investigated with the same depth as that of Zambia, the attempt to compare the three countries yields interesting and fruitful insights and begins to lay a foundation for further comparative work in this field.

The similarities of Zambia, Kenya, and Zimbabwe allow some systematic comparisons to be made between the cases. The most important similarity is that the roots of wildlife policies in Zambia, Kenya, and Zimbabwe are found in British colonial administration. Thus, the development of wildlife policy had common origins in these countries, and this study in part seeks to explain their divergent paths. Each country also harbors abundant and diverse wildlife populations. This means that the wildlife issues confronting all of the governments are similar and important; the conservation politics of countries with smaller or less valuable wild animals would face quite different tensions. Each country has also experienced long periods of rule by strongmen – as most African countries had in the first decades of independence.

The wildlife policies and their outcomes for the three countries, however, have diverged over time. Zambia, for instance, would appear at first glance to possess the best conditions for effective wildlife policy. President Kenneth Kaunda was an ardent conservationist who enjoyed the strong, centralized powers of a one-party president. Yet, conservation policies and their outcomes in Zambia were arguably weak during Kaunda's regime. President Moi of Kenya has played a dangerous policy game that attempted to balance his party's demand for greater illegal access to wildlife with the tourist monies that correspond with less illicit use. President Mugabe of Zimbabwe was neutral if not hostile toward wildlife conservation, and yet wildlife conservation policy was more effective in his country than in Zambia.

Additionally, because wildlife has been of long-enduring importance in Zambia, Zimbabwe, and Kenya, enough data exist to start comparisons of their wildlife policies. Reports from government agencies concerned with wildlife and tourism, newspaper accounts of wildlife-related crises, and information from nongovernmental organizations are available for an extended period in these countries.

Important institutional changes occurred in Zambia, Zimbabwe, and Kenya that allow for a detailed comparison of the effects of institutional change on wildlife policy. All three countries' political institutions changed with their independence from colonial rule. Afterward, Zambia and Kenya moved from a multiparty democracy to a one-party state, whereas Zimbabwe has remained a de jure multiparty system with one dominant party. In each of these three countries there have been changes in the institutions that deal with wildlife policy as well. Such variance over institutions allows the testing of how institutional change affects continuity and alteration of wildlife policy.

Because the activities that produce and result from wildlife policy occur at multiple political levels, a more complete understanding of the outcomes generated by institutions on wildlife policy also requires a multilevel approach. Such an approach allows us to see how different layers of institutions affect outcomes at the same and different levels. A multilevel approach also allows for a more complete account of the politics of wildlife policy, linking presidents to poachers and back again.

This book, then, includes analyses at the legislative, bureaucratic, and local levels. In each chapter, a detailed study of a particular aspect of Zambia's wildlife policy at a given level is followed by selected comparisons with Kenya and Zimbabwe at the same level.

PLAN OF THE BOOK

This book has three parts that correspond to the legislative, bureaucratic, and local levels it explores. Part I deals with wildlife policy at the legislative level, exploring how politicians seek to create laws to capture the benefits of wildlife resources for themselves. Chapter 2 features the construction of Zambia's initial wildlife policy during the country's multiparty First Republic (1964–1971). Despite an extraordinary shift in the institutional environment – from colonial administration to self-rule – the Zambian government retained most of the unpopular provisions of the colonial wildlife policy. By featuring the incentives offered to various politicians by the electoral and party institutions of the First Republic, and the distribution of benefits offered by wildlife policy to key individuals, this chapter explains why President Kaunda and the ruling United National Independence Party (UNIP) established such an unpopular policy. This chapter then examines how politicians in Kenya and Zimbabwe, confronting generally similar political conditions in their transition to independence, also retained the unpopular wildlife policies of the past.

Chapter 3 continues the examination of wildlife policy at the legislative level by exploring the distributive effects of two dramatic shifts in the 1972–1982 period: Zambia's switch to a one-party state and the rapid increase in the relative value of wildlife products. President Kaunda declared a one-party state in Zambia in 1972, attempting to thwart his political enemies by abolishing opposition parties and augmenting UNIP's powers. At the same time, Zambia's economy collapsed while international demand for wildlife products skyrocketed. This chapter examines how the incentives of these new political institutions and wildlife's increased value motivated parliamentarians to fight against President Kaunda's attempts to pass stronger wildlife laws. The similar institutional structures of Kenya's one-party state generated a corresponding political dynamic: Increasingly valuable wildlife products greased the wheels of a patronage system and made it few politicians' interest to favor conservation. Illegal use in Zimbabwe, by contrast, did not escalate to the same degree, because of the existence of other domestic loci of political power and a relatively stronger economy.

Part II moves to the bureaucratic level of wildlife policy. Chapter 4 assesses how politics affected bureaucrats who shaped policy in the 1980s and early 1990s in Zambia, Kenya, and Zimbabwe. In Zambia, individuals and groups who favored strong conservation policy secured new resources and employed them to create institutions to mitigate the predatory incentives of the one-party state. Two new wildlife programs emerged – the Luangwa Integrated Resource Development Project (LIRDP) and the National Parks and Wildlife Service's (NPWS's) Administrative Management Design for Game Management Areas (ADMADE). Although both programs sought to conserve wild animals by incorporating the participation of rural residents in their activities, they were constructed far differently than those necessary to achieve "efficient" community-based conservation. Instead, ADMADE and LIRDP's designers strategically responded to the incentives furnished by the institutions of the one-party state. Data from Kenya and Zimbabwe support the argument that agency designers construct their organizations with great regard for the pattern of political uncertainty and public authority generated by a country's political institutions.

Part III shifts the focus to the local level by examining the choices made by rural residents regarding wildlife resources. Chapter 5 details the distributive effects of wildlife policy at the local level. ADMADE and LIRDP, while possessing considerably different institutional designs, shared similar assumptions about the behavior of hunters, traditional rulers, and wildlife scouts in the field. As a result, the programs presented individuals similar incentive structures at the local level. This chapter indicates, however, that the programs' designers generally failed to address the decision problems confronted by local actors; LIRDP and AD-MADE administrators chose structures that primarily benefited their programs. The outcomes of "community-based" programs in Kenya and Zimbabwe follow similar patterns: Because property rights remain vested in the state, rural dwellers are skeptical of new, "decentralized" programs. Individuals tend to enjoy whatever benefits new programs can offer and continue to hunt, although their hunting practices often change as a result of the increased levels of enforcement that programs generally produce.

In the Conclusion (Chapter 6), I review the central lessons of this study. In all the periods examined, different sets of individuals attempted to gain access to wildlife resources. Individuals and groups sought to create policies advantageous to them. Their strategies for constructing favorable policy reflected the incentives spawned by the extant institutional arena. As political institutions changed, so did the strategies followed by individuals and groups, and so too did policy. Such policy did not necessarily lead to good conservation outcomes, but reflected the multiactor, multilevel, dynamic nature of African politics itself. This study of wildlife policy in Africa thus serves not only to increase our understanding about a particular and neglected aspect of African governments and citizens, but helps us to understand African politics more generally.

PART I

---

*The National Politics
of Wildlife Policy*

2

Unkept Promises and Party Largesse: The Politics of Wildlife in the Independence Period

The man who looks at an animal and sees beauty is a man who has eaten well.
University of Zambia employee

Contrary to promises made by future President Kenneth Kaunda and other Zambian nationalists during Zambia's independence movement, the government of the ruling United National Independence party (UNIP) did not revoke the much-despised wildlife policy they inherited from their British predecessors. In fact, immediately after independence in October 1964 Kaunda began to make radio broadcasts and public speeches about the need to protect wild animals as an integral part of Zambian history.[1] His government submitted a new wildlife bill to the National Assembly in 1968 that closely followed the proscriptions of the colonial ordinances while conferring even more authority over wildlife on the central government. By the end of 1971 the UNIP government had declared eight statutory instruments that detailed the laws regarding trophies, hunting license requirements, protected animals, and legal methods of hunting.[2] That same year President Kaunda signed an order that created thirty-two game management areas, and his minister of lands and natural resources introduced a motion into the National Assembly to declare a system of eighteen national parks within Zambia.[3] Like their colonial predecessors, the new government's administrators shunted aside calls for granting locals access to wildlife. Despite the widespread dislike for their similar colonial-style wildlife conservation policies, politicians in Kenya and Zimbabwe also chose to maintain the status quo.

This chapter explores why these African governments failed to follow preindependence calls to give their citizens greater access to wildlife resources, and how they survived this widely unpopular stance in multiparty systems with universal franchise. I argue that the structures of these countries' political institutions created incentives for ruling parties to ignore the electorate's desire for greater hunting. In Zambia, three important factors emerge. First, President Kaunda, who held considerable power over policy, favored a strong conservation policy. Second, electoral and party rules did not reward those parliamentarians who represented their constituents' calls for greater access to wild animals. Rather, the rules punished members of UNIP – the dominant party – for opposing Kaunda and UNIP's Central Committee. Thus, members of parliament (MPs) followed President Kaunda's preference for strong wildlife conservation and did not represent voters' desires. Third, by establishing government control over the wildlife sector through the National Parks and Wildlife Act, UNIP used wildlife to reward its followers, distributing jobs, game meat, concession areas, and trophies to supporters and only selectively enforcing the act's provisions. These benefits mitigated some of UNIP's political costs for establishing the colonially inspired wildlife policy.

Like Zambia's, the structures of Kenya and Zimbabwe's postindependence political institutions did not favor changing the status quo policies. Although these two countries did not boast a proconservation president, they did enjoy far greater income streams generated by the wildlife sector. These income streams would predispose many politicians to maintain the inherited wildlife policies despite the electorate's general animosity toward such measures. Political and electoral institutions enabled legislators to withstand public opprobrium generated by their policy position.

The chapter begins by reviewing briefly the history of wildlife policy in Zambia to demonstrate the deep antipathy that Africans had for the conservation laws that had removed their legal access to the benefits of wildlife. African nationalists used the popular discontent with colonial wildlife restrictions to foment resentment against the settler regime. The chapter proceeds to explore the institutional context of Zambia's First Republic, which fostered party discipline rather than constituency service and helped to shape the structure of political competition over wildlife policy. A parliamentary debate regarding the 1968 National Parks and Wildlife Bill illustrates how party and electoral rules influenced parliamentarian behavior. The chapter concludes by comparing the Zambian case with the experiences of Kenya and Zimbabwe.

A SHORT HISTORY OF WILDLIFE POLICY IN ZAMBIA

The importance of wildlife is nowhere more apparent than in Zambia. Although it is a land-locked country composed mostly of a high plateau (see Maps 1 and 2), the fact that Zambia's topological variation does not correspond exactly with rainfall patterns means that the country possesses great ecological diversity in its five major ecological zones and

Map 1. Zambia and the region. *Source*: D. Hywell Davies, ed., *Zambia in Maps* (London: University of London Press, 1971).

ten vegetational zones[4] (see Maps 3 [ecological zones] and 4 [vegetational zones]). Such habitat variation allows Zambia to be home to well over 100 species of mammals, nearly 700 species of birds, and more than 150 species of fish.[5]

The abundance and variety of Zambia's wildlife made it central to the country's colonial and postcolonial history. As with other African countries, the edible and nonedible products of wild animals were essential parts of diets and social relationships: Missionaries, adventurers, and administrators depended on wildlife to subsidize their activities; wildlife has affected farmers' decisions; and game meat was and continues to be part of the rural dweller's household economy.[6] And wildlife connected the area with international markets; for example, ivory from the ele-

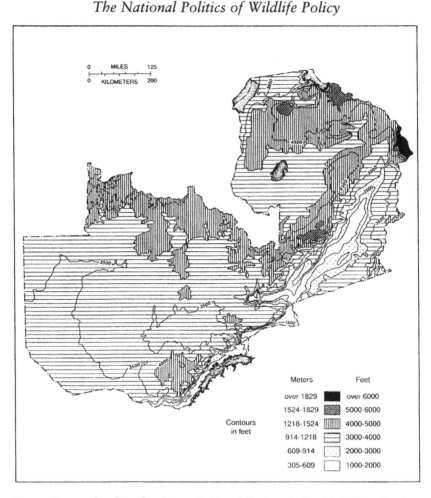

Map 2. Topography of Zambia. *Source*: D. Hywell Davies, ed., *Zambia in Maps* (London: University of London Press, 1971).

phant herds of the Luangwa Valley in eastern Zambia entered the world market as early as the seventeenth century; the valley's elephants continue to be targeted for their ivory today.[7]

Gaining control over wildlife was central to the plans of Northern Rhodesia's colonial administrators. The British South Africa Company (BSAC) sought to dominate the lucrative ivory trade in the late nineteenth and early twentieth centuries. To prevent widespread hunting, the BSAC administrators passed laws that restricted African ownership of firearms, founded a few game reserves, and established some game regulations.[8] As the age of explorers and adventurers passed, and the new

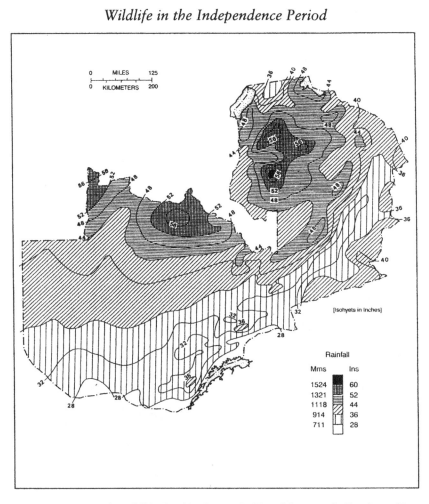

Map 3. Mean annual rainfall in Zambia. *Source*: D. Hywell Davies, ed., *Zambia in Maps* (London: University of London Press, 1971).

era of settlers began, wildlife policies also changed. Farmers demanded that the governments of the BSAC and the later Northern Rhodesian Protectorate establish measures to control the tsetse fly (which causes trypanosomiasis – sleeping sickness – in both humans and cattle) and wildlife's damage to crops and stock.[9] Sportsmen and conservationists called on colonial administrations to protect certain species of wild animals and create more extensive game reserves. The Legislative Council of Northern Rhodesia responded to these interests by adopting the 1925 Game Ordinance, creating game licenses and protected areas that limited both European and African hunting.[10]

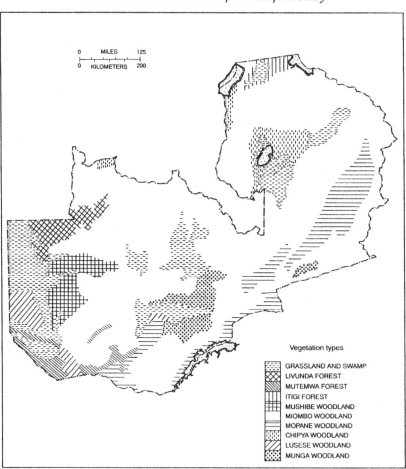

Map 4. Vegetation of Zambia. *Source*: D. Hywell Davies, ed., *Zambia in Maps* (London: University of London Press, 1971).

Although elephant control officers had been operating in the protectorate since the early 1930s, the central government's limited funds precluded the founding of a separate agency to execute the provision of the Game Ordinance until 1942, when the Department of Game and Tsetse Control began operation.[11] Although the new director of the department apparently supported some African access to wildlife, stating that "in a country where vast rural areas carry small populations, the wildlife in one shape or other is a main economic force just as much as the soil or the water supply," the initial terms of reference for the department followed closely the demands of the European settler population. The department's priorities were the control and preservation of game, with "the main theme being protection of cultivated land and help in the control of animal diseases." The department would preserve game only in "suitable areas with particular reference to the benefit and enjoyment of the public – the function of national parks." Furthermore the department would pursue the eradication of tsetse fly, which required that game reserves be located far from cattle and agricultural interests. The department also sought to control African hunting, for the "rationalisation of game-meat supplies . . . for what are, sociologically speaking, still hunting communities."[12]

The Legislative Council of Northern Rhodesia, the governor, and the civil servants of the Game Department made various marginal changes to wildlife policy over the next twenty years: The Fauna Conservation Ordinance (Chapter 241 of the Laws of Northern Rhodesia) provides an example of the powers the central government had assumed over wildlife by the early 1960s.[13] The governor could declare game reserves, game management areas, or controlled hunting areas or withdraw such recognition. The minister could authorize individuals to hunt even in contravention to promulgated hunting regulations and could revoke any license without reason. The director of the Game Department could prohibit or control the number, species, and gender of animals that could be hunted through an elaborate system of licenses that had evolved since the first BSAC game laws. The ordinance also outlawed various methods of hunting, including the use of pitfalls, snares, poisons, bush fires, automatic weapons, spears, and nets. All trade in game meat was prohibited, except for the barter of a legally procured animal between Africans in the same area, or as designated by the minister. Trophies, too, could be processed and exchanged only with government permission. The ordinance issued even stricter rules regarding the acquisition and trade of ivory and rhinoceros horn.[14]

The colonial government also designated vast tracts of land as protected areas. By 1959, 43 percent of Northern Rhodesia came under some restriction: The Kafue National Park (no hunting except by special license) covered 8,650 square miles; game reserves (no hunting except by special license) occupied another 10,080 square miles; controlled hunting areas (hunting of game animals by license) accounted for an additional 105,530 square miles.[15] The government moved entire villages in order to create some protected areas.[16]

Africans chafed at these laws. They continued to kill protected species. They fished and hunted in game reserves.[17] They also set bush fires and used snares, dogs, pits, and spears.[18] And they used conservation laws to their advantage. Under the legal provisions that allowed the killing of "crop raiders," they planted gardens directly on well-known hippopotamus trails and called in control officers whenever an elephant got near village gardens, knowing that the meat from such kills was distributed locally.[19] Finally, Africans vigorously opposed any expansion of protected areas.[20]

Conflict between Game Department staff and rural residents was continuous and sometimes lethal.[21] Arrests, fines, prison terms, and department efforts to "educate" residents about the benefits of conservation did little to stop Africans' use of wildlife resources.[22] Some colonial officers took the side of the local African and tried to protect local residents' access to wild animals.[23] Many Game Department members realized the incentives that lay behind African hunting: "To him (the African), game has only two aspects: a much-needed meat supply, and a foe to his crops. If he does not kill, the next man will, so he kills as much as he can whenever he can."[24] Nevertheless, the department pushed for additional staff and protected areas, believing that Africans "must learn that there is no longer 'plenty more round the corner'; somebody else has already been there, and if he destroys all that is left in his own area there will soon be none left to him at all."[25]

Wildlife conservation policies became an important issue that local African politicians throughout Northern Rhodesia used to incite opposition to colonial rule.[26] The restrictions placed on hunting bred contempt for colonial administration. In some of the more remote areas of Northern Rhodesia, the arrests made by wildlife officers were the only direct contact that locals had with government. African nationalists understood the costs imposed by wildlife policy and exploited them in the drive for Zambia's independence. In Eastern Province, political advancement became associated with the removal "of all sorts of irksome restrictions, so that the day of independence is seen by the villager as the day on which he will enjoy complete freedom to hunt."[27] In Luapula Province, activists organized large-scale protests against fish guards trying to enforce net regulations.[28] In Copperbelt Province, entrepreneurs continued to defy laws against the sale of game meat by shipping truckloads of lechwe, buffalo, and impala meat to sell to miners in urban areas.[29] In Southern and Central provinces, local activists used "two things calculated to stir up the Ba-Ila [an ethnic group]: questions affecting land and hunting rights. By unfortunate coincidence, new and severe measures for protecting red lechwe coincided [with] the impact of external politics and provided the disaffected with a first class grievance to exploit."[30] And local politicians from all over the protectorate condemned the taking of land for the creation of game reserves.[31]

National–level African politicians also denounced the colonial government's wildlife policy. The future president, Kenneth Kaunda, "enthusiastically encouraged" Africans to kill any wild animal they desired, and to resist – by force if necessary – their arrest if caught hunting by officials.[32] He called European restrictions on African hunting a legal and cultural absurdity.[33] Leaders of both UNIP and the African National Congress (ANC) made speeches with similar themes.[34] By the time of the 1964 elections, political activists had led Zambians to believe that independence would give them the right to hunt without restriction. In the months that followed, however, wildlife policy did not change: The incentives generated by the political institutions of the First Republic and Kenneth Kaunda's preference for conservation conspired against such hopes.

ZAMBIA'S MULTIPARTY FIRST REPUBLIC

During Zambia's First Republic, President Kaunda exerted a strong influence over government policy. His influence derived both from the specific powers conferred on the chief executive by Zambia's independence constitution and the period's particular constellation of electoral and party rules.

Political Institutions

In January 1964, Zambia experienced its first election with universal suffrage. UNIP dominated the polling for the new multiparty, Westminster-style parliamentary system that included an executive president. UNIP garnered 69.6 percent of the popular vote, securing fifty-five of the sixty-five main roll seats in the National Assembly; its main opposition, the ANC, mustered only 30.5 percent of the vote and ten seats.[35] This result bore witness to the superior organization of UNIP, which had established a countrywide presence for 1964 elections. But UNIP's organizational effort also contained contradictions: It aspired to be both a mass party that espoused democracy and a centralized party based on strict party discipline.[36]

UNIP's Central Committee was the most important administrative organ of the party. According to the party's 1967 constitution, the Central Committee had the right to formulate and implement policy, to exercise disciplinary control over party officials at all levels, and to propose a list of candidates to replace its own membership. The committee could also call sessions of the National Council (which could determine party policy and review decisions made by the Central Committee, but whose numerous members made it unwieldy) and the General Conference (the largest executive body of the party with hundreds of delegates representing all of Zambia's regions who could review policy, elect Central Committee members, and amend the party constitution). Importantly, the Central Committee selected candidates for both parliament and local government offices, which would then be forwarded to the secretary general of the party – Kaunda – for approval.[37]

In reality, the process was reversed: Kaunda selected candidates and the Central Committee gave the list their approval. (The National Council eventually gave Kaunda the formal authority to choose candidates in 1968.) The process started with party officials from the provinces submitting lists of suitable candidates. An individual could also apply personally to the president. The qualities most often rewarded with nomination were loyalty and length of service to the party.[38]

The ANC, on the other hand, was not a mass organization. It had no paid officials at the local level. Almost all of the party's power was vested in the person of Harry Nkumbula, and successive ANC constitutions merely formalized this arrangement.[39] Nkumbula appointed all national, provincial, and district officials. He also appointed the majority of the members to ANC's National Assembly, which had the power to expel people from the party. It is not surprising, therefore, that Nkumbula exerted a strong influence on the choices over parliamentary candidates. Although the ANC constitution did not specify any formal process for choosing candidates, generally those party members interested would write a letter of application to ANC party headquarters, where they were short listed and interviewed. As with UNIP, loyalty to the party was the most important criterion of candidate selection.[40]

Despite the disparity of methods and organization, the institutions of both parties engendered strong party discipline.[41] UNIP and ANC considered their constituencies not as areas represented by individual MPs, but as party property.[42] A change in electoral rules reinforced the already strong incentives for party discipline: After 1966, any MP who changed parties immediately forfeited his National Assembly seat and had to contest a by-election to retain it.[43] An MP's electoral chances after crossing the floor were not good: All of the first seven MPs who changed parties after the rule change lost their subsequent by-elections, and the practice diminished thereafter.[44]

One casualty of party rules was the representation of constituency interests. Because constituency service did not get candidates on the ballot, most parliamentarians did not strengthen their ties to the electorate. MPs rarely visited their constituencies. Although most were "local men," they often had little or no political base in the area. (It was not until 1972 that the idea of establishing an office in their own constituency became acceptable to MPs, the result of prompting by the UNIP executive and the new electoral rules under the one-party state.)

Electoral rules further undermined MPs' incentives to serve constituents' interests and made political stands on particular issues unimportant. Given that only one candidate per party could stand for election in each constituency, and that parties had strong geographic identities, the electorate confronted a choice over parties, rather than individuals.[45] As a result, although electoral surprises occasionally occurred, most seats were not marginal.[46] Nowhere was the strength of party label more starkly illustrated than when Mr. Hugh Mitchley, a white European who had previously belonged to an all-white party, affiliated with the ANC and won in the 1968 election in the Gwembe North constituency, an ANC stronghold. Constituency service and position taking on issues, therefore, did not generate significant electoral gains to candidates; party label alone generally determined the outcome of the vote.[47] Thus, rather than press their demands on their parliamentarians, constituents chose easier and more effective means like entreating local party and government officials in their area.[48]

Policy Making in the First Republic

Although Kaunda did not possess as many formal powers during the multiparty First Republic as he would in the one-party Second Republic (see Chapter 3), Zambia's independence constitutions granted its chief executive broad powers. Kaunda used this authority to press forward his preferred policies. If he felt strongly about an issue, and most other senior party and government officials (especially in the Central Committee and cabinet) did not vehemently object, Kaunda's policy preferences were likely to be introduced as government-sponsored bills to the National Assembly.[49]

UNIP front-benchers and backbenchers were reluctant to criticize government policy. They had the opportunity to discuss bills in UNIP parliamentary caucuses held before each session.[50] They did not need to persuade opposition members on the merits of a bill since UNIP held an overwhelming majority of seats. And their political futures depended on the favor of Kaunda and the Central Committee, who wanted MPs to toe the party line in public. Thus, if pressing for one's constituency meant questioning government, such a tactic was risky, even for ministers: Those who did often failed to get renominated as candidates.[51] Unquestioned loyalty rather than parliamentary participation paved the way to higher office.

Even if members chose to champion their constituents' interests, voters were unlikely to hear about it. Media coverage of parliamentary proceedings was nearly nonexistent. The percentage of constituents with access to radio or newspapers at this time was low. Constrained by the control that the party executive exerted over nominations, and electorally unrewarded by a political strategy that pressed for constituents'

needs, most UNIP members only reluctantly spoke in the National Assembly.[52] So pervasive was this tendency that, ironically, even President
Kaunda decried the lack of parliamentary debate.[53] Constituents' widespread loathing of wildlife laws, therefore, did not translate into parliamentary action to change the policy inherited from the colonial period.

The disorganization of the ANC, together with the institutional incentives described, led to little formal opposition and the lack of any coher-
ent set of policy alternatives.[54] Because the ANC's electoral strategy
reflected more of a desire to hold on to their few seats rather than to
woo UNIP members or voters, ANC MPs – when they debated at all –
mostly attacked UNIP positions, in largely inflammatory language. With
few funds, weak party organization, and no full-time officials, rumor
was one of the few political weapons the ANC possessed.[55] Even these
highly colored attacks likely had little effect on public opinion.[56]

THE POLITICS OF WILDLIFE IN THE FIRST REPUBLIC

Structure of Competition over Wildlife Policy

Few Zambians besides Kaunda favored conservation during this time.
Despite Game Department goals, the safari hunting and tourism industries had not yet begun to earn significant amounts of revenue. Game
cropping schemes had not convinced many politicians or rural residents
about the value of protecting wild animals to "rationalize" meat supplies.[57] The traditional supporters of conservation, European farmers,
did not have many members in government; neither could they offer
either the ANC or UNIP a significant number of voters.

The parliamentary debate over the 1968 National Parks and Wildlife
Bill offers a partial test of the political logic of wildlife policy during this
period in Zambia. Given the party and electoral rules of the First Republic, we would expect UNIP members not to speak out against the bill,
even though its provisions were widely unpopular with most Zambians.
MPs received no electoral advantage from presenting their constituents'
preferences and could lose their seats by criticizing the government. We
would also expect little opposition from ANC members, because assail-
ing of the ruling party did not generally reach the ears of the electorate.
If ANC members did choose to speak against the bill, we would expect
their criticisms to be in the form of attacks without policy alternatives.
European MPs, however, would likely speak in support of the wildlife
bill: Not only were they more likely to support conservation as individuals, but their election from the reserved roll meant that they represented
a European electorate as well.

Wildlife in the Independence Period

The 1968 National Parks and Wildlife Bill

The UNIP government introduced the National Parks and Wildlife Bill in 1968, and its contents reflected President Kaunda's strong personal preference for wildlife conservation and his strong role as policymaker within the country. In laying out the bill's contents, Sikota Wina (minister of local government and acting minister of natural resources) described a wildlife policy strikingly similar to that of the colonial period. Like the concern of the Northern Rhodesian government, Wina asserted the overall goal of the UNIP government was the "preservation of our national heritage" and capacity for wildlife conservation to "pay its own way."[58] The government expected to manage wild animals according to the latest methods (hence the changing of the label *game* to *wildlife*), it also hoped to induce more tourism and foreign exchange.[59]

Minister Wina expressed awareness of the "negative outlook" possessed by most Zambians toward wildlife policy. His government intended to foster a "positive approach" through the "correct management and utilisation" of natural assets. The new bill allowed rural inhabitants to hunt. It abolished and reduced the size of certain protected areas and reclassified them as "open" to hunting. It eliminated former provisions for private game areas used by European farmers to protect their lands from outside hunters.[60] And it established a district license, sold by local authorities who would be allowed to keep the revenue.[61]

In the vast majority of ways, however, the new bill closely resembled the old game ordinances. It retained a system of licenses, hunting methods, and protected areas that excluded most Zambians from hunting. Ownership of all animals was vested in the president, on behalf of the citizenry. To support the "Government's declared policy of protecting its fauna from the depredations of law breakers and poachers," penalties for offenses against the new bill were "considerably more severe" than under the colonial laws.[62] The minister asserted that Zambians "of all age groups" needed to be "educated" to "appreciate the facts and principles" of wildlife management.[63] Echoing the intense feelings of colonial game officers, Wina ended his presentation of the bill by saying that "the only people who will oppose this Bill are the poachers."[64]

Besides Wina, the only overt supporters of the bill were Europeans.[65] Elected on the reserve roll, and reflecting the general tendency among Europeans to support wildlife conservation, these members extolled the new bill's virtues. Mr. Mitchley (Midlands constituency) claimed the bill, among other things, would "protect the finest game parks in Africa," allow people areas where "they could get away from it all," and "earn foreign revenue." None of the European members discussed the distributive bias the bill had against rural Zambians. On the contrary, Mr. Burnside (Zambezi) was "delighted" to hear that the government was training "zealous" scouts that "examined the meat being cooked in the pots" of rural dwellers.[66]

The only parliamentarian to speak out against the 1968 wildlife bill was Harry Nkumbula, leader of the ANC. Nkumbula used inflammatory language in his opposition to the bill, attempting to disparage UNIP before the 1968 general elections, which would take place in six weeks. Nkumbula criticized the amount of protected land in Zambia, reserving special ire for the lands of the Kafue National Park, which abutted the heart of his party's stronghold in the Southern Province.[67] He doubted the wildlife tourism would ever amount to much in Zambia. He regaled the National Assembly with stories about game guards harassing innocent citizens. He drew the politics of race into the debate by calling those who supported the bill "honorable English squires."[68] Finally, Nkumbula linked the wildlife bill directly with the upcoming election. He said that citizens in the rural areas sang songs with lyrics like the following:

When the general election comes, we shall see who we shall vote for . . . the ruling party, which is UNIP, is protecting animals more than they protect human beings. Therefore, on the polling day we shall vote for those people who protect human beings. And those who protect animal life shall ask animals to vote for them.[69]

The European members and several government ministers assailed Nkumbula's performance, claiming he was "dragging red herrings" and the shadow of elections into a debate about a bill that "has no political connotation whatsoever."[70] After telling Nkumbula to quit "preaching from his anthill," UNIP members passed the bill easily.

In subsequent legislation, the UNIP government fleshed out their wildlife policy with statutory instruments that regulated hunting licenses and fees (Statutory Instrument No. 2 of 1971), hunting methods (Statutory Instrument No. 4 of 1971), game animals (No. 5 of 1971), and human activity in national parks (No. 9 of 1972). With the approval of parliament, President Kaunda declared seventeen new national parks in 1972 (No. 44 of 1972). In a speech that would have caused an uproar among Zambian nationalists in the preindependence period, Solomon Kalulu, minister of lands and natural resources, told the National Assembly that he would allow his game guards "to shoot at people who may be there in the country poaching."[71]

The debate surrounding the National Parks and Wildlife Bill largely conforms to our expectations about parliamentarian behavior and illustrates how UNIP could afford to pass legislation that was widely disliked. Because of party and electoral rules, party loyalty rather than an

34

appreciative constituency determined parliamentarians' political careers. Thus, despite the bill's continuation of a system that legally excluded most Zambians from using wild animals, UNIP backbenchers did not utter a word during the wildlife debate, and government ministers supported the line taken by Kaunda. The ANC's resistance, as manifested in Nkumbula's attempt to point out the bill's negative impact on the common Zambian, had little effect on the legislation's fate.

Predictably, wildlife – like most local issues – did not feature prominently in the candidates' speeches in the run-up to the 1968 parliamentary and presidential elections.[72] Electoral rules also did not penalize parties for the positions they took on particular issues. Zambians voted for the party they thought would give them the most overall benefits, not particular policy positions. Consequently, Zambians were unlikely to switch their allegiance to an opposition party like the ANC even though they detested constraints on their access and use of wildlife.

DISTRIBUTIVE USES OF WILDLIFE POLICY

Despite the general lack of enthusiasm within the electorate for a conservation policy based on the colonial code, such a centralized, exclusionary system provided the ruling party control over valuable goods. The National Parks and Wildlife Bill of 1968 continued the colonial legacy of locating legal authority over Zambia's wildlife estate within the agencies of the central government. By claiming this authority, UNIP was then free to use it with discrimination, rewarding its followers with employment, licenses, and access to wild animals. Indeed, conflict between the civil servants of the Game Department and UNIP politicians illustrates that the government understood the value of wildlife as a distributable benefit.

Employment

Buttressed by increasing revenues from copper, Zambia's most important export, the well-funded UNIP government increased its spending sixfold from 1964 to 1971.[73] UNIP focused its investment on expanding government services, diversifying the economy away from copper, and boosting employment opportunities.[74] Enlarging the civil service would not only address each of these goals, but also meet, in part, UNIP's promises of rapid development and higher standards of living. Thus, government jobs became a principal means to distribute political largesse after independence. In 1964 the civil service establishment was 22,561; by 1969 it had reached 51,497 and was still growing.[75]

Although UNIP secured political support through its employment policies, the government's rapid expansion of the civil service also confronted significant obstacles, not the least of which was finding qualified personnel. European settler rule in Northern Rhodesia had failed to train significant numbers of Africans: Although Zambia had a more solid financial base than many other countries on the continent at independence, it faced one of the smallest pools of citizens qualified to implement government policies.[76] As late as February 1964, Zambians held only 38 of 848 administrative and professional positions. At independence, less than 0.5 percent of the country's 3.5 million inhabitants had completed primary school.[77] The issue, then, was how UNIP could employ relatively unskilled citizens within government.

The Department of Game and Fisheries provided one answer. Given its largest amount of funding ever, the department, like other government agencies, expanded staff numbers quickly.[78] At the time of independence, 265 "subordinate" Zambian staff supported the approximately two dozen European "incumbents" who held professional and clerical positions.[79] In the year following independence (1965), the department increased its subordinate staff by 38 percent; the next year (1966), by an additional 32 percent. The department did not just allow more Zambians to be hired, but was able to employ those Zambians the UNIP government had the most difficult time placing: the undereducated.[80] To perform as a game scout, an individual did not need a great deal of formal education. After recruitment, candidates received basic training at a government camp; they were then deployed. It was precisely in these less-skilled jobs that the major growth of department positions occurred. In 1964, 253 of the 265 Zambians employed as subordinate staff were employed as game guards, game scouts, and vermin hunters. When the department swelled to 367 subordinate staff in 1965, 356 held these low-skill positions. The pattern endured through 1967 (492 guards out of 509 subordinate staff), when total appointments finally leveled. Not only did the department allow the UNIP government to distribute jobs, but it focused on expanding the number of jobs that required the least qualifications.[81]

One former wildlife officer remembers only one policy guiding the department at that time: to hire as many people as possible.[82] In addition to the regular civil service posts, the department hired hundreds of day laborers for capital projects such as clearing and maintaining roads and building staff houses and firebreaks. The number of Zambians hired at higher levels increased as well, filling the positions abandoned by Europeans as the agency "Zambianized." Even with their aggressive employment policy, the department experienced a "flood of applications."[83]

Wildlife in the Independence Period

Ministerial Powers over Wildlife

Along with creating jobs for followers, UNIP's wildlife policy gave the minister in charge of wildlife – and thus, Kaunda and UNIP – significant powers over both the benefits and costs of wildlife. Initially, however, the wildlife officers who drafted the bill did not give the minister, a political appointee, certain crucial prerogatives. Instead, they had conferred this authority on their director of the wildlife department, a civil servant.

In the original National Parks and Wildlife Bill presented to the National Assembly, the minister could, inter alia, regulate all activities in national parks, add to or subtract from the list of protected species, prescribe the terms and conditions of hunting licenses, and limit the use of specified weapons or methods of hunting. Of great significance was the minister's ability to issue special licenses to individuals, allowing them to shoot any animal anywhere, without regard to the quotas or protected status given to certain species by the wildlife department (Sec. 59). The minister used this power to supply UNIP party functions held in the rural areas with game meat, to give certain chiefs licenses to hunt elephant, and to furnish other cabinet members with special licenses.[84]

But the three wildlife department officers who drafted the bill did not bequeath all of the most critical powers over wildlife to the minister. In the form originally presented to the National Assembly, the bill designated the director of the wildlife department – not the minister – as the highest authority regarding appeals related to license refusals, suspensions, or cancellations (Sec. 66,71); trophy dealers' permits (Sec. 98); the export of game meat or trophies, including ivory and rhino horn (Sec. 122); the disposal of confiscated items, including trophies, firearms, or vehicles (Sec. 145); and appeals related to such forfeited items (Sec. 145). Control over these provisions was valuable: Friends or supporters could be given the right to deal in animal trophies; those who had been arrested could have their case dismissed upon appeal. Enemies, alternatively, could have their appeal refused and have their goods confiscated.

The UNIP government recognized what the wildlife officers' draft had accomplished and set out to revise the original bill. Through Act No. 65 of 1970, the UNIP government amended the National Parks and Wildlife Act, firmly establishing the superiority of the minister over civil servants in matters concerning access to the most valuable aspects of wildlife resources.[85] In his statement about the amendment, the minister of lands and natural resources, Solomon Kalulu, admitted that the original bill did not stipulate that "in all instances" the director of the wildlife department was "subject to the directions of the Minister." Kalulu wanted "to make it abundantly clear that the Minister has the final say."[86]

One of the bill's drafters lamented the reversion of these powers to the minister.[87] He believed that politicians should not be allowed the authority to intervene in these important matters, because their motivations lay in pleasing their political supporters, and not professionally managing of wild animals. Civil servants, on the other hand, would be less likely to use their control over wildlife as a resource for patronage. If able, this drafter would have switched these provisions back to the purview of the director of the wildlife department.[88]

Enforcement of Wildlife Laws. The UNIP government confronted a dilemma when it adopted Kaunda's preferences for a centralized wildlife policy: How could it tell Zambians not to hunt after having labeled wildlife conservation an oppressive colonial scheme that only benefited Europeans?[89] We have seen that such a policy had little bearing on a parliamentarian's electoral chances. But the overall image of UNIP would not be enhanced with the electorate if the Game Department aggressively enforced wildlife laws with its newly enlarged force of scouts.

The evidence suggests that the department did not. The UNIP government was reluctant to assign a high priority to the enforcement of game regulations, fearing local opposition.[90] The department did not receive instructions from any government or party officials to augment enforcement in the field. During this period very few scouts made more than one arrest per year, and given the amount of illegal hunting that prevailed in the countryside, this level of detection is extremely low.[91] Responding to these efforts, poaching rates increased dramatically in the period immediately following independence. Zambians seemed to be unmoved by arguments that wildlife protection was now for the benefit of their country and future African generations: There was "little evidence of any abatement in poaching activity throughout the Republic"; rather, it was increasing at an "embarrassingly accelerated rate."[92] In 1968, the department received "reports from all Commands" that "the ordinary people of Zambia do not appear to regard poaching as a serious crime, and are not deterred from the pursuit of this past-time by the punishment that they receive when they are caught and prosecuted."[93]

For the UNIP government there was little political cost of weak enforcement of wildlife regulations. Domestically, most Zambians enjoyed the fruits of low enforcement levels. Internationally, conservation organizations had not yet gained the influence with the media to call attention to the feeble implementation of Zambia's wildlife. Besides, the great wave of poaching that would wash across the continent did not start until the early 1970s. In the 1960s, by contrast, almost no wild animal confronted imminent extinction in Zambia – there were "plenty of animals back then."[94]

Kaunda's Principal–Agent Problem. Part of the weak enforcement resulted from a disjuncture between the preferences of President Kaunda and those of other UNIP officials, a situation that can be investigated by principal–agent theory. Principal–agent theory analyzes the process by which a principal contracts with an agent to act to produce an outcome desired by the principal.[95] Many relationships common to society reflect this situation: lawyer/client, broker/investor, doctor/patient, or, in the most general form, employer/employee. After agreeing to the contract, however, there is no guarantee that the agent will choose to pursue the principal's interest or pursue it efficiently. On the contrary, the agent will pursue her own goals, unless the contract imposes some type of incentive structure so as to make it in her interest to pursue the principal's interests. The principal's task is to design a structure that creates this convergence of interests. The difficulty of constructing such a contract is that the information about the agent's effort is difficult to obtain. The agent may put effort into those tasks that only appear as if she is fulfilling the contract (namely, moral hazard). Consequently, the principal needs to write a contract with provisions for monitoring as well as inducing the agent to reveal information about her behavior. The perfect contract would overcome this informational asymmetry and conflict of interest by concocting incentives that encourage the agent to act as if she were the principal in every possible situation.

Mechanisms such as time clocks, output quotas, and profit sharing, however, do not completely eliminate the information and motivation gap.[96] Recent scholarship regarding principal–agent theory indicates that monitoring and sanctioning do not completely resolve the contracting problem resulting from dissimilar preferences.[97] Where more than one agent is involved in the production of a good, it becomes exceedingly difficult to measure an individual's contribution to total output. Although it is theoretically possible to devise schemes to induce agents to perform, such schemes are prohibitively costly and do not lead to the maximization of total profit.[98]

Principal–agent problems between a policymaker and an implementing bureaucracy can take two forms: shirking and slippage. *Shirking* refers to the noncompliance resulting from the conflict of goals described. *Slippage* refers to institutionally induced problems; that is, even when bureaucratic agents and policy making principals share policy preferences, institutional arrangements within their bureaucracy may militate against choosing this most desired policy.[99] The challenge for the policymaker/principal is to design decision-making rules within the bureaucracy so as to mitigate the problems of agency.

Although Kaunda may have favored strict enforcement, he relied on others to implement his preferences. As in any principal–agent situation, slippage occurred. Moreover, because the government and party officials on whom he relied would have had little reason to antagonize the electorate unnecessarily with vigorous enforcement, individuals would be likely to shirk as well. With hundreds of officials and staff scattered across the country responsible for the implementation of wildlife measures, it was next to impossible for Kaunda to monitor his agents' actions effectively.

Furthermore, Kaunda himself had reasons for not monitoring the implementation of wildlife policy more closely. First, he may have been unaware of or unalarmed by the level of poaching during the 1960s. Although the department reported some increase in illegal hunting, little international scrutiny of his wildlife policy existed. In fact, during this period Kaunda basked in the glow of the international recognition he received from establishing one of the largest systems of national parks in the world.[100] Second, Kaunda had other important concerns that crowded his political agenda at this time, such as the pace of development, the infighting among members of the party's executive, the diversification of Zambia's economy away from the mining sector, and his relationship with Ian Smith's regime in Rhodesia. Without any domestic or international watchdog groups raising alarm, and with other concerns on his plate, Kaunda had less immediate motivation to invest political capital in monitoring the implementation of his wildlife policy. But as wide as the gap between his preferences and those of other officials was at this time, we will see it would grow vastly wider during the 1970s as the value of noncompliance increased.

WILDLIFE POLICY AND INDEPENDENCE POLITICS IN KENYA AND ZIMBABWE

The shared colonial origins of Zambia, Kenya, and Zimbabwe's conservation policies created remarkably similar trajectories for their wildlife policies in their colonial and early independence periods. As in Zambia, independence leaders in Kenya and Zimbabwe used colonial wildlife policy to foment antigovernment sentiment and promised change once their parties came to power. And, as in Zambia, these promises went unfilled: Both Kenya and Zimbabwe kept and eventually extended the centralized and exclusionary wildlife policies established under white rule.

Wildlife in the Independence Period

Kenya

During Kenya's colonial era, different sets of European authorities sought to preserve wildlife, but only as long as such pursuits did not hinder economic progress. In the early colonial period, the British East Africa Company (BEAC), like the BSAC in Zambia, created wildlife policies to control the ivory trade in Kenya, which had been long dominated by Arab traders. Both the hunting of elephants and the exportation of ivory were taxed and regulated.[101] When the British Foreign Office, which had prodded the BEAC to construct hunting quotas and license fees, took over Kenya's administration in 1895, it increased the number and type of regulations regarding the hunting of wildlife and established the country's first two game reserves. But the Foreign Office also adjusted its desire for conservation (a result of a growing conservation lobby in Britain) to fit the needs of white settlers who hunted for food, for profit, and for the protection of their domestic herds.[102] Hunting regulations were waived or amended for certain Europeans; game reserve boundaries were moved for the expansion of settler plantations.[103] And whereas the Game Department's creation in 1907 heralded an increased institutionalization of wildlife policy enforcement, most of these laws were ignored or easily evaded at the time.[104]

Like that of Zambia, one of Kenya Game Department's more important goals in the first half of the twentieth century was "animal control." Increasing numbers of European settlers and displaced Africans made reaching this goal illusory, as wider agricultural use of land meant more unwanted interactions with wildlife. Predators presented a significant obstacle to profitable farming and ranching.[105] Both European and African farmers adopted a strong antiwildlife position. The Game Department's position both to preserve and to control wildlife was thus difficult – especially as it funded itself on ivory and rhino horn sales in the 1920s and 1930s.[106]

Unlike in Zambia, however, the activities of a small domestic pro-conservation group in Kenya succeeded in generating a valuable tourism industry based on wildlife by the end of the 1950s. This group worked hard to overcome European farmers' antipathy toward wildlife (some still advocated the total elimination of wild animals) and to create alliances with the newly emerging international wildlife organizations (especially the Society for the Protection of the Fauna of the Empire, which was instrumental in paying for wildlife survey missions and lobbying activities).[107] These efforts resulted in colonial government support for the establishment of four national parks immediately after World War II. These national parks quickly drew large numbers of tourists: Whereas in 1946 only a few hundred international tourists visited Kenyan game reserves, by 1955 over 100,000 flocked to the reserves and national parks.[108] Significantly, none was situated in an area highly valued by Europeans. As a result, these efforts transformed the heretofore small voice for wildlife conservation in Kenya – one that had been lobbying a relatively uninterested colonial government for decades – into dozens of conservationists. Importantly, many of these conservationists were European business owners who began to make significant monies in the tourism industry by the mid- to late 1950s. And the central government also benefited through taxes on tourism-related receipts.

As usual, the vast majority of Africans in Kenya received few of the benefits of the tourism trade or of wildlife policy more generally. They resisted and resented game laws, especially because colonial-style policies meant their exclusion from land or constraints on its use. National parks were especially vilified, because – according to the international model of national parks – any Africans who lived within the park boundaries had to be resettled elsewhere. Consequently, conservation and tourism were seen to benefit the European while punishing the African. Nationalists fueled such sentiments. If one views poaching as an expression of opposition to colonial policies, such opposition was "mind-boggling" during the independence campaigns of the 1950s and early 1960s.[109]

But black Kenyans' antipathy toward wildlife conservation did not translate into different policy in the postindependence period, for many reasons. As in Zambia, the electoral institutions did not favor issue voting. Kenya's first independent, multiparty election featured single-member districts in a first-past-the-post format. Such a system favors voting for parties, not issues.[110] Kenyan political parties at independence were not distinguishable so much by platform as by region and ethnic group, catalyzed by the political and economic institutions that the British administration itself had created. (Until the 1960s, colonial policies prevented Kenyan politicians from campaigning outside their own district in order to prevent any strong national political group.)[111]

If Kenya's transition could be characterized by one issue, it was rights to land. With over 80 percent of Kenya's land unsuitable for extensive agriculture, black Kenyans demanded access to the better lands held by European settlers. This concern pushed political parties toward ethnic regionalism, and thus ethnic politics.[112] Rather than other substantive policy issues like access to wildlife, the land question – with the bloody insurrection of the 1952 Mau Mau rebellion as a reminder – dominated the thoughts and plans of the politicians involved in the postindependence government.

Kenya's political and economic institutions, thus, furnished little incentive for most politicians to favor a radical change in wildlife policy after independence in 1963. Despite most people's dislike of conservation laws, conservation was just one of a number of policy issues that parties could address, and it was not considered the most important at the time. Those who were affected most by wildlife's transgressions were, as in Zambia, scattered and unorganized. The land question, the most important political issue, did not significantly affect conservation policy directly, because protected areas occupied less than 10 percent of Kenyan land and were located in the least agriculturally desirable locations (white settlers had consistently opposed locating wildlife sanctuaries in productive areas).

Although President Jomo Kenyatta neither held a strong stand on conservation nor enjoyed the level of control over his ruling party (the Kenya National African Union [KANU] was very decentralized at the time), the status quo policy offered Kenyan politicians benefits in a way that Zambia's conservation policy during the postindependence period did not. Kenya's tourism industry produced significant and growing returns to both private and public coffers.[113] Kenyatta and his party were not searching for ways to give up the centralized powers over such sectors as wildlife that they had so recently received from the British; in fact, quite the reverse occurred.[114] Given this institutional setting, the protests of poor and scattered Kenyans against conservation went unheard.[115]

Zimbabwe

Zimbabwe's colonial experience (as Rhodesia) with conservation policy followed the rough outlines of that in Zambia and Kenya. Early pioneers and explorers used wildlife to subsidize their activities. As European settlers replaced their more adventurous precursors, wildlife began to be seen as an impediment to agriculture and ranching. Efforts to conserve wildlife fell under the exclusionary pattern: The colonial government passed laws that limited hunting and created reserves. Although the laws may not have discriminated against black Zimbabweans, few understood the legislation, few had access to firearms, and most forms of trapping were declared illegal.[116]

Because Rhodesia was a settler colony more along the lines of Kenya than of Zambia, the opinion of the white farmers is key to understanding the extent of wildlife conservation in the colonial period – and that opinion, as in Kenya, was decidedly negative. Given the push for European settlement, the most important domestic issue in Rhodesia was land. Only 37 percent of land in the country receives more than the seven hundred millimeters of rain necessary for semi-intensive agriculture, and in most parts less than a third of this total is arable. Consequently, more than 75 percent of the country is subject to conditions that make nonirrigated agriculture very risky.[117] Although the efforts of British metropolitan interests like the Society for the Protection of the Fauna of the Empire and Rhodesian domestic hunters and conservationists succeeded in getting wildlife reserves established, these were few in number.

As the settler populations grew, the few game ordinances that existed were increasingly despised by white Rhodesians. A cheap landholders' permit allowed farmers to shoot as many animals on their land as they liked in order to "protect their livelihoods," but neither the meat nor skins of animals could be sold after Rhodesia became party to the International Convention for the Preservation of African Fauna and Flora in 1933.[118] Farmers complained about having to "farm in a zoo."[119] Ranchers lost significant numbers of domesticated animals to wild carnivores. Many also believed that game, as a host of the tsetse fly, was responsible for spreading sleeping sickness in cattle and humans and advocated the complete destruction of wild animals.[120] As a result, vociferous debate accompanied wildlife-related legislation, especially the creation of game reserves: "We must make up our minds whether we are going to keep this Colony as a game reserve or whether we are going to make it a Colony of white people."[121] Even the domestic proconservation lobby conceded that conservation should not encroach on agricultural priorities.[122] On balance, game preservation was subordinated to agricultural and ranching interests.

Resentment of the restrictions in the game ordinances was, of course, even greater among the black Africans of Rhodesia. The Land Apportionment Act of 1930 moved them off the best land in the high veld and onto land reserves much less suitable for cultivation. These lands were also more likely to host populations of wildlife, increasing the probability of human–animal interactions.[123] Africans found it more difficult to obtain permits and licenses for legal uses of wildlife. Even those killing crop–damaging animals for their white employers were harassed by game department staff.[124] And the instruments that African farmers might use to protect their own crops – snares, traps, nets, and others – were outlawed completely.

The trajectory of Rhodesia's wildlife policy, however, shifted away from the exclusionary model that Zambia and Kenya had followed. A Rhodesian High Court judge – who happened to be a leading figure in the hunters' association – ruled that the natural vegetation on a ranch could be considered private property, and that landowners could protect that vegetation by shooting wild animals that could eat it.[125] This effectively made all herbivores subject to elimination on private land. The Wildlife Conservation Act of 1960 allowed landowners to obtain permits to trade in wildlife.[126] Wildlife, once a cost to settlers, became valuable, and the wildlife utilization industry developed rapidly.[127] Wildlife populations outside parks and reserves began to recover quickly, indicating that white farmers had been killing a great deal of wildlife previously. The Department of National Parks and Wildlife Management (DNPWM) witnessed this growth of the private wildlife sector and subsequently wrote it into law: The 1975 Parks and Wildlife Act transferred effective control over wildlife on private lands from the central government to landowners. The act allowed the minister to give "appropriate authority" over wildlife to holders of private property. Like other colonial laws, the act benefited white commercial farmers and ranchers most: Africans in the communal land gained nothing from this momentous shift away from the preservationist concepts of the "King's Game." The DNPWM did mount an effort to gain the support of Africans by giving revenue and game meat from certain cropping operations to rural communities, but the policy ended largely in failure.[128]

Like the political milieu of Kenya, the land issue dominated Zimbabwe's independence period. In fact, many observers argue that the recovery of land lost to white settlers was a central reason why the guerrilla war in Zimbabwe was successful.[129] At the time of independence, half of Zimbabwe's best land was owned by a small group of white farmers.[130] To calm the fears of the landowning whites, a critical element of the war-ending Lancaster House agreement prevented government usurpation of private land for a period of ten years. Even with this constraint, each of the two leading African parties for the independence elections featured land resettlement schemes prominently.[131]

Although land was the most important substantive issue, independence politics still reflected the Africans' exclusion from the benefits of wildlife. Leaders of Zimbabwe's independence movements encouraged Africans to defy conservation laws as a means of protest against settler rule.[132] A wave of elephant poaching swept through Zimbabwe; game department staff attributed it not to the ivory trade but to political resistance.[133] Newly elected Zimbabwean parliamentarians voiced a general displeasure with wildlife conservation policies, especially those that seemed to favor white farmers (the twenty white MPs in the new parliament were much more likely to speak out for conservation than their black colleagues).[134] And the government moved to strip power from a white-dominated advisory board that had previously blocked public works projects in the name of conservation.

Despite the presence of wildlife conservation as an issue in the revolutionary and independence periods, policy itself did not change substantially. First, as in Zambia and Kenya, electoral institutions did not favor voting for parties based on policy differences. Although the system used in Zimbabwe's first independence elections – proportional representation with multimember districts – might favor such party differentiation, voters could not evaluate parties' legislative histories because no such record existed. By the second general election in 1985, Zimbabwe changed to a first-past-the-post system with single-member districts, an electoral system that does not encourage voters to distinguish parties by specific policy issues.[135] Because national parks and reserves generally were not located on the most desirable land, the cry for resettlement onto lands inside conservation areas was also not great at this time.[136] (Only 12 percent of Zimbabwe's area had been designated as a park or reserve – far less than the extent of Zambia's protected lands.)

Second, by allowing farmers to benefit from wildlife through the 1975 act, domestic conservationists and the DNPWM had gained powerful allies among some of the largest farmers in the country. Certain business interests also had footholds in the lucrative tourism industry based on wildlife. These groups wanted to maintain the significant revenue flows from tourism and wildlife utilization schemes and thus had no incentive to agitate for different wildlife policies.

Third, the central government benefited from its control of wildlife resources.[137] For example, even though the Wildlife Act favored white landowners, after independence this group was forced to apply for wild-life-related permits to the minister of a black government, who could then reward supporters and punish enemies by controlling access to wildlife. As in Zambia and Kenya, the newly independent government of Zimbabwe retained the power to distribute the benefits derived from the status quo policy. Given the immediate concern for land among black Zimbabweans, a relatively strong domestic lobby for the status quo policy, and the centralized power of wildlife held by the government, few politically important groups in postindependence Zimbabwe favored altering the colonially inspired policy.

CONCLUSION

President Kenneth Kaunda consistently advocated conservation as Zambia's leader.[138] Over the years, he told countless visitors about his own wildlife experiences; in one story, Kaunda described his home village, where, as a youth, he enjoyed the large trees and scores of animals that surrounded it. His father would often hunt duiker (a small antelope) "for the pot," without thought of the long-term consequences. But when Kaunda returned to the area years later, the president found the place "in ruins." The trees had been destroyed. No animals were left – not even the flocks of guinea fowl that had been so common before. Shocked by the environmental ruin, Kaunda became even more convinced of the need for strong wildlife conservation measures in Zambia.[139]

Wildlife in the Independence Period

In his first term as president, Kaunda translated this and other experiences into one of the most comprehensive wildlife conservation policies on the African continent. The 1968 National Parks and Wildlife Bill included far-reaching regulations on all aspects of the hunting and trading of wildlife and allowed for the establishment of a far-flung network of protected areas.

This chapter has highlighted how the political institutions of Zambia's, Kenya's, and Zimbabwe's independent republics allowed governments to maintain unpopular wildlife laws with little political cost. In Zambia, given UNIP's majority and the rules that fostered party discipline for parliamentarians and party identification for the electorate, the ruling party faced little observable opposition to the wildlife bill, despite the popular resistance to such restrictive measures that had been so prominent before independence. Similar patterns can be found in the early stages of the independence periods of Kenya and Zimbabwe.

The chapter has also demonstrated that wildlife was far from having "no political connotation whatsoever" in these countries, as white politicians in Zambia had tried to claim during this period. Establishing and maintaining extensive government control over the wildlife sector allowed each of the three independent governments to use such authority with discrimination. Wildlife resources became another source of goods that an incumbent party could distribute. In Zambia, for example, UNIP filled hundreds of jobs that it had created through the Department of Game and Fisheries, dispensed countless special licenses, and selectively enforced wildlife laws. As Chapter 3 will show, the political use of wildlife resources would intensify in Zambia's and Kenya's one-party states, as the relative value of wildlife products increased along with the need for sources of patronage.

The preceding analysis has presented evidence for the theory of institutional change outlined in Chapter 1. The political fight among civil servants, interest groups, and politicians over the control of wildlife policy illustrates that political actors in all three countries regarded the primary benefits of wildlife policy to be distributive goods, and not the collective good of conservation. The institutional context for each of these countries provided sets of incentives that influenced politicians' choices about wildlife policy. Under the electoral and party rules of the First Republic, Zambia's Kaunda was able to establish his most preferred policy. Parliamentarians, on the other hand, could not afford to support openly their constituents' desire to hunt and trade wild animals. The rules also protected UNIP candidates from electoral defeat, as party label motivated voter choice. Given the widespread disaffection for wildlife regulation in Zambia at this time, a set of institutions that rewarded position taking by politicians could be expected to change the country's wildlife policy, as we will see in Chapter 3, with the advent of a single-party "participatory" democracy.

The evidence from Kenya and Zimbabwe suggests dynamics and patterns similar to Zambia's. Contrary to the fears of the conservation establishment around the world, the newly independent governments did not dismantle colonial conservation policies, despite popular resentment against these laws.[140] Neither country sought to reverse the centralization of authority over wildlife. Neither degazetted parks and reserves. And neither sought to grant significantly greater access to wildlife resources to citizens. Control over wildlife presented new independent African governments with a valuable asset. And unlike Zambia's, Kenya's and Zimbabwe's wildlife sector produced enough income to generate some domestic support for the status quo policies, obviating the need for the explicit advocacy of any "strongman."

Electoral and political institutions did not facilitate domestic backlash against such policy. Few, poor, and scattered in the most remote regions of their countries, the rural dwellers who paid the highest costs of living with wildlife had little chance of collectively influencing policy. As in the colonial era, one way these Africans continued to express their discontent was through poaching. And as we will see in the next chapter, the decline of many African economies and the construction of one-party states in the 1970s and early 1980s motivated politicians and bureaucrats to join in the hunt.

3

The Political Logic of Poaching
in One-Party States

Mr. Speaker, when the registration of voters was taking place, I did not hear of any animal being asked to go and register as a voter; I heard the campaigners ask only human beings. Maybe the animals were asked in a different language.

The Honorable J. M. Kalenga, addressing the National
Assembly, 10 December 1982

The institutional environment of Zambia's First Republic did not last long. Threatened by the electoral gains of opposition parties, Kenneth Kaunda declared a one-party state in Zambia in 1972, concentrating power in the office of the president. Along with this dramatic change in political institutions, a fall in the price of copper significantly decreased the Zambian government's revenues in 1975. Subsequent government policies and a growing international demand for wildlife products increased wildlife's value for most Zambians, and a wave of poaching swept through the country.

Kaunda responded to the upsurge in poaching with a broad array of actions, including the introduction of stronger antipoaching legislation to the National Assembly. Unlike in Zambia's First Republic, however, President Kaunda faced active opposition to his wildlife policy during the early years of the Second Republic: Members of both the party and the government sabotaged his calls for stiffer penalties and broader regulation.

In this chapter, I explain how the incentives generated by the new political institutions encouraged politicians to oppose Kaunda's preferred wildlife policy. I argue that Zambia's one-party state's party and electoral rules tied parliamentarians and party officials more closely to their constituents than did the institutions of the country's multiparty First Republic. These rules and wildlife's increased value motivated politicians to fight Kaunda's proposals to augment wildlife conservation laws.

The fate of wildlife in Zambia from 1972 to 1982 also challenges some conventional wisdom about the politics of African one-party states. One-party presidents, despite their extensive constitutional powers, do not always achieve their policy preferences. One-party parliaments are not always moribund. One-party parliamentarians can represent their constituents on some issues. And one-party elections can make a difference in the composition of national assemblies and the behavior of their members. In Zambia's Second Republic, institutions created incentives that induced politicians to resist the power of a one-party president.

Political institutions also affected poaching rates in Kenya and Zimbabwe. A domestic economic crisis in Kenya had starved the patronage system of the one-party state; wildlife became a valuable good in efforts to maintain patron–client relations. During the same period, Robert Mugabe and his party had not constructed such an extensive patronage system. Countervailing domestic institutions also helped to prevent the complete centralization of power. These factors, along with a relatively stronger economy, produced better conservation outcomes.

This chapter begins by exploring how the institutions of the one-party state in Zambia combined with a declining economic environment to generate a widespread shadow market in wildlife. Not even Kaunda's vast new powers could restrain increases in illegal hunting. These changes also affected political competition over wildlife policy and decreased the ruling party's interest in favoring conservation. The new incentives motivated Zambian parliamentarians to oppose publicly proposed legislation intended to combat poaching increases. The chapter concludes by comparing Zambia's experience with that in Kenya and Zimbabwe and discusses how incentive structures faced by politicians in these three countries affected their behavior and policy outcomes.

ZAMBIA'S ONE-PARTY STATE

Political Institutions

The United National Independence party government entered the 1970s flush with revenue generated by the highest copper prices in Zambia's history.[1] Despite such fortune, electoral losses to the African National Congress (ANC) and United Progressive Party (UPP) in the 1968 elections threatened the political hold of the ruling party. To prevent the further erosion of its support, UNIP banned all formal opposition: President Kaunda announced the establishment of a one-party state on 25 February 1972.[2]

Both the 1973 Republic of Zambia and UNIP constitutions further concentrated power in the ruling party generally, and in the president specifically. Party structures were supreme over their counterpart government bodies, so that the secretary general of the party outranked the prime minister.[3] As the cabinet managed the daily affairs of government, the Central Committee (the executive committee of the party) deliberated and adopted policies before sending them on to the cabinet for implementation. Government bureaucracies could advocate policy positions, but the Central Committee possessed the authority to make national policy.[4]

As head of both state and party, the president dominated national politics more than ever. His constitutional powers included the appointment of the secretary general of the party and the prime minister. The president chaired and nominated members to the Central Committee and appointed all cabinet ministers and district governors, the key party officials at the district level. The president became the chairman of the Zambia Industrial and Mining Corporation (ZIMCO), the state holding company, and thus selected a large number of senior management and board members in the parastatal sector.[5] Finally, the president had the right to detain any person without trial under the Preservation of Public Security Act. When exercising any function conferred upon him by the constitution, the president "was not obliged to follow the advice tendered by any other person or authority."[6]

Zambia's single-party system allowed for only one candidate to stand for the office of president during general elections. The candidate, to be chosen by the UNIP's General Conference, had to receive the majority of votes cast. The constitution imposed no term limits.

Under the one-party state, parliamentarians elected from single-member districts expanded from 105 to 125, with the president allowed to appoint another 10 members. Candidates also had to pass through primary elections before running for parliament. To contest primaries, candidates had to be members of UNIP and had to pay a refundable deposit and obtain signatures from nine registered voters. An electoral college consisting of all party officials at regional, constituency, and branch levels in the parliamentary constituency voted during primaries. The electoral college then forwarded the three candidates with the highest votes to the Central Committee for confirmation or rejection for the general election.[7] If the Central Committee removed a candidate, the next highest vote getter took his place.[8] For general elections, the party-approved candidates paid a nonrefundable fee and gathered the signatures of another nine registered voters in their constituency. The local district governor and party officials had the responsibility for conducting the campaigns of all three candidates.

The National Politics of Wildlife Policy

Policy Making in the One-Party State

The centralization of power in the office of president made Kaunda by far the preeminent policymaker in Zambia. His addresses to UNIP General Conferences, National Council, and Central Committee meetings, as well as his various announcements from State House, included major and minor policy decisions. Government and party officials generally accepted these statements as policy directives.

Most scholars model Zambian decision making during the Second Republic as a process in which other groups merely reacted to the decisions reached by Kaunda and a small coterie of advisers.[9] The president appeared unwilling or unable to delegate authority, discouraged independent actions by reversing decisions made by others, and used his considerable arsenal of patronage to reward compliance with his decrees.[10] Those politicians seeking to rise to the top of the party "did best by striving to emulate the preferences of its leader."[11]

Scholars generally find the Zambian National Assembly had comparatively little influence over policy, because UNIP held credible threats over the political careers of current and aspiring parliamentarians. Local UNIP officials ran campaigns, the Central Committee vetted dissenting parliamentarians, and party officials decided on the distribution of government largesse. Most research also asserts that although some parliamentarians occasionally used their seats to express displeasure at government schemes, members did not "change the content or direction of government policy."[12] Scholars consider the Zambian National Assembly, like other one-party state legislatures, during this period as "residual" to the policy making process.[13]

THE DEMISE OF THE ZAMBIAN ECONOMY AND THE RISE OF POACHING

Although Kaunda and UNIP solidified their political power by creating a one-party system of government, the country lost a great deal of economic strength when the market for copper crashed in 1975. This crash also made Zambians relatively poorer, motivating many to enter the growing market in wildlife products. The National Parks and Wildlife Service (NPWS) could not stem the subsequent increase in illegal hunting: It had suffered some of the most severe budget cuts made by the UNIP government. Consequently, the benefits of wildlife were distributed widely in Zambia.

Poaching in One-Party States

Zambia's Economic Decline

At the time of independence in 1964, Zambia boasted one of the highest per capita gross national products in Africa. The Zambian government's ability to finance its ambitious industrial, agricultural, and social spending outlined in the First and Second National Development Plans depended mainly on the receipts from only one source: copper. From 1970 to 1975 copper accounted for an average of nearly 30 percent of the country's gross domestic product (GDP) and 40 percent of government revenue. Together with cobalt, copper represented over 90 percent of the country's export earnings.[14]

The plunge of world copper prices in 1975 undermined the government's ambitious developmental goals. Copper lost 40 percent of its value, its terms of trade fell by 50 percent, and its contribution to Zambia's GDP fell to 13 percent the same year.[15] Copper prices never fully recovered, confining real GDP growth to an average of 0.3 percent from 1974 to 1985.

In an effort to stave off declines in consumption levels, the government curbed its expenditures and accumulated debt.[16] The latter action led to inflation: Zambia's annual rate of inflation averaged 17.3 percent from 1975 to 1985, and reached 37 percent by 1985 compared with only 6 percent from 1964 to 1974.[17]

The economic crisis caused by the decline of copper prices reverberated throughout Zambia's economy. While copper production shrank to an average −2.7 percent growth rate during 1975–84, the agricultural sector also staggered, as a result of the combination of drought and government policies that favored urban consumers over rural producers.[18] The UNIP government decreased producer prices for maize, which had previously accounted for over 70 percent of marketed agricultural production in Zambia. Maize production fell to an average of 50 percent from 1975 to 1984.[19] Evidently, the price offered by the government fell below the market clearing price, as surveys made during this period indicate many rural households quit producing for the market.

These policies played havoc with rural incomes. Jansen estimates that smallholder incomes dropped 58 percent per year from 1974 to 1983.[20] The terms of trade for rural residents also fell precipitously in 1979: bartered fish and charcoal received only 70 percent of the goods received seven years earlier.[21]

Urban incomes also declined, despite the positive effect of maize meal subsidies on urban consumers. Formal employment declined 2.4 percent from 1975 to 1980, despite a 40 percent increase in the urban population.[22] High income urban residents averaged income losses of 13.2 percent from 1975 to 1985. Poorer urban residents' faced income declines ranging from 1.6 to 2.1 percent for the same period.[23] Civil service workers, who represented approximately two-thirds of all formal sector employment, saw prices outrace government wage increases.[24]

Nearly all Zambians experienced income losses during this period; many individuals chose to supplement their income by hunting wildlife.

The Rise of the Wildlife Market

Almost simultaneously with the collapse of Zambia's domestic economy, several international forces combined to foster a thriving trade in wildlife products. The flush of petrodollars from the Organization of Petroleum Exporting Countries' (OPEC) successful cartel and increasing incomes in some Asian countries stimulated demand for animal products, especially elephant ivory and rhinoceros horn.[25] Decreased incomes within Zambia also stimulated the domestic market in game meat. As a result, hunting activity in Zambia expanded quickly.

Ivory prices dramatically increased beginning in the early 1970s, multiplying sixfold by the late 1980s.[26] In response, hunters killed 75 percent of Zambia's elephants from the late 1960s through 1989.[27] In Zambia's Luangwa Valley alone, poachers shot an estimated 40 percent of the elephants from 1972 to 1979.[28] Others calculate a 60 percent fall for the period 1975–1986.[29] Whereas Zambia exported $10 million worth of legally documented ivory from 1979 to 1988, nearly $172.8 million left illegally.[30]

Strong international demand ignited a similar explosion in the prices, trade, and hunting for rhinoceros horn, except that the price for rhino horn exceeded that of ivory by a factor of 10.[31] Zambia experienced some of the heaviest rhino poaching on the continent.[32] Robinson estimates that 50,000 black rhinos lived in the Luangwa Valley in 1972.[33] The horn size of rhino noticeably decreased in 1978, and NPWS reduced the hunting quota for the species. By 1981, only two thousand rhino were left in the valley.[34] Tourists still saw rhino as late as early 1984, but probably fewer than a dozen, if any, were alive by 1992.[35]

Zambia's economic decline also stimulated a market for game meat, a significant part of many Zambians' diets, especially in rural areas.[36] After 1975 hunters seeking game meat killed species such as buffalo, hippopotamus, lechwe, warthog, and impala in unprecedented numbers.[37]

The Response of the National Parks and Wildlife Service

The escalating relative value of wildlife products like ivory, rhino horn, and game meat made poaching an attractive activity to Zambians. After 1975, because of the enormous cuts in the budget of the National Parks and Wildlife Service (NPWS), poaching became a less risky strategy as well. NPWS never possessed the manpower or the finances to enforce Zambia's wildlife laws; in the mid-1970s, it had drastically decreased resources.[38]

The NPWS budget suffered some of the largest reductions of any government department after the 1975 copper shock.[39] While the government's total expenditures fell an average of 6.7 percent from 1975 to 1978, NPWS's dropped by an average of 23 percent each year.[40] The NPWS portion of total government expenditure from 1970 to 1974 averaged nearly 0.5 percent. In the period 1975 to 1982, its share dropped to an average of 0.2 percent; it never subsequently exceeded 0.3 percent.

As discussed in the last chapter, NPWS had enjoyed strong budgetary support from the UNIP government in the period following independence. It had hired hundreds of general laborers for capital projects, operated a fleet of five aircraft, sponsored internationally renowned scientific research, and experimented with programs designed to demonstrate the possible economic returns of wildlife. Although department officers believed poaching continued after independence, they hoped that despite the "basic motives of human nature" and the incessant conflict between agriculture and wildlife, the department could bring most forms of poaching under control.[41] In 1973 the North Luangwa National Park, soon to be a favorite hunting ground of elephant poachers, contained the country's highest density of elephant.[42]

The collapse of copper prices and government revenues resulted in the withering of NPWS operations after 1975. In 1977 NPWS cut 30 percent of its general labor force and did not start any major capital projects. The department did not initiate any major scientific projects that year, mustering resources for just one animal count. Only the contributions of the Wildlife Conservation Society of Zambia, the safari companies, and the Honorary Rangers sustained antipoaching efforts. Without this support, the NPWS director believed, it would have been "impossible to deal with" the increased poaching.[43]

In 1978, the Ministry of Finance refused to release appropriated monies to the NPWS capital account, reducing this budget, already cut by 38 percent in real terms from the year before, a further 50 percent.[44] In response, the department suspended most of its capital projects.

Activities funded by the recurrent budget also deteriorated. The number of antipoaching patrols declined because NPWS could not pay the Civil Service Commission's mandated subsistence allowance for scouts on patrol.[45] Only one aircraft operated at this time, down from the five used in 1974, and its flying hours were almost eliminated. The department also suspended staff attendance at international conferences.

The National Politics of Wildlife Policy

Interest groups and businesses stepped in to help fund NPWS. The Honorary Rangers, a newly formed nongovernmental organization called Save the Rhino Trust (SRT), and safari companies became important financiers of antipoaching operations. The contributions promised by SRT to the department augmented the official budget by nearly 14 percent.[46] Circuit Holdings, a subsidiary of Zambia Consolidated Copper Mines (ZCCM), supported NPWS patrols near the ZCCM-owned resorts at Kasaba Bay and Nkamba Bay.[47] But despite this injection of monies, the department continued its decline: Unable to maintain its only helicopter, NPWS returned it to the Wildlife Conservation Society of Zambia (WCSZ). Critically short of funds, the department eventually encouraged safari companies to provide it with vehicles in exchange for hunting concessions. In fact, NPWS wielded so little clout that when it finally received an allocation of eight vehicles, Zambian security forces confiscated four of them for their own use.[48]

Although reductions in expenditures affected all departmental activities, those requiring relatively more expensive items such as fuel, vehicles, firearms, and ammunition – the material heart of enforcement operations – were hardest hit.[49] Countries that successfully protect their wildlife spend approximately one hundred dollars per square kilometer on enforcement; some conservationists believe four hundred dollars per square kilometer is necessary to save rhino from poachers. In 1983, Zambia spent four dollars per square kilometer and had a field presence of about one poorly equipped scout for every 350 square kilometers of protected territory.[50]

The NPWS implemented new policies it hoped could meet the growing crisis without great financial cost. The NPWS directorate, for example, established a Prosecutions Unit within the department in 1979 to overcome the ineffective investigations and weak prosecution record of the Zambian police in matters concerning wildlife. Although this led to a few more convictions, the increase did little to affect the extent of hunting.

The New Distribution of Wildlife's Benefits

The heterogeneity of poachers in Zambia spread the benefits of wildlife resources widely. The increasing relative value of wildlife encouraged a wide cross section of Zambian citizens to participate in the market, including rural and urban residents, chiefs, business owners, police and military personnel, NPWS staff, and politicians.

Economic shocks and government policies greatly increased the incentives for rural residents to hunt. Government pricing policies resulted in declining returns from agriculture. Government had cut jobs and services in the rural areas after the copper crash. With fewer opportunities to earn income, rural residents found that petty trade in game meat and the benefits of alliances with ivory and rhino horn poachers offered ways to augment a household's income.[51] Some villagers expanded their hunting, made easier by the decline of NPWS enforcement; others routinely covered up commercial poachers' activities in return for meat or consumer products like flour, sugar, salt, cooking oil, and cloth.

Chiefs in rural areas also increased their hunting activities and collaboration with poachers. The traditional rulers benefited from their residual power over resources in the area, power enhanced by a decline in wildlife policy enforcement. A chief often settled for little in exchange for his permission to hunt and the help of his assistants, sometimes just a case of beer and a leg of buffalo.[52]

Urban residents enjoyed the growing market for game meat. Government economic policies had discouraged or redirected a great deal of economic activity in urban areas: Currency controls hurt businesses producing for the export market, inflation induced investment in enterprises with short-term production cycles, and formal sector employment stagnated under government fiscal and monetary policy. The low costs of hunting and the strong demand for game meat in the cities, as well as ivory and rhino horn in the international market, made poaching a profitable response to Zambia's economic environment.[53] And it was relatively easy for someone in Lusaka to buy a hunting license from NPWS headquarters in Chilanga (a fifteen minute drive). Hunting quickly became a valuable addition to the portfolio of many urban-based business owners after 1975.[54]

Members of the Zambian military and police units, also suffering from income declines, possessed the weapons and authority to support a great deal of illegal hunting activity. A 1980 report by the Wildlife Conservation Society of Zambia found well-documented incidents of army personnel setting up roadblocks at game park entrances. Later, army vehicles drove away, laden with meat and tusks.[55] Even if not directly poaching, soldiers and police regularly allowed other Zambians to borrow, rent, or purchase their official weapons, transport, or ammunition.[56]

Some Zambian politicians also exploited wildlife resources. Politicians hunted for economic profit, sport, distribution of favors, and their own consumption of game meat. The evidence available suggests a pattern of political involvement: Officials made regular trips to their regions to hunt without licenses, ministers demanded licenses in excess of NPWS quotas, and district governors roamed game management areas in search of buffalo.[57] Politicians implicated for wildlife illegalities include a secretary general of UNIP, district governors, parliamentarians, ministers of state, provincial members of UNIP's Central Committee, party officials, and members of the Office of the President. A member of the National Assembly told colleagues that when government officials visited to his constituency, it "turned into a hunting camp."[58]

Staff of the National Parks and Wildlife Service sat at the center of poaching controversies. Economic decline reduced scouts' incomes, and other perquisites of a government job – like housing – were sometimes never allocated. The government might pay salaries months late. NPWS budget cuts had reduced the number of hours spent by supervisory staff in the field. These difficulties resulted in an ineffective NPWS with little control over its own employees. Villagers, chiefs, other civil servants, safari hunters, government ministers, and conservationists all decried the quantity of illegal hunting done by NPWS scouts and the trafficking in illegal trophies by NPWS officers. The department carried out few actual arrests against its own staff from 1973 to 1983.[59]

THE POLITICS OF WILDLIFE IN THE SECOND REPUBLIC

International demand and domestic economic catastrophe helped create a strong market in wildlife products. A wide variety of Zambians benefited from the new market. Budget cuts had left the NPWS weak, disorganized, and unable to cope with escalating poaching activities.

Members of the UNIP government and the National Assembly knew about the alarming increases in illegal hunting; some even participated. Their political responses to this crisis were far different from those in the multiparty First Republic. The institutional incentives of the one-party state induced politicians to sabotage Kaunda's policies designed to resolve the upsurge in poaching.

The Structure of Competition over Wildlife Policy

While the demands of a stagnant economy absorbed most of the president's attention after 1973, Kaunda's strong support of wildlife conservation and his newly expanded political powers led him to pursue numerous strategies to curb the growing poaching crisis.

Despite his belief that businessmen from Senegal and Mali had instigated the serious poaching in Zambia, reports from newspapers and NPWS officers convinced Kaunda that many members of his own party and government participated in the wildlife market. In an effort to end their clandestine activities, he "talked a great deal about these issues" with members of the Central Committee, the cabinet, and the security forces. Eventually, he put a "blanket stop" on all hunting, legal or otherwise, by members of the Central Committee.[60]

The president's exasperation with the extent of illegal hunting grew to the point where he issued circulars in 1978 threatening to dismiss anyone in the civil service or the party who were caught poaching. Many politicians thought the policy was unconstitutional, but nobody initiated a legal challenge. Even NPWS officers disagreed with the circular, believing that the individuals accused would be able to win easily in court.[61]

Kaunda became increasingly disenchanted with the effectiveness of NPWS and sought various ways to circumvent the agency. Representatives of nongovernmental organizations such as the World Wildlife Fund and the Wildlife Conservation Society of Zambia as well as international donors had no difficulty in getting appointments with the president to talk over conservation projects at State House.[62] The president publicly supported the extensive efforts of Save the Rhino Trust (SRT), whose members supplied and directed intensive antipoaching operations near two national parks using NPWS scouts beginning in 1979.[63]

A significant result of this open-door policy was that conservationists persuaded Kaunda to back a policy that would establish a new government agency designed specifically to investigate wildlife–related offenses. Ministers, SRT staff, prominent conservationists, and safari operators met with the president several times in 1982 to discuss the design and powers of the new agency, suggesting that it follow the structure of the Special Investigative Team into Economy and Trade (SITET), a unit set up during the 1970s to investigate currency and trade between Zambian and Rhodesian companies and answerable only to President Kaunda.

Kaunda used his authority over state-owned industry to bypass the "cheaters" at NPWS, instructing Zambia Consolidated Copper Mines (ZCCM) to get into the business of tourism and wildlife "because they are effective and get things done."[64] Kaunda's directive eventually led to a ZCCM-owned safari business, ZCCM-sponsored antipoaching patrols, and ZCCM purchase of tourist resorts at Nkamba and Kasaba bays. Using his constitutional powers to alter the boundaries of national parks, Kaunda even degazetted part of Sumbu National Park to facilitate ZCCM's development plans for Kasaba Bay.[65]

The president, as commander in chief of Zambia's armed forces, also directed the military to participate in two extensive antipoaching operations. The largest military intervention occurred in 1981, when hundreds of Zambian army troops, supported by dozens of military vehicles and three helicopters, made a wide sweep through villages in the Luangwa Valley to make arrests and confiscate weapons and wildlife products.[66]

Kaunda did not give up entirely on his own government's bureaucracy: In an effort to strengthen wildlife legislation and its enforcement, he appointed individuals with legal experience to head the Ministry of Lands and National Resources in the early 1980s. Fitzpatrick Chuula, the former attorney general, pushed hard for additional legislation that would increase the punishments for poaching offenses. And, unlike his predecessor, he successfully introduced such an amendment to the floor of the National Assembly. The next minister selected by Kaunda, Fabiano Chela, a former police inspector general, enjoyed a reputation for cleaning up corrupt government agencies.[67]

Despite his expanded constitutional powers and patronage resources, the president's actions had little effect on the wildlife crisis. Any policy advocated by Kaunda still depended on the support of the party and its government for effective implementation. But wildlife conservation benefited few in either bureaucracy. Rather than promoting conservation, government and party members used wildlife to augment their systems of patronage.

Interest groups likely to support stronger wildlife conservation policy did not include Zambia's urban residents, the new core of UNIP supporters. The Wildlife Conservation Society of Zambia's adult membership was almost entirely European and consisted of commercial farmers and businessmen, precisely those groups whom the party had fought during independence.[68] As in the First Republic, the suspicion and hostility continued as European commercial farmers frequently contested the UNIP government's agricultural policy. Such distrust grew during the Second Republic: UNIP perceived European farmers as unrestrained profiteers seeking to undermine the goals of the one-party state; European farmers, in contrast, perceived a progressively interventionist state – a state in which they had no official representation – manipulating the prices of agricultural inputs and production to hurt their economic interests. Such an adversarial relationship did little to further the party's interest in the European farmers' concerns, including wildlife conservation.[69]

Other groups with strong interests in conservation included the growing number of individuals associated with businesses connected to wildlife, such as lodge owners, professional hunters, and game area concession holders. Like the commercial farmers, these groups were numerically small and predominately non-African. The criticism of these non-African business owners as profiteers only increased after the UNIP government began currency controls in the late 1970s.[70] Because tourism relied almost exclusively on wild animals and was one of the few industries that dealt directly in foreign exchange, businessmen scrambled to obtain companies related to wildlife. The competition over access to tourism and hunting enterprises intensified when the government allowed companies to retain half of the foreign exchange they earned from 1983. Many NPWS and ministry staff believed the owners of wildlife-related companies consistently defrauded the government by under-reporting the foreign exchange earned and overcharging tourists and hunters.[71] Government and party members resented the activities of these groups.[72] Because their membership was non-African, many Zambians believed conservationists wanted to continue the colonial agenda of removing Africans from control over wildlife.[73]

Adding to this stew of antagonism was the NPWS perception that Zambia's Europeans believed the department to be an incompetent manager of wildlife resources. Rumors of President Kaunda's search for a European director of NPWS and a promise from conservationist groups to pay his salary if selected increased the bitterness of Zambian bureaucrats and party members toward the domestic conservation movement.[74]

On an individual level, party and government personnel gained little from conservation policy. It was unpopular: With the increase of wildlife's relative value, Zambians were even more antagonistic toward policies that excluded them from these resources; an increasing number believed the only beneficiaries of conservation were European tourists.[75] And its legal benefits were costly: Few Zambians could afford the prices for legal safari hunting or vacations in tourist lodges.

Party and government members did, however, increase their use of the more valuable resource to reward their friends and supporters. Examples are legion: The minister of lands and natural resources, completely disregarding the quotas established by his civil servants in NPWS, distributed licenses to fellow ministers and other politically powerful individuals; the minister dominated the committee that decided who received concessions for increasingly valuable hunting blocks. While NPWS pushed the criterion of sound game management, the common factor of most recipients of hunting areas was strong party support or friendships with powerful politicians; the minister gave certain chiefs permission to hunt one elephant a year as a gift of UNIP; wildlife scouts looked the other way when politicians entered hunting areas without licenses; government and party officials handed out game meat after returning from illegal hunts; and local party functionaries expected NPWS staff to supply political rallies with game meat.[76]

Kaunda's Growing Principal–Agent Problem

Kaunda's formal and informal powers could not overcome his party and government's aversion to conservation policy; the institutions of the one-party state and the economic environment exacerbated the principal–agent dilemma he faced.

Even greater shirking and slippage characterized the implementation of Zambian wildlife policy in the Second Republic than in the First.[77] Kaunda favored stronger conservation measures. Party and government members preferred using the increasingly valuable wildlife as a commodity for patronage and were individually rewarded by a weaker policy. Given the divergent preferences of Kaunda and his followers, combined with the lack of a powerful domestic conservation lobby, party members and bureaucrats failed to devote much energy to, and actively frustrated, attempts by conservation groups and Kaunda to strengthen wildlife policy. Kaunda's measures to mitigate these principal–agent problems were insufficient. The UNIP government was able to cut the NPWS budget without antagonizing the party's core constituents, urban dwellers.[78] Wildlife conservation never made the final drafts of UNIP policy documents, let alone the government's series of five-year development plans. Kaunda's circulars led to the dismissal of only two civil servants.[79] The government never fully supported the European-led SRT operations.[80] Ministers, senior police officers, and party officials successfully waylaid the proposed independent wildlife investigative agency. Military support for antipoaching operations was intermittent and surrounded by suspicions that soldiers notified their poaching friends before sweeps began.[81] The director of public prosecutions dropped ivory cases against "top leaders."[82] And ZCCM's efforts focused more on development of tourism than on wildlife management. The increased relative value of wildlife, and the premium placed on items needed to sustain patronage under a one-party state during troubled economic times, led party and government members to use wildlife according to the logic of distributive politics.[83]

The Response of Parliament

Even parliamentarians fought against attempts to augment conservation policy. Despite the loss of its policy making power and the centralization of control over parliamentarians' political careers, the incentives created by the political institutions of the one-party state encouraged National Assembly members to risk opposing the wildlife policy agenda of the most powerful politician in the country – Kaunda.

Given the government's dominant position in Zambia's economy, election to parliament offered the possibility of substantial economic and political gains to the individual member. The new rules of Zambia's one-party participatory democracy removed opposition parties from politics but did not eliminate the benefits of and thus competition for National Assembly seats. In fact, the reforms allowed for increased political participation at both the local and national levels. An increase in the number of constituencies meant the possibility of more candidates and better representation of local interests. The removal of rival political parties led to an increase in the number of districts with more than one candidate.[84]

(Previously, opposition parties would either decide not to run in regions of UNIP dominance or be prevented from doing so.) And more people ran for each office.[85]

The electoral rules also created a new constellation of relationships between local party officials and parliamentary candidates. During the multiparty First Republic, the national party executive would choose candidates and sponsor campaigns. The one-party Second Republic, in contrast, gave local officials the power to choose three candidates in primary voting and then run their campaigns during the general elections. Local officials used their resources and personal influence to support certain individuals' campaigns, and they also solicited votes from other members of the electoral college during primaries. Such activities could enhance or sabotage candidacies, as individuals running without the backing of the local party machine stood no chance of being selected to take part in the general election. As a result, candidates frequently used bribes to secure nominations, and local officials expected the favors to continue after elections. Eventually, electoral malpractice became so widespread under the primary system that President Kaunda himself publicly complained about the "sinful" practice of bribe taking by local party functionaries.[86]

The more competitive general elections also tied candidates to local voters in new ways. Because each candidate at this stage had been approved by the Central Committee as a UNIP party loyalist, candidates had to differentiate themselves from their opponents along other dimensions, such as constituency service. Citizens began to expect that their member of parliament should be from, and aware of problems in, their area. Any candidate who did not understand the new constituency logic of the Second Republic could expect cries such as "Tabumoneka!" (We have not seen you [here]!) during campaigning and a loss at the polls.[87] Voters wanted a share of the benefits that went along with a seat in the National Assembly. In the words of a local, "Why should we vote for you? You will go off to Lusaka and make money. We will be left here, same as before."[88] As in other one-party multiple candidate systems in Africa (e.g., Kenya and Tanzania), constituents frequently voted out parliamentarians who failed to deliver local benefits, unlike the politics of the multiparty First Republic.[89]

New rules in the National Assembly also reinforced the logic of constituency service. The Chona Commission, appointed to report on the changes necessary to implement a one-party state, recommended that MPs should be able to speak and vote on any issue introduced to the National Assembly; the government agreed to this measure.[90] MPs began to articulate local needs and criticize the implementation of government policy. Some UNIP officials decried the new trend of criticism, and

President Kaunda pushed to install the party's own disciplinary rules as part of Parliament's Standing Order. Members, however, continued the practice of questioning government.[91] Sometimes, even front-benchers maligned government policy.[92]

Such public activity may not have influenced the average voter; it is unlikely that many citizens bothered reading the transcripts of parliamentary debates. Testimony about parliamentarians' behavior did, however, reach the ears of local party officials, who were now responsible for candidate selection and campaigns. These officials acted against MPs who failed to articulate and meet local needs: Local party officials ousted twelve incumbent MPs during the 1978 primaries.

The new political logic of the one-party state made wildlife a salient issue for parliamentarians. Wildlife laws restricted access to a wide cross section of people over most of Zambia. Of the Second Republic's 125 total constituencies, 27 included national parks, where hunting is prohibited. Forty-six had game management areas within their areas, where hunting is very restricted. Over half (64) of Zambia's constituencies included or abutted a national park or a game management area. People had always cared about access to wildlife; institutions now motivated them to direct their concerns to their elected representatives.[93]

As previously discussed, most Zambians, especially rural residents, detest wildlife laws. Citizens feel they possess a right to hunt and believe that foreign safari hunters and not "hunting for the pot" endangers wildlife populations. Villagers also express a strong dislike for NPWS staff who interfere with their hunting practices.[94] The collapse of Zambia's economy and its resultant impact on incomes exacerbated the demands of citizens for wildlife resources.

Parliamentarians visiting or campaigning in their constituencies faced numerous complaints regarding wildlife policy.[95] Villagers griped about the few and costly hunting licenses, overzealous wildlife scouts, and lack of alternative sources of protein in their regions.[96] Some rural citizens thought the drop in animal populations resulted from a movement of wildlife to national parks, and not poaching. (In fact, villagers demanded access to these fugitive animals as well.) Family members often pleaded the cases of relatives jailed for violating wildlife laws. Urban constituents protested the high prices for licenses and beef and urged parliamentarians to legalize the trade in game meat. Such complaints were not new.[97] But, as a result of one-party political institutions, these grievances meant more to members of the National Assembly, who now needed local support.[98]

In addition to constituents, parliamentarians felt pressure from the rural and urban elite who had taken advantage of the burgeoning wildlife market. Those individuals involved in commercial meat, rhino horn, or ivory enterprises could be valuable friends or powerful enemies. Even influential Zambians wanting to sport hunt without infringement made their case to their politicians. "Every (National Assembly) member had at least one friend" pressing for low penalties and greater access to wildlife.[99] Consequently, both constituency service and patronage politics conspired against wildlife conservation.

THE CASE OF THE 1982 AMENDMENT

The parliamentary debate over the 1982 Amendment to the National Parks and Wildlife Act offers strong support for the hypothesis that Zambian parliamentarians, acutely aware of their new economic and political institutional environment, acted to protect their political interests at the expense of the collective outcome of better wildlife conservation.

From 1975 to 1982 NPWS made three attempts to get the National Assembly to pass amendments to the National Parks and Wildlife Act of 1971 that would boost the punishments for poachers.[100] With President Kaunda's backing, one proposal finally made it to the National Assembly.

As described in Chapter 2, the 1971 Wildlife Act centralized authority over Zambia's wildlife resources.[101] The president enjoyed absolute ownership of wildlife on behalf of the citizens and could declare or void game management areas. The minister in whose portfolio NPWS fell could, among other powers, regulate hunting licenses and fees, prohibit the hunting of certain animals, and restrict certain activities (e.g., vehicle traffic, setting of fires, fishing) within national parks.[102] The director of national parks administered the day-to-day operations of NPWS and advised the minister on the legal changes NPWS staff thought necessary to improve wildlife conservation.

The minister of lands and natural resources used his powers to issue a number of statutory instruments during this period, covering subjects such as hunting licenses and fees, prohibitions from certain areas, and safari and camping fees. The minister could also influence hunting quotas, which were composed as an internal document of the ministry and the department.

But the crucial act of changing the penalties associated with violating wildlife laws required the National Assembly to pass a law. Mr. Mwananshiku, the minister of lands and natural resources, presented such a bill in August 1982, the only NPWS effort to stiffen poaching penalties that made it to the National Assembly.[103] Emphasizing how the party and its government supported wildlife conservation, and noting the rapid increase in illegal hunting and deplorable state of the underfunded yet hard-working NPWS, Minister Mwananshiku outlined the plan of the National Parks and Wildlife Bill Amendment of 1982 to increase poaching punishments. At that time, Capital Law 316 stipulated that individuals convicted of poaching elephants and rhino could opt to pay a fine, and most did because the amount was insignificant; individuals caught hunting in national parks could pay a fine or face a maximum five years in prison. At the heart of the new bill were three clauses: Clause 6 proposed that anyone convicted of hunting, wounding, or molesting elephants or rhinos would be sentenced to jail for fifteen years without option of fine.[104] Clause 7 proposed that anyone caught hunting illegally in a national park be subject to a sentence of no longer than ten years in jail without option of fine. And Clause 9 was intended to force the court to confiscate all the weapons and trophies of the convicted.

A two-sided debate over the bill emerged. Front-benchers (ministers, ministers of state, and district governors), all dependent upon President Kaunda for their positions, asserted that the amendment would protect wildlife resources for future generations, help NPWS with its fight against poachers, save the animals necessary to spark a more lucrative tourism industry, and prevent the extinction of elephant and rhinoceros. In other words, those members who had been appointed as government officials supported a conservation view closely aligned with that of President Kaunda, but that ignored the interests of most rural and urban residents. Backbenchers, on the other hand, passionately condemned the amendment. If passed, the bill, which "must have been designed by expatriates," would "protect the animals at the expense of the people," "protect animals so that only people from developed countries can see them," turn Zambia from "man-centered to animal-centered," "prosecute traditional practices," and reduce Zambians to "subhuman beings."[105] Amazed at the avalanche of dissent, the speaker of the National Assembly exclaimed, "The whole House wants to speak!"[106]

Members of the National Assembly themselves recognized the political incentives that separated front-benchers and backbenchers.[107] The backbencher L. B. Hantuba alluded to the fact that the front bench district governors present should have been attending another meeting but had flown in to Lusaka "to come and defend the animals."[108] W. H. Banda launched a direct attack on the sympathies of Kaunda's appointees:

If the House is going to allow this law to pass in its present form, Sir, it will be the most unfair law to be adopted by this August House. I am appealing, Mr. Speaker, particularly to the Members of Parliament who are District Governors and Ministers of State. I know that they are ready for other promotions but they should not use this proposed Bill as a means of influencing the appointing authority for promotion.[109]

Members understood front-benchers' conflicting incentives.[110] Speaking out for the amendment might have pleased Kaunda, but hurt an individual's electoral chances. The best strategy for some was silence in the National Assembly, "quietly praying that the Bill is defeated."[111] Backbenchers exposed ministers who whispered that "once this Bill goes through Parliament, half" of their constituents "will die in prison."[112] Most Kaunda appointees chose neither to oppose nor to support the amendment during debate. Only six front-benchers spoke for the bill, less than a tenth of their total numbers in the National Assembly.

Backbenchers made clear the link between wildlife and elections in three ways. First, dissent focused primarily on the potential effects of the bill on constituents, not on the collective goods it might produce, such as conservation and tourism receipts. Parliamentarians expressed concern about "punishing those who put us in power," and felt the bill would "humiliate innocent people" as well as jeopardize citizens' access to wildlife.[113]

Second, backbenchers pointed to the shadow of the upcoming 1983 elections. W. H. Banda expressed concern about the effect of the 1981 military antipoaching operation in his area on elections: "Parliamentary elections are very near. Indeed this incident . . . early created dissension in Malambo Constituency and other areas. Some people even threatened not to take part in the elections and declared that animals would vote instead."[114] Harking back to the statements made by the ANC leader, Harry Nkumbula, against the original National Parks and Wildlife Bill, L. B. Hantuba claimed that political songs "have already been composed in various districts that this Government favors animals more than human beings."[115] Backbenchers felt that they needed to articulate to the government "the true feelings of the people of Zambia" because they had to contest "difficult" elections against "about six other opponents"; they worried about how to interpret the legislation before the House to voters.[116]

Third, dissenting parliamentarians highlighted the basic political fact that people – not animals – vote: "When the registration of voters was taking place, I did not hear of any animal being asked to go and register as a voter; I heard the campaigners ask only human beings. Maybe the animals were asked in a different language";[117] "I hope they (those who vote for the amendment) will have the strength to tell their people in their constituencies that they favor animals more than people";[118] "At no time did rhinoceros or elephants participate in the fight of our independence."[119] With an election on the horizon, parliamentarians feared the anger of voters if the bill augmenting the status quo wildlife law passed.

Backbenchers used various techniques to fight the 1982 amendment. Rancorous debate caused the government to withdraw the bill after its second reading. When the bill reemerged four months later, its provisions had been significantly watered down: The minister had reduced the prison sentences for rhino and elephant hunting and stipulated that the harsh sentences were aimed at "traffickers." The minister also replaced the provision for mandatory jail terms for first-time violators of hunting in a national park with the option of a fine for first offenses.

Even though the government weakened the bill's intended penalties, parliamentarians continued to vent their frustration with the punitive intent of the bill. Several members claimed the government did not care about citizens because it enjoyed a "dictatorial" majority of frontbenchers in the National Assembly and threatened to walk out of parliament to delay the bill's passage.[120] To ameliorate the tense emotional setting, the interim speaker rescheduled the bill to last on the agenda. The prime minister attended the final session and urged members not to abandon their duty by leaving the chambers, hinting of possible retaliation against those who might dissent. Despite these appeals and warnings, backbenchers walked out of the proceedings, an unprecedented event. Front-benchers quickly passed the bill without their back bench colleagues in attendance.[121]

The parliamentarians' success at weakening the bill had significant consequences for wildlife policy enforcement. Government officers had a difficult time proving that the people they caught with rhino or elephant products were indeed "traffickers" and thus subject to imprisonment. In 1987, Save the Rhino Trust officials arrested a woman from Botswana who had acquired two rhino horns. State prosecutors were unable to convince the magistrate that she had been "trafficking" in these products, and she received only a small fine.[122]

To make a more systematic test of these assertions about parliamentarian behavior, I construct a statistical model to account for parliamentarian position taking on the 1982 amendment. Because the National Assembly did not record votes, I code the statements made by parliamentarians during the debate on the 1982 amendment discussed. Thus, the dependent variable of the model measures whether the parliamentarian spoke against the bill (SPEAK = 1) or spoke either in support of the bill or not at all (SPEAK = 0) during debate.[123]

I construct independent variables to capture the incentives motivating parliamentarians to speak against the 1982 amendment. The variable GOVT accounts for whether a parliamentarian is a front-bencher (GOVT = 1) or a backbencher (GOVT = 0). Given their dependence on Kaunda for their positions, I hypothesize that front-benchers would be more likely either to speak for the bill or to remain silent. Backbenchers rely less on Kaunda, and thus would be more inclined to speak out against the bill.

REGION seeks to measure the extent to which wildlife policy reflects a regional bias. Scholars have long characterized Zambian national politics as regional in nature, especially the tension between politicians from rural and urban areas.[124] Because protected areas are scattered throughout Zambia, however, I hypothesize that a regional variable should be insignificant. The provinces are grouped into urban and rural categories.[125]

The variable MARGIN attempts to measure the influence of the parliamentarians' margin of victory in the last parliamentary election (1978) on their behavior regarding the amendment. MARGIN is the difference between percentage of the vote received by the incumbent and that by the next closest candidate. I hypothesize that the smaller the margin of victory, the more likely a parliamentarian would speak out against the 1982 amendment in order to appease constituents.

PROTECTED AREA seeks to account for the influence of wildlife protected areas (both national parks and game management areas) on parliamentarian behavior. If a constituency harbors no protected area, PROTECTED AREA = 0; if less than 50 percent of the constituency is covered by a protected area, PROTECTED AREA = 1; if 50 percent or more of the constituency, then PROTECTED AREA = 2. I hypothesize that as the percentage of a constituency that is protected increases, a parliamentarian grows more likely to speak out against the amendment.

The variable INTERACT represents the interaction between MARGIN and PROTECTED AREA. I theorize that the margin of victory and area of constituency protected interact in the following manner: The closer the margin and the more land protected in a constituency, the more likely the MP will oppose the 1982 amendment. The larger a parliamentarian's margin of victory in the last election, the less concern he or she will have with position taking on the bill (and less likely the need to risk incurring Kaunda's wrath), whether or not their constituency included a protected area. Because the dependent variable is dichotomous, I use logit analysis to assess effects of independent variables.[126] Table 1 presents the results of this analysis. Only one of the independent variables, REGION, is insignificant (and this corresponds to the hypothesis). The rest of the independent variables are significant. But to capture the effects of these variables requires calculating the change in the dependent variable's probability that results from changes in the independent variables.[127] In Table 2, I present the estimated probabilities of the dependent variable, at different values of the independent variables. These probabilities support most of the hypotheses elaborated.

The first hypothesis predicted that members of the government would

Table 1. *Position taking on the 1982 amendment*

(Standard error)	
Intercept	−2.42**
	(.65)
GOVT (front-bencher)	−2.16*
	(.89)
MARGIN	.05*
	(.02)
PROTECTED AREA	1.77**
	(.65)
INTERACT	−.07*
	(.03)
REGION	−.03
	(.58)
N	125
Pseudo R^2	.17
Log likelihood (LL)	−.42.56
$2 \times (LL_1 - LL_0)$	17.92**

*Significant at .05 level.
**Significant at .001 level.

Table 2. *Probability of speaking out against the 1982 amendment*

		Probability	Change in probability
Front-bencher		.032	
Backbencher		.22	−.19
Electoral margin			
0%		.09	
21%		.10	
45%		.13	+.04
Protected area			
0		.09	
1		.12	
2		.15	+.06
Electoral margin × protected area			
0	0	.04	
21% (means)	0	.09	
45%	0	.23	+.19
0	1	.17	
21% (means)	1	.12	
45%	1	.07	−.10
0	2	.55	
21% (means)	2	.15	
45%	2	.02	−.53

be less likely to speak against the bill. In the first two rows of Table 1, the probability of a front-bencher's speaking against the amendment is .032. The probability of a backbencher's speaking out is .22. Thus, the probability of a backbencher's speaking out is 19 percentage points greater than the equivalent probability for a front-bencher.[128]

As predicted, the independent variable REGION is insignificant, lending support to the hypothesis that the concerns of politicians over wildlife were countrywide.

According to the third hypothesis, MPs should be more prone to speak against the 1982 amendment if they fought in a close race in the last parliamentary election. The estimated effect of the electoral margin is only 4 percent, but it is not in the expected direction; that is, as an MP becomes electorally safer, he or she becomes more likely to speak out against the bill.

The fourth hypothesis asserted that the more land in a constituency was protected, the more likely its MP would oppose the bill. The estimated effect of this independent variable is also small: The MP with the most protected areas is only 6 percentage points more likely to speak against the bill than the MP without a protected area in his constituency.

Incorporating the interaction of these two variables, however, produces stronger and more interesting results. For those MPs with greater than half of the constituencies covered by protected areas (PROTECTED AREA = 2), changing the electoral MARGIN variable from one standard deviation below its mean to one standard deviation above its mean decreases the probability of speaking against the bill by 53 percentage points. For MPs with less than 50 percent of their constituencies covered by parks (PROTECTED AREA = 1), the probability of opposition falls by 10 percentage points when changing MARGIN from one standard deviation below to one above the mean.

For those members who have no park within their constituencies, however, the estimated probabilities show an unexpected result: As the electoral margin increases, these MPs were *more* likely to oppose the amendment. This unexpected behavior can be partially explained by examining the eight particular individuals whose actions run counter to the hypothesis.[129] Four of these MPs, while representing urban constituencies, came from families who resided in rural areas; these individuals were also enthusiastic hunters.[130] Thus, their own interests, and the interests of their families, might have motivated them more than fear of Kaunda's possible reprisals. One MP had a long-dominant position in the economic and political affairs of his constituency. He is rumored to have a great many illegal dealings with Angolans and would have an incentive to vote against any bill that might increase any type of law enforcement in his area.[131] Another MP, Dawson Lupunga, consistently opposed the UNIP government on a variety of issues, apparently enjoying the dangerous game of being contrary.[132]

The logit procedure and estimated probabilities generally support the theory that parliamentarians cared about wildlife policy as an electoral issue. Front-benchers, owing allegiance to President Kaunda for their positions within government, were less likely to speak against one of his favored pieces of legislation. The regional background did not matter much to those MPs who took a public stand against the 1982 amendment, because protected areas cover parts of all Zambia's provinces and were therefore of concern countrywide. More significant to the MP was how much of the constituency contained lands on which hunting was limited by the wildlife code, and how close the previous election returns had been. If MPs with a great deal of protected area who fought tough elections were much more likely to speak out against the bill, this indicates that Zambian voters cared about their access to wildlife, and that politicians were aware of the electorate's concerns.

POLICY RESPONSES TO THE POACHING IN KENYA AND ZIMBABWE

Kenya

Kenya endured poaching on a scale similar to Zambia's in the 1970s and 1980s. Even with a significant proconservation lobby in Nairobi, and a profitable and growing tourism industry based on wildlife, the political institutions of Kenya's one-party state and an economic downturn increased wildlife's role as a source of patronage goods. The political equilibrium caused by these factors was powerful, and policy change resulted only from the outside pressure of donor organizations.

Although Kenya did not legally become a one-party state until 1982, the Kenya African National Union (KANU) enjoyed de facto one-party rule when their last opposition party was outlawed in 1969. As in Zambia, parliamentarians became tied more tightly to their constituents. Candidates seeking parliamentary seats needed the approval of local party members, who expected returns from their endorsement.[133] Successful candidates had to survive very competitive elections with up to fifteen individuals running per seat. Delivering benefits to constituents dictated whether an MP could expect to stay in office; incumbents failing to secure political pork lost elections regularly.[134]

By the time of his death in 1978, Jomo Kenyatta had successfully concentrated power in the office of the president and had used it to increase his political support. After 1968, KANU's rules required that the party nominate presidential candidates, meaning that Kenyatta – and his successor, Daniel arap Moi – ran unopposed in the general elections. The president chose his ministers and bureaucrats primarily on the grounds of loyalty rather than competence. He directly selected state officials at all levels of government, from the directors of parastatals to the country's forty nonurban district commissioners. And he expanded the number of those reliant upon the state: By 1971, the Kenyan government was the country's largest employer.[135]

Three important consequences emerged from these actions. First, alternate locations of political power, from local government to the parliament, were stripped of power.[136] By the late 1970s MPs in legislative session rarely even voted. Second, the frequent shuffling of civil servants led to low levels of expertise, and high levels of indifference and corruption. And third, the system depended on resources for distribution between patrons and clients.[137]

The economic downturn in Kenya in the 1970s and 1980s severely reduced the supply of these resources. Import substitution policies, the world oil crisis, poor agricultural performance, and inflation combined to squeeze the Kenyan economy: State and individual incomes declined quickly. State expenditures were cut severely. The president could no longer afford to purchase his popularity with government revenue.[138]

Given their lack of alternative resources and the increase in the value of certain wildlife products such as ivory and rhino horn, many Kenyan politicians turned to wildlife to help meet their need for patronage resources.[139] By the middle 1970s, bureaucrats, ministers, local and national politicians, as well as their friends and relatives, were profiteering in wildlife. Unlike President Kaunda, who had a strong conservation ethic, President Kenyatta had no such commitment. At one point, he even asked a cabinet minister to give an export permit for fifteen tons of ivory to his daughter. And Kenyatta's fourth wife was one of the principal ivory traders in the country.[140]

The officials responsible for animal conservation were also heavily involved in the illegal wildlife trade. Two assistant ministers responsible for wildlife management participated in ivory sales. Park wardens from Kenya's Wildlife Conservation and Management Department (WCMD) skimmed from national park gate fees (which were collected in foreign exchange), and game guards accounted for a third of all rhino kills. When a reform-minded wildlife officer tried to fire dozens of WCMD personnel for corrupt acts, most were reinstated by their political patrons.[141]

Kenyatta did not respond with the same effort as Zambia's President Kaunda to the poaching crisis. In fact, there was little reason to do anything. Party and government officials at every level enjoyed this new source of income in a time of economic difficulties. Communities living in wildlife areas did not mind the increased hunting – they benefited from both the decrease in game as well as the money from their own participation in the wildlife trade. While international and domestic conservationists pressured Kenyatta's government for change, their political clout did not compete with that of the vast majority of Kenyans who enjoyed the fruits of wildlife. And, importantly, this increase in poaching did not hurt Kenya's tourism revenues at this time.

It took external pressure to disrupt this political equilibrium. The World Bank, which was implementing a program to develop Kenya's tourism sector, pushed Kenyatta to act. The president's response was to ban all hunting in 1977. Although dramatic, this actually accomplished little, because the problem stemmed from illegal, not legal, hunting. More importantly, it did little to dismantle the role of wildlife in patronage politics. The following year the government banned the sale of all wildlife products. This did discourage some from the wildlife market – curio markets, for example, were hit hard by the policy change – and the wildlife market was forced underground. President Moi launched an anticorruption campaign that also decreased some of the larger-level wildlife activities, but Moi's actions were designed to remove rivals from power, rather than to clean up patronage politics.[142] Poaching and the wildlife trade continued.

A second external shock helped to change Kenyan wildlife policy more radically. In September 1988 international newspapers published reports highlighting Kenya's poaching problems, and these stories began to affect Kenya's image as a tourist destination.[143] The threat was significant: By 1980, 360,000 foreign tourists visited Kenya and spent $20 million in foreign exchange; by 1988 the figure had increased to $350 million.[144] President Moi knew he needed to shore up Kenya's wildlife image with the international community in order to sustain the country's lucrative tourism industry. In April 1989, a day after two tourist minibuses were attacked by poachers, Moi appointed Richard Leakey to head a new parastatal, the Kenya Wildlife Service. Leakey had no experience in wildlife management but possessed strong links to the international community. Moi's action received tremendous media coverage, and Leakey soon garnered commitments for over $150 million in aid for wildlife management.[145]

Zimbabwe

Zimbabwe did not suffer from the same rapid increase in poaching as Zambia and Kenya. When the poaching wave hit Zimbabwe's borders, its economy was doing relatively well, despite the international boycotts against the white settler regime of Ian Smith. The relatively well-paid staff of the country's wildlife department continued to pursue its system of protection, which featured wildlife management by landowners (the result of the 1975 Wildlife Act, discussed in the previous chapter). Although Robert Mugabe's Zimbabwe African National Union (ZANU) party was dominant, political institutions in the early 1980s did not favor the construction of a widespread patronage system. The result of these factors was a wildlife policy that, although sustaining some losses in poaching, did not confront the same levels of corruption or poaching as endured by Zambia and Kenya. In fact, the Zimbabwean wildlife industry grew, despite the suspicions of black politicians who viewed wildlife conservation as a luxury enjoyed by whites.

At independence in 1980, Prime Minister (later President) Mugabe inherited an economy that had actually diversified and broadened under Ian Smith's regime. From the years 1965–1980, Zimbabwe's manufacturing sector had grown from 18.6 to 22.5 percent of the gross national product. Agriculture had successfully shifted to export crops such as tobacco. In the immediate postwar period, the country's GNP expanded, with gains in both manufacturing and agriculture.[146] In general, the economic mood of the country and its government was very optimistic.

While his party was clearly dominant, several factors prevented Mugabe and his Zimbabwe African National Union (ZANU) from constructing an elaborate system of patronage politics as in Zambia and Kenya. The new Zimbabwean constitution provided for a multiparty republic.[147] As a result, some residue of multiparty competition remained through 1990, reducing the degree to which unfettered patronage politics could be practiced. Bureaucracies were subject to some oversight.[148] Additionally, powerful domestic interest groups in farming and industry helped to decentralize Zimbabwean political influence to a greater extent than in Zambia or Kenya.[149]

The Department of National Parks and Wildlife Management (DNPWM) in Zimbabwe, unlike the more demoralized, ineffective, and corruption-ridden agencies in Zambia and Kenya, was able to pay its staff and to continue with its policy of constructing partnerships with landowners for the comanagement of wildlife resources.[150] In a crucial move to establish greater support for wildlife conservation in the rural sector of Zimbabwe, the DNPWM along with other domestic groups worked to have "appropriate authority" status – which had been previously reserved for landowners – given to district councils in the country's communal areas. As we will see in the next chapter, this move would increase the political support given to wildlife conservation, because African communities now stood to benefit from wildlife resources as had white farmers since 1975.

Wildlife conservation was still unpopular: Individuals in some communities still felt their land had been stolen from them to create national parks and wanted this land back. They hunted illegally. They helped outside poachers. And they elected district councillors to forward this message to the government.[151] National–level politicians also viewed the wildlife industry with distrust: Conservation groups were generally dominated by whites. Those who received the bulk of the monies from wildlife–related industries were white hunters, white lodge owners, and white owners of tourism businesses.[152] Black officials thought that commercial white farmers were using conservation provisions to prevent the state from acquiring "underutilized" lands for resettlement programs.[153]

The new single-member, first-past-the-post electoral system installed in 1985 seemed to have facilitated the same type of constituent-service opposition to conservation as the Zambian case. In a rare fight against a government-introduced bill, members of the Zimbabwean parliament condemned legislation designed to introduce new, more restrictive regulations on the snaring of wild animals. MPs claimed that it was just another attempt at increasing white commercial farmers' control over their lands, while "ignoring the food requirements of rural peasants."[154] The bill ultimately failed to pass.

Despite such signs of opposition by parliamentarians, the wildlife industry provided a great deal of foreign currency to Zimbabwe, had good backward and forward linkages to other segments of the economy, and was often more profitable on marginal lands than cattle ranching.[155] And the DNPWM was working to include the residents of communal areas in the decentralization of wildlife management.

CONCLUSION

This chapter has explored how Zambia's change from a multiparty to a one-party state and an exogenous economic shock affected the country's wildlife policy from 1972 to 1982, as the political institutions of the Second Republic altered the pattern of benefits accruing to politicians and shifted their subsequent choices. Unlike in the First Republic, individuals in the Second Republic had great incentive to battle Kaunda's preference for more extensive wildlife conservation policy. The result was a wildlife policy that, although unchanged de jure, created significantly different de facto outcomes: More individuals hunted more animals with less fear of being caught by NPWS.

This result defied President Kaunda, whose new powers within the one-party state were considerable. After all, no Zambian politician during this period openly suggested weakening wildlife laws, despite such a move's potential popularity with the electorate. But, this chapter has demonstrated that Kaunda's new authority also had limits, which allowed parliamentarians to oppose bills that augmented poaching penalties and UNIP officials to make cuts in the NPWS budget and sabotage new conservation agencies. Additionally, no government officials made any attempt to inform magistrates of the new provisions of Act 32 of 1982; the future director of the wildlife department was fined for contempt of court when he criticized a magistrate over the small fines meted out to a person caught with two rhino horns.[156]

The evidence presented in this chapter calls into question many commonly held assumptions about the politics of one-party states in Africa. Scholars have indicated that in African one-party states parliaments were composed of members with few ties to the electorate, offering scant opposition to government policy.[157] Most observers tend either to ignore the role of elections under one-party rule, or, when they are mentioned, to characterize them as vehicles to ensure centralized party control over political recruitment.[158] Further, researchers assert that dominant one-party presidents and their advisers easily manipulate constitutional provisions and government policy.[159]

This chapter has presented evidence that parliaments in a one-party state can be relatively independent of the executive on certain issues. Parliamentarians can be strong representatives of their constituents and be motivated by electoral competition even when such action challenges the preferred policy position of a one-party president. The case of the 1982 amendment revealed that parliamentarians under Zambia's one-party state succeeded in modifying a president's policy position.

Four characteristics of wildlife policy facilitated the Zambian parliament's opposition. First, the effects of wildlife policy were widespread. Most of Zambia's electoral constituencies contained or abutted a game management area or national park. Those constituencies that did not, usually urban areas, still included Zambians interested in wildlife as a business or supply of meat. Second, the evidence suggests parliamentarians viewed wildlife as an electoral issue. Although certain economic policies pursued by the government may have more seriously damaged the livelihood of the average rural resident, such laws were difficult to understand. In contrast, villagers knew precisely the cause of their exclusion from wildlife resources and continually sought greater legal access. Pressuring parliamentarians and poaching emerged as two of their strategies to obtain such access. Third, the benefits politicians received from preventing greater enforcement of wildlife conservation accrued to them individually, obviating the need for collective action. Policies that required group solidarity would be more vulnerable to a breakdown in support. Monitoring and sanctioning mechanisms would need to be constructed and maintained. And such a group would also be an easier target for a one-party president. Finally, parliamentarians could oppose

President Kaunda's policy preferences by doing nothing; rather than expose themselves politically by advocating policy change, they could hide behind supporting the status quo, which was, in effect, Kaunda's old policy. These four characteristics of wildlife policy allowed a so-called rubber-stamp parliament to foil a one-party president's goals.

This chapter has also demonstrated that the case of Kenya presents some striking similarities to that of Zambia. Political institutions and economic decline fueled a widespread illegal wildlife market. Without a President Kaunda to impose any limits, Kenya's politicians and officials – hungry for patronage resources – obtained any benefits they could from the increasing value of wildlife products. Parliamentarians neither had to introduce legislation to help their constituents gain wildlife's benefits, nor to battle a conservation–minded president in order to reap political reward. On the contrary, one reason the "poaching equilibrium" was so stable was that politicians did not have to do anything to gain economic and political advantage.

Zimbabwe's experiences were quite different from Kenya's and Zambia's. Not confronting severe economic contraction, and not possessing the type of patronage politics found in well-entrenched one-party systems, Zimbabwe did not endure poaching to the same extent. Aside from large losses to its rhino populations – which most observers attribute to cross-border hunting by Zambians – Zimbabwe's wildlife populations remained relatively intact. Nevertheless, as in Zambia the structure of Zimbabwe's post-1985 electoral system offered incentives to parliamentarians to question the augmentation of wildlife enforcement.

While exploring the politics of wildlife policy in Zambia, Kenya, and Zimbabwe, this chapter has emphasized deeper issues of institutional creation and change. It has shown that alterations to the institutional arena had significant effects on the distribution of resources and, consequently, policy outcomes. Zambia and Kenya each endured serious economic decline at the same time that the international demand for wildlife products was increasing. These external shocks, combined with the political institutions of the one-party states in Zambia and Kenya, which emphasized the distribution of patronage resources, resulted in a dramatic increase in the illegal hunting and marketing of wildlife. Poor conservation results motivated Kaunda to try to modify wildlife policy. But the shift in resource endowment and institutional incentives motivated other Zambian political actors to maintain status quo institutions, despite the economic and biological losses due to rampant poaching in the country. Presidents Kenyatta and Moi of Kenya did not make serious efforts to disturb the political equilibrium of poaching until external forces threatened to disrupt their extremely important tourism market. Zimbabwe was characterized by different political and economic features, which resulted in lower levels of illegal wildlife use. Conservationists frequently claim that wildlife staff in Zimbabwe were "just less corrupt" than their colleagues in Zambia and Kenya; this chapter has explored the institutional reasons for such behavior.

In the 1980s, the poaching crisis in parts of African generated some consensus among African wildlife managers, donors, and nongovernmental organizations that local communities should be more involved in the management and benefits of wildlife conservation. Groups in Zambia, Kenya, and Zimbabwe all espoused this new decentralized approach. Part II explores how national bureaucracies in these three countries contended with this new policy emphasis. Political institutions provided constraints to the choices of wildlife managers and help to account for the content and outcomes of the countries' wildlife policies.

PART II

The Bureaucratic Politics
of Wildlife Policy

4

The Conservationists Strike Back: "Community-Based" Wildlife Policy and the Politics of Structural Choice, 1983–1991

The project [LIRDP] has originally planned to become sustainable after five years, that means the middle of 1993. But experience is showing that this will not take place. . . . In the budget for 1992, the project's own income is estimated to cover 4% [of its budget].

Magne Hallaraaker, LIRDP Fourth Annual Meeting,
December 11, 1991

The previous chapter demonstrated that political institutions provided incentives for politicians and civil servants in Zambia to maintain a wildlife policy that advanced individuals' political and economic goals, but failed to conserve animals. The political logic of an economically crippled one-party state thwarted those individuals and groups who wanted to augment wildlife policy in Zambia – President Kenneth Kaunda, the Zambian National Parks and Wildlife Service (NPWS), international donors, and local conservationists.

These actors employed new strategies after 1982 to circumvent the impediments presented by members of the party and government. NPWS officers created the Administrative Management Design for Game Management Areas (ADMADE), a new program of "community-based" wildlife management primarily financed by the United States Agency for International Development (USAID). European conservationists, backed by President Kaunda, established the Luangwa Integrated Resource Development Project (LIRDP), a new public agency supported by the Norwegian Agency for International Development (NORAD).

Both LIRDP and ADMADE sought to conserve wild animals by incorporating rural residents in decisions over and benefits from wildlife resources.[1] But the political institutions of the one-party state induced LIRDP and ADMADE's designers to construct programs far different from those necessary to implement their goal of efficient, community-based conservation.[2] The programs' designers worried about possible interference by Zambian politicians seeking patronage resources. They

83

prepared for bureaucratic turf battles with other Zambian public agencies, recognized their potential rivalry over control of Zambia's wildlife estate, and most importantly, understood the advantages and disadvantages posed by an alliance with President Kaunda: His favor could provide decisive support to a program's struggles to survive; his disapproval could prove fatal to a bureaucracy.

This chapter features an examination of Zambia's wildlife policy from 1983 to 1991 by focusing on the construction of ADMADE and LIRDP. The structure of both programs resulted from their designers' desire to expand their program's resource base subject to two constraints: (1) the pattern of political uncertainty generated by Zambia's system of government and (2) the designers' political resources, specifically their share of public authority. Rather than construct organizations to pursue their promulgated goals of conservation, local participation, or bureaucratic "efficiency," ADMADE and LIRDP designers' primary objective was to create structures that secured additional resources for their programs. The political uncertainty spawned by a one-party state and the designers' control over public authority compelled them to build particular sets of structures to secure and to insulate program resources.

In Kenya, Richard Leakey enjoyed both the strong support of President Moi and the public authority afforded by being the director of the Kenyan Wildlife Service. These assets allowed Leakey great latitude in his construction of an agency insulated from other politicians. But as Moi's support wavered, Leakey was left completely exposed to the patronage-seeking politicians of Kenya's one-party state. Unlike in Kenya and Zambia, which were characterized by a pattern of political uncertainty, wildlife bureaucrats in Zimbabwe faced a de jure multiparty political arena composed of many important politicians and interest groups. The staff of Zimbabwe's wildlife department responded to this environment by putting their efforts into building a coalition of domestic and international groups to pursue its policy agenda, which featured a broadening of its base of support to include Zimbabweans living in communal areas.

This chapter begins by reviewing concepts provided by research on the politics of structural choice and employing them to understand the incentives confronting bureaucrats in an African one-party state. These insights are then applied to the cases of ADMADE and LIRDP in Zambia, where bureaucrats' knowledge of the Zambian political landscape greatly influenced how they structured their public agencies. As a result, ADMADE and LIRDP designers made decisions over political sponsors, financing mechanisms, and decision-making structures to augment their resources while insulating these resources from political uncertainty. The chapter continues by applying the insights of the structural choice approach to examples from Kenya and Zimbabwe. The last section concludes by discussing the contributions of the politics of structural choice to the study of bureaucratic politics.

THE POLITICS OF STRUCTURAL CHOICE

Researchers have made great strides in their study of bureaucratic behavior. In early public administration tradition, bureaucrats had been characterized as apolitical individuals with exogenously derived goals, operating within their exogenously crafted organizational structures. Such a view made behavior merely a matter of selecting the most efficient action to carry out an agency's mandate.[3] The messy reality of politicized bureaucracy forced scholars within the field of public administration to wrestle with the dichotomy of administration and politics.[4]

Although scholars of bureaucracies and the environmental policy of industrialized democracies have increasingly injected more politics into their work,[5] most studies concerning environmental policy in developing countries forward Wilsonian solutions to bureaucratic problems: more money, more staff, more equipment, better training, and so on.[6] Where politics is not ignored in discussions of bureaucratic behavior, it is often introduced only incidentally.[7]

Some recent studies of bureaucracy by political scientists, however, may offer important tools for those seeking to explain bureaucratic behavior in non-Western countries. This research – especially that which employ economic methods and agency theory – characterize bureaucrats as possessing their own preferences and operating in an arena composed of other important political actors. A growing body of research regarding bureaucrats in the United States characterizes these individuals as seeking their own policy goals,[8] responding to external influences such as the president,[9] the U.S. Congress,[10] and the courts.[11]

This new line of inquiry assumes that well-informed politicians, interest groups, and bureaucrats compete to structure public agencies in ways to achieve their own particular goals. The approach indicates that two core characteristics of politics profoundly affect the strategies of political actors competing over the design of public agencies.[12] First, politics is about the exercise of public authority, the ability to allow political winners to impose their preferred government structures and policy on the entire polity, often at the expense of political losers. Rather than view the supply of a public agency as a contract between interested groups seeking to remedy a collective action problem, the politics of structural choice conceptualizes public agencies as the result of groups seeking to control public authority for their own benefit.[13]

Second, politics makes the exercise of public authority temporary.

This uncertainty drives the creators of public agencies to choose institutional designs they would never select if pursuing technical efficiency alone. Because political victory allows incumbents only temporary control over public authority, they attempt to protect their agency from their political opponents, who could gut or dismantle the agency tomorrow. The fleeting nature of political control may even motivate incumbents to insulate their agency to an extent that even their own exercise of public authority is impaired.

If politics is conceptualized as the temporary exercise of public authority, the distribution of public authority under a system of government critically influences the strategies chosen by today's political winners to protect their agencies from tomorrow's uncertainty.[14] For example, the separation-of-powers system found in the United States encourages actors to bury "their" agencies in layers of legislation. Because passing laws is difficult in this system, it makes sense for those wanting to protect their agency to formalize its mandate and activities by passing a web of detailed laws. Even if opponents happened to secure a legislative majority in the future, the United States's powerful and independent president and lack of party discipline make change laborious and uncertain. The separation-of-powers system also promotes political compromise, allowing political opponents the chance to hamstring at the outset those public agencies they dislike. The result is a highly constrained, complex, and formalized American bureaucracy.[15]

The political institutions of a parliamentary system, on the other hand, offer a different set of incentives to those wishing to control public authority and shield it from political uncertainty. Parliamentary politics makes it easier to pass laws, because a party or coalition usually dominates both executive and legislative branches of government. Consequently, writing legislation to hide a public agency from its future enemies is less effective. Parties and groups would seek other strategies, such as constructing independent commissions or government corporations.[16] Thus, in both the separation-of-powers and parliamentary systems, bureaucratic structures can be partially explained by examining political actors' choices vis-à-vis the distribution of public authority in a particular system of government.

THE POLITICS OF STRUCTURAL CHOICE
IN A ONE-PARTY STATE

New institutionalists' insights about the politics of structural choice in industrialized democracies can be extended to other political settings. Individuals and groups seek to control the exercise of public authority in all countries, not just industrialized democracies. And democratic elections are not the only source of political uncertainty – it springs from phenomena common to all political systems, such as shifting alliances, fluctuating levels of political resources, and changing political opportunities. This section attempts to model how individuals would construct their most-preferred government agency under a one-party state with a strong executive, the system of government so common in postindependence Africa.[17]

At the apex of the one-party system stands the head of state and party, whose concentrated political power makes for a potent ally and formidable enemy.[18] One-party presidents generally dominate government and party institutions. They appoint important government and party personnel.[19] They control most decision-making processes. And they wield unparalleled influence over choices regarding state revenue and expenditure.

Groups interested in expanding their public authority and resources under any political system must beware those actors who seek to use public agencies for their own ends. But groups operating under a one-party state have a distinctive concern: They must contend with the one-party president. At a minimum, groups must ensure that the interests of the one-party president are not threatened. Moreover, if the group wants to secure strong political or budgetary priority, they need the president's active support. The benefits of the president's patronage, however, also pose considerable costs, because his monopoly over public authority allows him to intervene capriciously in government affairs.[20] A group that secures the president's backing must also worry about his future use of power, which could alter or destroy their agency.[21] Consequently, some groups may shun a president's assistance if they can survive without it, preferring to avoid the potential costs of presidential intervention.

Those groups needing the president's support would seek ways to limit his intervention in their agency's affairs. One way is to control the information the president receives about the agency. By regulating this flow, the group may help shape the president's preferences and choices, thereby reducing the possibility of his more capricious and damaging actions.

At first glance, another way to blunt presidential intervention would be to seek those domestic allies who may help defend the agency from the president. This strategy is likely to be relatively ineffective, however, because most politicians and officials do not have independent and unassailable sources of political power under such a system of government. Whereas parliamentarians, ministers, and other party and government officials could help an agency acquire additional services and funds, the president's dominant position allows him to dismantle most of these relationships if desired.

Because this government system makes protection from *domestic* sources ineffectual, groups may seek security from *international* sources for their agency. A foreign patron could alleviate political uncertainty caused by the one-party president by tying his hands through bi- or multilateral agreements about the agency's structure and mandate. Aid contracts could be written to specify the agency's mandate, hiring procedures, funding mechanisms, and decision-making processes. Monitoring mechanisms – such as review missions, required reports, financial audits, and annual meetings of the government and donor – could be included in the agreement to keep the agency protected from the president and other domestic politicians aspiring to use it for their own goals. By gaining international support, a group also succeeds in linking the president's reputation to their agency. The president's acceptance of an agreement with a donor confers some international significance on their bureaucracy. Failure to perform the actions agreed upon may damage his credibility and thus threaten his access to other forms of international aid.

Groups seek to augment and insulate their public agencies under any system of government; a one-party state forces them to consider specific mechanisms to limit the capricious inclinations of a powerful president as well.

CONSERVATIONISTS AND THE SEARCH FOR NEW WILDLIFE PROGRAMS IN ZAMBIA'S SECOND REPUBLIC

Individuals and groups interested in conserving Zambian wildlife had little success in changing policy or programs from 1973 to 1982 (see Chapter 3). President Kaunda, the National Parks and Wildlife Service, and international and local conservationists could not overcome the incentives generated by Zambia's political and economic institutions for party and government members to oppose conservation measures. The institutional environment changed, however, with an influx of ideas and financing from international sources.[22]

Using these new resources, two proconservation groups emerged within Zambia. Both attempted to create programs they most preferred. Both sought the resources necessary to extend their own authority over Zambia's wildlife estate. And both had to contend with the political uncertainty generated by Zambia's one-party state. Their fear of Kaunda's possible interventions drove them to choose some parallel strategies of insulation. But their strategies and resultant agency structures diverged because they possessed different levels of public authority at the outset.

Wildlife Policy and Structural Choice

The Emergence of Two Conservation Factions

In the late 1970s and early 1980s a researcher from the United States found that human activity such as farming, bush burning, and legal and illegal hunting significantly altered the movements and foraging habits of elephants in the Lupande Game Management Area of the Luangwa Valley.[23] The researcher's studies brought him into daily contact with villagers and traditional authorities. It became clear to him that rural residents paid the costs of conservation policies without receiving much benefit. The abundance and variety of wildlife in national parks and game management areas favored tourists and licensed hunters; wild animals did little to augment legally the daily living standards of the villagers.[24]

Motivated by his observations, and his conflicts with a local chief, the researcher, with the help of NPWS and the nongovernmental organization Save the Rhino Trust, arranged for a conference of wildlife managers, conservationists, government officials, and donors to discuss the problems regarding resource use in the Lupande Game Management Area. The Lupande Development Workshop convened on 18 September 1983 to develop strategies to combat the increasing depletion of natural resources in both the Lupande area and Zambia's other protected zones. Participants in the Lupande Development Workshop represented precisely those groups whose conservation interests had been stymied by members of the party and government in the preceding decade.[25]

The Lupande Development Workshop's proceedings, resolutions, and aftermath would change the face of Zambian conservation policy for the next decade. Participants agreed that Zambia needed a new program of wildlife conservation. They agreed that a project should be established to develop the Luangwa catchment area as a model for the efficient management and utilization of wildlife.[26] They agreed that both domestic and international funds were necessary to support the proposed research and more effective antipoaching efforts. And they agreed the project should also include "people of the Luangwa Valley GMAs [game management areas]" in the "development and management of the catchment's natural resources."[27]

But participants strongly disagreed over the proposed project's design. Two different factions within this proconservation lobby emerged. One group, led by Europeans from international development agencies and the Zambian conservation community, favored a large-scale program that incorporated the management of all natural resources. They argued that the contingent nature of villagers' resource use required an integrated resource development project (IRDP). Importantly, this bloc also expressed a desire for the new institution to be independent of the normal course of Zambian politics, which had stymied their attempts to change policy in the past. With complete control over all natural resources in a particular geographic area, these conservationists believed, their IRDP could mitigate some of the political meddling caused by politicians' and bureaucrats' search for patronage resources. Many in this group also privately expressed their long-standing desire to create a structure free of the influence of NPWS, an agency they considered lacking in integrity and capacity.

Another group, led by NPWS officers, expressed apprehension about such an institutional design.[28] They voiced concern about how the IRDP might replace their legislative authority over wildlife. They believed NPWS could provide the expertise needed by any wildlife conservation scheme, and they wondered how such a large program could effectively include the needs of the local resource user, supposedly the goal of any new policy. Other government officials sided with NPWS's concerns. Although all departments generally favored the benefits of donor-funded development schemes, they remained wary about the roles that their respective agencies might play in such a structure.

The National Parks and Wildlife Service: Reestablishing and Extending Authority through ADMADE

NPWS officers understood the threat posed by the European bloc and their proposed IRDP. Without an effective counterstroke, NPWS stood to be replaced as the manager of wildlife resources in the Luangwa Valley. Worse, given President Kaunda's early support for the IRDP concept and his own deep distrust of NPWS, the department feared they could be removed as Zambia's principal wildlife manager throughout the country if the IRDP proved successful.[29] The NPWS responded by creating their own pilot conservation program, which aimed to increase their control over wildlife resources while shielding these efforts from political interference.

The NPWS possessed a resource that critically influenced its strategies: It already enjoyed a share of public authority. The department had a legislative mandate to manage Zambia's wildlife estate. Further, it controlled an organization that, though weak, existed nationwide. These assets allowed NPWS to develop and implement a new program under its own auspices, without forming alliances with other public agencies or politicians, which might foster future intervention or takeover. These assets also marginally reduced politicians' ability to intervene in NPWS's affairs, because they would incur transaction costs if they decided to change the department's policy or structure (as seen in Chapter 3). NPWS's share of public authority allowed it to construct a new program that, at least in its infancy, was relatively insulated from political meddling. Most important, these assets allowed NPWS to pursue its program without direct dependence on President Kaunda.

NPWS's Initial Actions: A Pilot Project. As a first response to the disconcerting support that many of the workshop's participants gave to a large-scale project, NPWS sped up plans to establish their own pilot wildlife management project in the Luangwa Valley.[30] Their design emphasized three organizational goals for the pilot project: first, to increase the department's revenue and shield it from governmental control; second, to increase the number of NPWS staff, without depending on other departments if possible; third, to create popular support for the project. Throughout the process of designing the new project, NPWS avoided involving Kaunda.[31]

The NPWS needed revenue to establish its program. To this end, it successfully persuaded the Ministry of Tourism (NPWS's parent ministry) to declare the Lower Lupande Game Management Area as a safari hunting concession under the pilot project's control. The department also convinced the Ministry to implement a new tax on safari companies.[32] Formerly, those companies had paid two fees to engage in the hunting business: a fee (in dollars) for the hunting rights to a particular area and a game management area permit (in kwacha), both amounts accruing to the central government. Despite these taxes, many NPWS officers maintained that safari companies paid relatively little when compared with the amount of profit that could be earned during the hunting season. They believed that the companies would be willing to pay more for the hunting rights to an area as popular as Lupande. They also knew that it would be difficult to appropriate any share of the extant fees on safari hunting that the central government currently received. To provide the project with financing while staying clear of political fights that could cause intervention, NPWS officers suggested an entirely new safari concession fee.[33] The NPWS soon established the new fee at a rate of two thousand dollars for each fourteen-day safari.

It was one thing for NPWS to gain new sources of revenue; it was another to insulate the newly acquired funds from politicians and bureaucrats, who were ever hungry for patronage resources. The financial freedom desired by NPWS for their pilot project was greatly facilitated by the department's extant Wildlife Conservation Revolving Fund (hereafter the Fund). Because of the mounting fiscal problems confronting the government budget in the 1980s, the party and its government had decided to allow public agencies to create revolving funds, in the hope that some agencies could operate on the revenue they earned. Although such funds actually did little to reduce the demands for financing that agencies placed on the central government, they did allow the agencies great financial latitude.[34] Revolving fund managers rarely submitted the annual reports required by the Ministry of Finance, so little was known about the revenue or expenditure of these funds.[35] NPWS, which had acquired its own revolving fund in January 1983, began to use it more intensely for their pilot project: All the new safari fees were paid directly to the Fund. This allowed the department flexibility and speed for its expenditures.[36] It also helped shield the project and its revenue from oversight.

The NPWS's second goal was to use the pilot project to increase their staff in the field, thereby enhancing the department's control over Zambia's wildlife estate. Before the pilot project, the NPWS faced two constraints to hiring employees: a legal limit to their department's numbers and the lack of money necessary to pay new personnel. The NPWS came up with a clever solution to these problems; they convinced their minister to designate classified employees as wildlife officers.[37] This permitted the NPWS to hire local residents, normally unqualified to be civil servants, to act as wildlife scouts for the pilot program. Classified employees could be paid a fraction of the wages of regular civil servants. This tactic allowed the NPWS to staff its program at relatively low expense, it provided the local community with the tangible benefit of employment, and gave the NPWS more flexibility in hiring and firing staff, because classified employees did not receive the wages or protection of the Zambian civil service code. Classified employees could be terminated for nonperformance – unlike regular NPWS civil servants – providing the project with motivated and loyal personnel.[38]

The NPWS's last goal was to gain grass-roots support for the pilot project. Such support would reduce both the costs of implementing the project and the likelihood of any political attempt to cancel it. Delivering tangible benefits to locals was also one of the policy changes advocated by the NPWS and others at the Lupande Workshop. Consequently, NPWS worked hard at gaining grass-roots support for their program.[39] They established a cropping station to provide employment, meat, and revenue for local residents and gave the local community 50 percent of the profits the station earned from the sale of meat, skin, and tusks.[40] In addition, the NPWS gave the community 40 percent of the revenues it collected from the new safari concession fee.[41] They also expedited the grading of the major road in the area, hiring local villagers as day laborers to complete the task. And to win the support of the local elite, the NPWS consulted Chief Malama about which individuals should be selected as village scouts.

The NPWS hailed its pilot project as a great success, claiming that in addition to generating revenue and jobs, it had caused poaching rates to decline 90 percent in the project's area over a three-year period, it had enabled local residents to buy game meat legally from the cropping station, and it had a staff of village scouts whose motivation exceeded that of regular NPWS staff.[42] Additionally, an NPWS survey of villagers' attitudes toward wildlife found with "convincing certainty" that individuals within the pilot project area had a more protective attitude toward wildlife than those outside it.[43] Critics of the program questioned many of these claims.[44]

But the NPWS also had clearly achieved its organizational goals. It had expanded and insulated its revenue base. It had extended its authority over wildlife through the village scout program. And it had gained a measure of support from the local elite, who had benefited most from the project's goods.[45]

Establishing a National Program. The NPWS, increasingly worried about the progress of their rivals' IRDP implementation, quickly adopted the pilot project's basic structures as departmental policy in 1987, calling it the Administrative Management Design for Game Management Areas (ADMADE). Like that of the pilot project, the NPWS crafted AD-MADE's design both to enhance the department's resources and to insulate them from political interference. Because it chose to keep AD-MADE within the legal mandate of the department, the NPWS avoided political conflicts with other Zambian bureaucracies and retained tight control. An examination of ADMADE's decision-making and revenue structures demonstrates these strategies.

ADMADE's Decision-Making and Revenue Sharing Structures. The NPWS designed ADMADE to keep all facets of the program under their control and to avoid external scrutiny. Overall responsibility for AD-MADE's design and implementation was in the hands of the ADMADE Directorate, which included only senior officers from the NPWS. Beneath this body, ADMADE established wildlife management units in certain areas of the country.[46] The NPWS appointed one of its own staff as a "unit leader" to direct the implementation of ADMADE policy in each unit.

For each unit capable of supporting its own wildlife management, ADMADE established a Wildlife Management Authority. The district governor chaired the Authority, and the district executive secretary served as vice-chairman. Members included the area's wildlife warden, the member of Parliament, unit leader, chiefs, and ward chairman. The Authority also allowed the managing directors of safari companies to become members if their business operations had a commercial interest in the unit's area.[47] Every Authority, in turn, contained a Wildlife Management Sub-Authority for each chiefdom in the unit. The local chief

93

chaired this body, whose members included village headmen, the unit leader, ward chairman, teachers, and a district council representative.

The NPWS had a twofold strategy for membership in the Authority and Sub-Authority. First, the NPWS wanted to use these bodies to garner support for ADMADE at the local level. Villagers had traditionally been the most antagonistic opponents of wildlife conservation policy. The NPWS officers believed if ADMADE could secure the favor of chiefs, headmen, ward chairmen, and teachers, their program could be implemented with less hostility from the local community and thus lower the department's enforcement costs. In the best case, local demand for AD-MADE would be high enough to thwart any political threat to the program.[48] Second, the NPWS specifically chose to include certain regional political actors within ADMADE's structure to enhance the department's access to government goods and services, while trying to limit the politicians' possible use of the program for their own ends.[49]

The choice to include politicians within the ADMADE structure did not come easily to NPWS officers; they greatly feared political intervention. Originally, they had planned to appoint their own wildlife wardens as chairmen of the Authority. But the Ministry of Tourism's permanent secretary advised them to ask district governors to chair the Authority, both to protect the program from local politicians seeking to hijack it and to use the governors' influence to expedite central government services.[50] The NPWS eventually agreed to this tactic.

The NPWS bequeathed only marginal powers to the authorities and sub-Authorities, and thus decreased the possibility of political interference. The Authority could only advise on decisions already taken by the NPWS staff regarding access to wildlife resources, that is, hunting quotas and hunting licenses. Additionally, ADMADE policy required the Authority and the Sub-Authority to help the NPWS fulfill its mandate of protecting Zambia's wildlife estate. The Authority should "monitor both legal and illegal off-takes of wildlife," "prepare a work plan for the unit's wildlife management program," and "enforce the National Parks and Wildlife Act, Cap. 316, and other relevant Acts through the office of that unit's leader." Among other things, the Sub-Authority should "monitor and solve wildlife management problems on the level of the chiefdom" and "facilitate the implementation of any programs, plans, projects, etc. approved by the authority."[51] The NPWS allocation of decision-making powers to nondepartmental people was slight; the department remained in firm control over the substance and implementation of the ADMADE policy.

The ADMADE Directorate also created a formula to distribute AD-MADE revenues that kept its interests paramount. In the original allocation, the NPWS gave itself 40 percent of ADMADE revenues to meet its management costs in each unit. The local community received 35 percent for development projects. The NPWS also awarded itself 15 percent of ADMADE revenues to run Zambia's national parks, even though ADMADE funds came predominantly from hunting in game management areas. The remaining 10 percent went to the Zambia National Tourist Board for the promotion of tourism.[52] The ADMADE Directorate changed the beneficiaries over time, increasing the NPWS's allotment. In 1990, they applied 15 percent to the NPWS to defray its overall costs of administering ADMADE.[53] By 1991, they retained the 10 percent portion as well, to support the costs they incurred for managing national parks.[54]

ADMADE and International Sponsors. Regardless of the precise allocation formula, it was clear to the NPWS that they needed more revenue to establish ADMADE nationwide. Partial funding from the World Wildlife Fund allowed ADMADE to be instituted in six (out of thirty-two) game management areas in 1988.[55] The new safari hunting concession fee they had established was lucrative but would fall short of the funds the Directorate believed necessary to beat back the threat posed by the European conservationists and their proposed IRDP, who had already received the enthusiastic backing of President Kaunda and were currently discussing funding with the Norwegian Agency for International Development (NORAD).[56]

The Directorate also knew they could not count on the Zambian government to fund ADMADE. The government had severely cut NPWS budgets over time. Given the general lack of political support (see Chapter 3), bureaucratic battles over budgets would not likely end in the NPWS's favor.

NPWS senior officers realized that donor monies might be more forthcoming that government revenue. Working through connections than the U.S. researcher had cultivated with U.S. embassy personnel, the NPWS achieved some of the financial security it had sought: a $3 million grant from the United States Agency for International Development (USAID). The money firmly established ADMADE as a major program in Zambia.

The U.S. support was more than just a financial boon for ADMADE; NPWS officers purposefully used the international agreement to protect the independence of ADMADE's decision-making, personnel, and financial institutions from domestic political intervention. First, the project grant agreement between Zambia and the United States acceded to ADMADE's established decision-making structures. The document's description of the membership and powers of the Authority and Sub-Authority mirrors ADMADE's prior policy documents.[57] The ADMADE Directorate, whose name changed to the ADMADE Coordinating Committee, continued to be composed of only NPWS officers.[58] Second, the Zambian government agreed to augment "substantially" the number of NPWS staff to reduce poaching.[59] In addition, the government committed to assigning ADMADE a land use planning officer, a senior natural resource economist, a senior wildlife ranching ecologist, an accountant, a senior wildlife warden, and "any other professional or technical personnel as may be required under the Project." To support the "continuation and growth" of ADMADE, the Zambian government also agreed to absorb these positions into their permanent civil service.[60] Third, the agreement produced and protected ADMADE's revenues. USAID's money allowed ADMADE to expand to nine GMAs, considerably enlarging the area over which the NPWS could exert effective authority.[61] The Zambian government agreed to contribute "all other resources required to carry out the Project effectively and in a timely manner."[62] In addition, Zambia agreed to transfer 50 percent of the revenues earned from hunting licenses and trophy fees to the Wildlife Conservation Revolving Fund to help cover the management costs in ADMADE GMAs; to begin to tax tour operators and give the levies to the Fund; and to allow ADMADE to retain the portion of income it had been giving to the Zambian National Tourist Board. And, because ADMADE depended primarily on revenues derived from the safari business, USAID obliged the Zambian government to maintain at least the current level of recreational safari hunting in the country.[63]

To ensure the future integrity of ADMADE, the United States and Zambia agreed on the need to establish an evaluation program as part of the project. Such evaluations would include the project's success in attaining its objectives, identification of problem areas or project constraints, and assessment of the overall development impact of ADMADE, helping to reduce the possibility of ongoing intervention by domestic political actors.[64]

USAID money breathed new life into the NPWS. But the ADMADE Directorate used the sponsorship to protect their program as well. The USAID agreement tied the Zambian government to the institutions designed by the ADMADE Directorate, which had been constructed to extend NPWS authority and insulate the ADMADE program from domestic intervention. And it backed ADMADE's institutional arrangements with the threat of international retaliation.

Conservationists, Kaunda, and the Birth of LIRDP

Crafting Institutions and Seeking Political Patronage. After the 1983 Lupande Workshop, the European-led group pursued its desire to create an IRDP in the Luangwa Valley. Facing the same set of political institutions as NPWS, the group's members, however, confronted a different task in setting up their program: They were not government officials; they did not currently run a Zambian public agency; they had no staff; and they controlled no funds. These factors forced the groups to choose different tactics in their efforts to gain control over Zambia's wildlife estate and to contend with the political uncertainty of the Zambian one-party government. Most important, it pushed them into an alliance with President Kaunda.

LIRDP's Original Design. Following the Lupande Workshop's proposals, the National Commission for Development Planning (NCDP) submitted a funding request to NORAD on 17 July 1984 for a feasibility study for an integrated resource development project on the Luangwa Valley.[65] NORAD and NCDP selected two consultants for the study: Thor Larsen (NORAD) and Fidelis Lungu (NPWS).[66]

Larsen and Lungu's recommendations for the new pilot conservation program – the Luangwa Integrated Resource Development Project (LIRDP) – followed closely the three major preferences of the European-led conservationist bloc of the Lupande Workshop.[67] First, Larsen and Lungu supported the multisectoral IRDP approach.[68] Like the European conservationists, they believed such an all-encompassing institution could best manage the contingent nature of resource use, despite the general trend in the development community to move away from large-scale projects, and despite their own lack of experience with development projects of this size.[69]

Second, both Larsen and Lungu distrusted the NPWS. Their proposed LIRDP virtually eliminated NPWS's authority over the most important wildlife areas in the country. Larsen and Lungu suggested that LIRDP gain control of the South Luangwa National Park, the "jewel of the NPWS crown," and the Lupande Game Management Area, home to some of the better hunting blocs in Zambia.[70] Not only did NPWS stand to lose the revenues from the sale of these areas to safari operators, but the transfer of authority would also seriously damage the department's prestige as the de jure protector of Zambia's wildlife.[71]

Third, despite rhetoric to the contrary, Larsen and Lungu mirrored some of the European conservationists' misgivings about devolving any real authority over wildlife resources to local Africans. The consultants' report devoted less than two of more than ninety pages to the role of local Zambians within LIRDP. Larsen and Lungu avoided making any concrete recommendations about the role of locals, leaving future LIRDP administrators to "determine how these ideas and principles can best be put into life under the LIRDP."[72]

Larsen and Lungu espoused a design for LIRDP that would enhance its insulation from political intervention. They suggested the LIRDP assume authority over all land-use and resource management projects in the proposed area, including control over all aspects of wildlife management that the NPWS currently exercised, such as determining hunting quotas, controlling harvesting, distributing meat, and patrolling for poachers. The consultants thought that LIRDP administrators should also be included in the decision-making processes of all government ministry programs in the project area. Further, the consultants' report recommended that LIRDP administration gain supervisory powers over all ministry staff seconded to the project.

To enhance LIRDP's financial freedom, the consultants advocated that the project be given its own revolving fund mechanism. All revenues from project activities would be put into this fund, including game license fees, safari license fees, national park entrance fees, and revenues generated from the sale of confiscated trophies (such as ivory and rhino horn). Larsen and Lungu proposed to give the LIRDP administrators complete control of this fund, so that they could authorize necessary expenditures without having to run the gauntlet of central government agencies for permission.[73]

Further insulating LIRDP was Larsen and Lungu's plan to confer strong powers on LIRDP's two directors. The codirectors would be responsible only to a Steering Committee.[74] Although the codirectors could be advised by members of the NPWS, the University of Zambia, the Wildlife Conservation Society of Zambia, six chiefs, four chairmen of the local UNIP wards, and "other relevant agencies," the codirectors had the power to choose which activities would be funded and which individuals would staff them.[75]

Consequently, Larsen and Lungu's recommendations reflected both the preferences of the European conservationists' bloc and the political institutions of Zambia's one-party state. Decisions would emanate from the top of a hierarchically organized, independent government agency that was unaffiliated with the NPWS. LIRDP administration would have authority over the projects and staff of other government agencies in its area, and control their own revolving fund. And although rural residents would benefit from the program, they were still removed from any meaningful decision-making power over wildlife resources and remained subject to the exclusionary impact of Cap. 316, the provisions of which LIRDP planned to enforce more diligently.

LIRDP's Need for Kaunda. Lungu and the European conservationists knew their proposal for a vast new bureaucracy would not fare well if left to the normal political process. Conservation was unpopular. The government was nearly bankrupt. And extant government agencies would resent LIRDP's attempts to usurp their share of public authority. Only one Zambian politician could provide the political backing necessary to carve out the niche that LIRDP sought: President Kaunda.

Larsen and Lungu used the influence of the Eastern Province member of UNIP's Central Committee and the leverage of Larsen's affiliation with NORAD to press for a private audience with Kaunda. During their discussions, the consultants also suggested that the president assume the chairmanship of LIRDP's Steering Committee. Kaunda enthusiastically accepted.[76]

Kaunda had several reasons to support LIRDP. Of course, one reason was that the president was a conservationist who had been frustrated by his previous efforts. Conservationists outside Zambia had criticized his handling of the protection of Zambia's wildlife, and LIRDP might succeed in protecting animals where other measures had failed. But LIRDP served other, more political, ends as well. LIRDP would channel funds, development projects, and employment to the Eastern Province, long known as a UNIP stronghold. Further, LIRDP could deliver these benefits without generating criticism about Kaunda's playing regional favorites: After all, the Luangwa Valley area was chosen because of its spectacular wildlife, and the monies would come from international donors, not government coffers. The program's core area, the Mambwe Subdistrict, happened to be the home of Kaunda's wife's family; his son Wezi would win the area's parliamentary seat in 1988. Supporting the LIRDP allowed Kaunda to meet conservation and political goals with little cost.

LIRDP began to benefit immediately from the patronage of the most powerful politician in Zambia. Unlike most development projects under the NCDP, Larsen and Lungu used Kaunda's backing to avoid presenting their proposals for scrutiny, and LIRDP's Phase I began without NCDP review.[77] Kaunda intervened directly to hire LIRDP's codirectors, writing to the Malawian president, Hastings Banda, to release Dr. Richard Bell from service as a consultant to the Malawian wildlife department. Kaunda also wrote a letter to the Ministry of Finance on 7 May 1986, formally initiating LIRDP and appointing Bell and Lungu as its codirectors.[78] And Kaunda began personal appeals to the prime minister of Norway for funding.[79]

Bell and Lungu used Kaunda's backing to build an organization insulated from other government agencies. After LIRDP's official start under the supervision of the NCDP's permanent secretary, the codirectors concentrated on developing the organizational structure, work programs, and funding proposals from late 1985 to early 1986. The permanent secretaries of an advisory committee, worried about LIRDP's future powers, encouraged the codirectors to discuss LIRDP with salient government departments, NGOs, and local communities.[80]

Bell and Lungu realized that government agencies would fear their program, because they had acquired Kaunda's backing and needed public authority that must come from the portfolios of extant ministries and departments.[81] In their first progress report, Bell and Lungu attempted to mollify some officials' initial worry about their spheres of influence. Explicitly stating that LIRDP "should not be regarded as a 'special project' with special privileges," the report asserts that although LIRDP may be a "novel" organization, it will develop to be a "mainstream component of the Zambian Government."[82] The proposed structure of LIRDP at this time appeared to place the project squarely under the authority of existing government and party officials. The Steering Committee, whose mandate was to give general policy guidance to LIRDP, included members of both the UNIP Central Committee and ministries in whose sectors or provinces LIRDP intended to operate; President Kaunda remained the chairman. Permanent secretaries formed an Executive Committee (formerly the Advisory Council), responsible for the implementation of policy. The director general of the NCDP chaired the Executive Committee.[83]

Despite these assurances, Bell and Lungu advanced a design that emphasized LIRDP's insulation from political and financial intervention. They recommended that all district-level government officers in their program area be seconded to LIRDP. They reiterated the need for a revolving fund under the day-to-day control of the codirectors.[84] And they asked the government to draft legislation to give LIRDP the legal status of an independent, self-managing Authority.

Permanent secretaries immediately objected to Bell and Lungu's proposal for the secondment of their district-level officers to LIRDP. Bell and Lungu retreated and tried to construct another way to maintain access to the government personnel they needed to run their program.[85] Eventually, they suggested the formation of technical subcommittees to the Executive Committee. These technical subcommittees, composed of both departmental and LIRDP staff, would develop and supervise the work programs of the sectoral department staffs in the project area, with funding through LIRDP.[86] Departmental staff would "remain responsible to their parent departments, which transmit to them the decisions of the technical subcommittee."[87]

The codirectors reported the progress of Phase I, which included their design for LIRDP, to a meeting of government officials and donors at Chichele Lodge in the Luangwa Valley in June 1987. Although not attending personally, Kaunda cast a long shadow over the proceedings: The permanent secretaries present eventually agreed to Bell and Lungu's revised LIRDP structure.[88]

Despite the presence of officials from the aid agencies of the United States, Sweden, and Norway at the meeting, major donor funding had not been secured by its end. To demonstrate his strong support for LIRDP, President Kaunda summoned all of the meeting's participants to his residence at Kasaba Bay on Lake Tangyanika for discussions – with the government picking up the tab for all transportation, meals, and accommodation. Government officials present for the Kasaba Bay meetings believed Kaunda intended to demonstrate to donors that LIRDP was worth funding because it had his personal backing.[89] Donors did make stronger commitments to fund LIRDP as a result of Kaunda's intervention: In October 1988, NORAD agreed to grant LIRDP $12.3 million over its first five years.

Seeking Insulation through NORAD.   Like the NPWS, Bell and Lungu used their affiliation with an international sponsor for more than just revenue. Though benefiting from Kaunda's patronage, they also feared it. One of their strategies to reduce the president's possible intervention was to keep him as head of the LIRDP Steering Committee, a relatively powerless position that would allow the codirectors both to monitor Kaunda's positions and to influence him to favor their goals. But the president could still squash the dreams of Bell, Lungu, and the European conservationists for an entirely independent conservation agency operating in the Luangwa Valley.

Consequently, the codirectors structured the agreement with NORAD to limit the possibility of political – especially Kaunda's – intervention. The agreement stipulates LIRDP's institutional design as the outcome of the Chichele lodge meeting and confirms the responsibilities and membership of the Steering Committee, the Advisory Committee, and the Technical Subcommittees, thus locking Kaunda, as well as other politicians, into certain well-defined roles.[90] The document also requires an annual meeting of NCDP, NORAD, and LIRDP and sets forth a minimum agenda, including discussions about ongoing activities and guidelines for the coming year's activities, work plans, and budgets. Such reviews would help the codirectors keep LIRDP on their preferred course, because their informational advantage could be used to sway NORAD and government officials. Norway also expected Zambia to "ensure that revenues from the Project are transferred to the LIRDP revolving Fund for investments and daily running of the Project," to "bear all expenses that may be required over and above the Grant for successful implementation of the Project," and to "promptly inform Norway of any condition which interferes with or threatens to interfere with the successful implementation of the Project."[91]

They hoped the institutions agreed to by the Zambian government with Norway would help mitigate Kaunda's possible intervention. They had placed him in a largely ceremonial position within the LIRDP hierarchy. They had secured a revenue base distinct from the Zambian government and Kaunda's direct control. They had agreed to annual meetings with NORAD, which would help prevent Kaunda from hijacking the program's activities. Most important, they had successfully linked President Kaunda's personal reputation with the survival of institutions designed by Bell and Lungu.

EXPANDING AGENCY AUTHORITY

Administrators of both ADMADE and LIRDP understood that the politics of structural choice never end. Even after the successful launching of their programs in the 1983–1987 period, the administrators realized their mandates could be restricted, their budgets cut, and their discretion curtailed. As a result, they continued to seek resources to protect and expand their authority from 1988 to 1991. Their initial share of public authority and the uncertainty produced by the one-party state continued to constrain their structural choices.

ADMADE: Authority and Resources through Insulation

NPWS senior officers chose ADMADE's structures to enhance significantly their agency's authority over Zambia's wildlife estate. Using their exclusive control over the Wildlife Conservation Revolving Fund and keeping all of ADMADE's decision making within the department, the program's Directorate enlarged NPWS staff, built capital projects, and spread the department's effective presence throughout the country. Insulating ADMADE's institutions and following only extant law allowed the NPWS to increase its resources while avoiding potentially costly bureaucratic turf battles with other government agencies.

The NPWS kept their revolving fund remarkably insulated from both external and internal scrutiny. Few NPWS officers other than the members of the ADMADE Directorate knew anything about its total revenues, expenditures, or procedures. Most professional hunters, unit leaders, and chiefs involved with the program did not understand how ADMADE generated or distributed the fund's monies.[92] And contrary to the ministry of finance's regulations, the NPWS chose not to submit annual reports regarding the fund to the government.[93]

The Revolving Fund's lack of transparency allowed the ADMADE Directorate great flexibility. As the Fund's beneficiary and fiduciary, the Directorate was able to make decisions that placed its interests before the preferences of local communities and the conservation needs of protected areas.[94] For example, in many cases the appropriate amount of money did not reach the ADMADE Sub-Authorities but was spent on items deemed more important by the department.[95] The directorate used monies donated to the Revolving Fund to pay for unauthorized activities.[96] They also actively protected their monopoly over financial information: Because local communities were never told the value of their wildlife, locals were preempted from any informed bargaining about the community's share of revenue generated in their area.[97]

Such financial freedom allowed the ADMADE Directorate to enlarge the department's institutional capacity. Most of the "spectacular results" reported by the NPWS for ADMADE's second year of operation (1989) referred to the expansion of departmental activities, not conservation outcomes: The village scout program approximately doubled NPWS staff in the field; ADMADE units recorded a record number of arrests (545) and confiscated firearms (140); the NPWS built more than 145 houses for village scouts; and 500 local residents obtained employment through ADMADE as either village scouts or day laborers.[98] Additionally, ADMADE's Revolving Fund allowed the NPWS to expand the department's capabilities in land-use planning, community development, resource monitoring, and scout training.[99] These accomplishments mirrored the type of goals pursued by the department for the previous fifty years. And, according to the Fund's own administrator, the NPWS swallowed 70 percent of the Revolving Fund's 1991 income to achieve these ends.[100]

These activities enabled the NPWS to increase its effective reach over the country's wildlife estate by establishing a much stronger presence in the field. Thanks to ADMADE, NPWS deployed scouts to reinforce the most lucrative safari hunting areas. The program also funded scouts in areas without significant wildlife populations, hoping that in time, these regions could also prove attractive to safari hunters. Additionally, ADMADE monies paid for the increased supervision of these scouts.

The ADMADE Directorate jealously guarded their decision-making powers, maintaining tight control over long- and short-term policy decisions. They supervised the program's daily implementation and controlled all financial disbursements, vehicle usage, hunting quotas, and wildlife monitoring activities. Indicative of their strategy to insulate the program and their decision making, the ADMADE Directorate created no mechanism to evaluate its operation over its first four years.[101]

The Directorate's pursuit of additional resources and insulation was often at the expense of its promulgated goal of a sustainable, participatory conservation program. ADMADE's data on animal populations were spotty and unreliable;[102] its hunting quotas were arrived at by guesswork;[103] it had mustered only one significant animal survey (of elephants), and only after USAID had agreed to pay for it;[104] it had made no progress toward getting the government to give local proprietorship over wildlife to local communities;[105] it had produced no hard evidence of decline in poaching;[106] and, most important, it had not yet established any self-sustaining wildlife management programs.

A review team also found ADMADE's Wildlife Conservation Revolving Fund in disarray. Rumors about illegal revenue transfers were rife. The fund's administrator could not account for a large amount of missing money.[107] The staff had no system for reconciling the revenue earned from licenses with the number actually issued, allowing inflated numbers to be sold.[108] They mixed the expenditures and receipts from ADMADE units, which made any assessment of each area's self-sufficiency impossible. They lost important financial documents,[109] wrote reports lacking crucial data, and made mathematical mistakes.[110] Rather than improve conservation, much of the insulation that ADMADE had achieved promoted mismanagement and a distribution of benefits to individuals.

LIRDP: Authority and Resources through Legislation

Because LIRDP had no legal foundation, its codirectors could not follow the same strategy of insulation employed by the NPWS. Without a legislative mandate, the codirectors remained dependent on Kaunda in the short run to acquire additional resources and authority, and yet they also wanted to eliminate the political vulnerability of being Kaunda's ward. Thus, armed with LIRDP's most significant powers, the codirectors followed a two-pronged strategy: to secure an independent financial base for LIRDP operations and to get legislation passed to establish LIRDP as an entity separate from the president and other government ministries.

LIRDP's organizational structure focused control of the program on the codirectors, Richard Bell and Fidelis Lungu.[111] The program's cumbersome committee structure prevented functional management or oversight of LIRDP's codirectors. The Steering Committee, chaired by President Kaunda, did little after its first meeting on 13 July 1988 to follow its mandate of giving policy guidance to the program.[112] The Executive Committee, composed of permanent secretaries, did not perform its role of implementing the program.[113] Neither committee had any legal standing, and no functional managerial relationship or coordination seemed to exist between the committees, their subcommittee, and the project's regular administration.[114] The codirectors filled this administrative gap and assumed significant personal control over both short- and long-term operations, dominating decision making about LIRDP's planning, staffing, and finance.

LIRDP's institutions quickly became identified with the persons of Bell and Lungu.[115] The codirectors delegated little authority to their administrative deputies, whom they considered ineffective and inexperienced.[116] The codirectors appeared at every committee meeting[117] and took over jobs they felt too crucial to entrust to their staff, such as managing the foreign exchange earned from LIRDP's safari hunting operations.[118] Eventually, lower level administrators relied on the codirectors for all initiatives, implementation, and decisions.[119] So dependent was LIRDP on its codirectors that NORAD officials feared the project would not survive if Bell and Lungu left their positions.[120]

The considerable political capital provided by President Kaunda's favor allowed Bell and Lungu to construct and control financial structures for LIRDP that remained remarkably free of oversight. As with AD-MADE, LIRDP enjoyed the financial freedom of a revolving fund. The contributions of the Zambian government and NORAD were placed directly into the fund. As a result of the influence of Kaunda, LIRDP retained 100 percent of the foreign exchange it earned from its projects in the Lupande area, in complete disregard of the regulations of the Exchange Control Act.[121] Kaunda also allowed LIRDP to establish overseas bank accounts.[122] Although the permanent secretary of the NCDP had overall responsibility for the fund, specific expenditures from the fund did not need NCDP approval.[123] NORAD had to approve extraordinary expenditures and ceilings for major categories, but the codirectors controlled expenditures within categories.[124] Like ADMADE's Revolving Fund, LIRDP's fund did not submit its reports to the Ministry of Finance as required by law.[125] As a result, Bell and Lungu governed the daily operation of the fund.[126]

In addition to establishing independent control over LIRDP's finances, the codirectors used the political umbrella provided by Kaunda to seek legal foundations for their program and expand its legislative authority.[127] One of their first attempts was to transfer control over wildlife resources in the LIRDP area from the NPWS to LIRDP through a statutory instrument.[128] At the time, NPWS scouts and officers were the only individuals legally empowered to manage and control wild animals in Zambia. To circumvent the "legal entanglements" that would have been generated by LIRDP personnel instructing NPWS staff, the Ministry of Tourism created a new NPWS command post with boundaries that coincided with LIRDP's area;[129] the warden of the new Mfuwe Command, although not officially seconded to the LIRDP, then worked with the codirectors to execute LIRDP's wildlife management activities (LIRDP administered its own village scout program, supported NPWS patrols, and created an investigation unit to combat poaching).[130]

This arrangement remained unsatisfactory to Bell and Lungu, who considered the personnel of the NPWS and the Ministry of Tourism ineffective and possibly corrupt. The codirectors castigated the Ministry of Tourism for overruling their decisions regarding the organization of safari hunting, tourism development, allocation of special hunting licenses, and National Park entry fees.[131] Using the authority granted by the resolution of the Kaunda-chaired LIRDP Steering Committee, which instructed LIRDP management to "investigate and make recommendations on alternative legislation with the object of strengthening and streamlining the operation," Bell and Lungu prepared a draft statutory instrument to give LIRDP complete control and management powers over wildlife in the program area.[132] LIRDP's Executive Committee approved the draft and forwarded it to the Steering Committee.[133] In an April 1989 meeting of the president and NORAD representatives, Kaunda gave assurances that "the matter would be rapidly resolved," intimating that LIRDP would be granted complete responsibility for wildlife in the program's area.[134] The Ministry of Legal Affairs argued later, however, that the proposed transfer of authority could not be accomplished by a statutory instrument (which presumably would not have been difficult for Bell and Lungu to obtain through Kaunda and his minister) but would require an amendment to the Wildlife Act, which required action by the entire National Assembly.[135] The finding forced Bell and Lungu to drop their efforts to achieve authority over wildlife through a statutory instrument.

But the codirectors had other legislative strategies, such as pushing for amendments to a new Wildlife Act that would increase LIRDP's authority over wildlife. The amendments offered by Bell and Lungu stipulated that the minister of tourism could establish integrated resource development committees (IRDCs) by statutory order. The IRDCs' powers were to include managing national parks and game management areas, as well as promoting and developing integrated approaches to the management of human and natural resources. The amendments also provided that the IRDCs could set up a fund to retain all the revenues generated by wildlife resources in their area.[136]

The amendments' provisions clearly mirrored the structure of the LIRDP program. Importantly, the amendments also placed the IRDCs in a more powerful position than the NPWS director in terms of the control and management of the national parks and game management areas.[137] Although the new laws regarding the IRDC would not fully eliminate LIRDP's conflicts with the NPWS or the Ministry of Tourism, because the minister retained the power to create IRDCs and appoint their secretariats, they could establish the foundations for IRDC supremacy over the NPWS in wildlife management. When the new Wildlife Act, complete with the IRDC alterations, passed in 1991, Bell and Lungu succeeded in providing legal grounds for the existence of LIRDP and its independent funds while partially removing some of the NPWS's ability to interfere with the program.

Another legislative goal for the codirectors was to gain Authority status for LIRDP.[138] An Authority "would have autonomous status capable of having corporate bodies to execute the powers entrusted to the authority."[139] Such status would make LIRDP completely independent of the line ministries, whose responsibilities would be transferred to the program by amending every parliamentary act that concerned control over natural resources and development in the LIRDP project area.[140]

Finally, the codirectors planned a legislative attempt to create a national version of LIRDP. Bell and Lungu proposed a National Integrated Resource Development Programme (NIRDP), based on the LIRDP model, and suggested a feasibility study be funded. Under the NIRDP, ADMADE would be incorporated into the NIRDP with a "minimum of adjustment," and the NPWS would be relegated to assigning one professional wildlife officer to each NIRDP project area.[141] In other words, the NIRDP would control Zambia's wildlife estate and have the ability to direct the activities of NPWS personnel. The NIRDP concept received "considerable campaigning" at the level of the LIRDP Steering Committee.[142]

The codirectors' strategies did not necessarily improve LIRDP's goals of conservation or community participation. Evaluators found many of LIRDP's structures appeared to exist only for political purposes.[143] Although chiefs, through the Local Leaders' Subcommittee, made decisions regarding development projects, reviewers questioned the extent of the codirectors' influence on the subcommittee's membership; no institutional mechanism seemed to balance the powers Bell and Lungu wielded as a result of their strong connections to local and national political leaders.[144] One review mission openly doubted that the codirectors used these political resources to enhance their accountability to the local community.[145]

Review teams also criticized Bell and Lungu for their attempts to insulate their program as well as expand its authority without regard for other government and nongovernment agencies.[146] The reviewers indicted the codirectors for not encouraging other projects in the LIRDP area, bypassing the local district councils, duplicating the efforts of other government agencies, and trying to undermine other institutions rather than strengthen them.[147] A "groundswell of resentment" had grown toward LIRDP as a result of their confrontational methods.[148] The evaluators reported that personnel of other government departments and ministries – especially the NPWS and Tourism – expressed deep resentment and felt "hijacked" by LIRDP.[149]

BUREAUCRATS AND STRUCTURAL CHOICE IN KENYA AND ZIMBABWE

Kenya

Richard Leakey's long tenure as the head of Kenya's museums had taught him that bureaucrats faced a highly uncertain political environment in his country. Politicians and civil servants confronted a one-party patronage system with President Moi at the apex. As the new director of the Kenya Wildlife Service (KWS), Leakey understood that his own political authority was directly related to his personal appointment by Moi. Like the creators of Zambia's LIRDP, who also faced a powerful one-party president and lacked public authority, Leakey used Moi's political support to construct a highly insulated public agency. In doing so, the new director risked political enmity by ignoring and challenging other Kenyan politicians and bureaucrats.

The first four years of Richard Leakey's tenure brought about a remarkable transformation of Kenya's wildlife management. Leakey fired more than two thousand employees and acquired updated equipment, uniforms, and better pay for the ones who remained. To the KWS pool of vehicles, which before 1989 did not have enough fuel for routine patrols, Leakey added many all-terrain vehicles and even two helicopter gunships. To demonstrate Kenya's commitment to the ivory ban, Leakey convinced President Moi to burn $3 million worth of elephant tusks. He provided better weapons to his scouts and pushed a "shoot to kill" policy against poachers – and made sure KWS got favorable publicity after any successful KWS field battle. Poaching decreased. Elephant populations increased. By 1994, Kenya's tourism produced $450 million of foreign exchange to the Kenyan economy.[150] Domestic groups associated with tourism and conservation in Kenya, as well as international conservation organizations, praised Leakey's rapid progress.

Leakey pushed for and enjoyed the fruits of a bureaucratic structure that allowed him wide latitude in administering wildlife policy. Given President Moi's need to shore up Kenya's international reputation as a tourist haven, and the reputation of the former Wildlife Conservation and Management Department (WCMD) as a corruption-ridden bureaucracy, Leakey possessed the leverage needed to demand considerable autonomy from regular governmental structures.[151] Under the new KWS terms, he was answerable only to President Moi, not the Ministry of Tourism, as had been the former WCMD. Moi's support of the new KWS parastatal allowed Leakey, among other things, to fire civil servants relatively easily, to accumulate and to distribute monies directly, and to pay some of his staff wages superior to those of their civil service colleagues. Assured of President Moi's backing, Leakey used these powers freely as he pursued a mix of wildlife policies aimed at protecting megafauna, obtaining international funds, and bolstering Kenya's image as a tourist destination. Leakey was also interested in creating policies that included local participation, the growing trend in African wildlife management.[152]

Although the KWS structure may have been efficient for the implementation of wildlife policy, it ran counter to many of the incentives generated by Kenya's one-party state. Kenyan politicians and bureaucrats disliked the KWS's insulation from line ministries: Leakey appointed and fired staff without regard to ministers or party officials. Politicians and bureaucrats resented having their access to wildlife resources curtailed: The KWS no longer allowed local councils to skim from the gate receipts of national parks, and officials lost some of the bribes they had formerly received from organized ivory poachers. And politicians and bureaucrats coveted the new resources Leakey had generated: Leakey did not share KWS's large influx of foreign funds and equipment with other politicians or bureaucrats.[153] Among others, Leakey had also directly crossed Nicholas Biwott, the government's chief fund-raiser, by denying him permission to construct an oil pipeline through the Nairobi National Park.[154]

Without Moi's political backing, Leakey was extremely vulnerable. Because Moi was at the apex of the patronage system, Leakey had not constructed alliances with other politicians in the country. The vast majority of Kenyans remained at best skeptical about the need for conservation laws. With a growing population and a scarcity of arable land, opposing conservation remained a safe political position in Kenya. Wild animals still presented a threat to some rural Kenyans' crops and lives (wildlife killed eighty-eight people in the Tana River district alone from 1980 to 1989). And because the majority of those who cared about or benefited from the conservation laws were white, the race card could be played easily in battles over wildlife policy. Politicians used all of these issues after Moi withdrew his support for Leakey.

Verbal attacks by the local government minister William Ole Ntimama, one of Moi's closest allies, signaled the end of Leakey's presidential support.[155] Ntimama claimed that Leakey used his scouts as a private army, ignored the plight of the Maasai families who lived cheek by jowl with wildlife, failed to give local councils their share of game park revenues, and discriminated against black Africans. Using language that would have been familiar to the independence politicians of Zambia and Zimbabwe, Ntimama declared that Leakey "has disregarded our human rights and upheld the rights of animals in order to kill us off."[156] Twenty-five local councils joined the public vilification. The minister of tourism, whose authority over wildlife had been bypassed with the creation of the KWS, launched an official investigation into the agency's activities.

In the face of these withering attacks, Leakey eventually resigned, placing his future as the director of KWS in the hands of his former supporter President Moi. Moi, caught between his political clients' desire to dispose of Leakey and the outrage of international and domestic conservation groups supportive of Leakey, demonstrated his own understanding of the politics of structural choice: Moi did not accept Leakey's resignation, but restructured the KWS so that (1) the KWS director would report to the minister of tourism, (2) 75 percent of KWS resources would be disbursed to areas outside game parks, (3) 25 percent of game park receipts would be given to communities, and (4) KWS's armed units would be answerable to Kenya's police force. Rather than accept these terms, Leakey resigned again. This time, Moi accepted.

Zimbabwe

Officers within Zimbabwe's Department of National Parks and Wildlife Management (hereafter the Department) did not confront the same type of political uncertainty as those in the wildlife departments of Zambia or Kenya. Although President Mugabe was powerful, his personal backing was not necessary for the success of an agency or its programs. Other domestic politicians and interest groups mattered in Zimbabwe's political arena, especially those involved in large economic sectors like commercial farming and the tourism industry. Neither did the Department need to establish its public authority, because, like the NPWS in Zambia and the KWS in Kenya, it enjoyed the legal mandate over wildlife in Zimbabwe. Instead, the Department went about building a coalition of domestic and international groups to pursue its policy agenda, which centered on broadening its base, especially among Zimbabweans living in communal areas.

The Department had successfully changed many commercial farmers' opinion about wildlife with policies that allowed landowners to gain commercially from hunting and trade in wild animals (codified in the 1975 Wildlife Act). But most of the country's conservation lands abutted communal land, not private land, and thus the majority of people who had interactions with wildlife were black and nonlandowning. The country's first black Zimbabwean government and its overwhelmingly black electorate retained their historical suspicions of wildlife conservation. For example, a 1989 political rally for the ruling party in a rural area had to be canceled as a result of the lack of an audience; some complained that the high-ranking party official scheduled to address the rally should address the wild animals of the area instead, as the animals represented the party's real constituency.[157] In some areas locals thought the Department arrived quickly at the scene of an elephant kill but responded painfully slowly to complaints of crop raiding elephants.[158] The government's ambivalence toward the Department was demonstrated in the severe staffing cuts it would endure as a result of a World Bank structural adjustment exercise.[159] Clearly, any Department effort to broaden their domestic political support or responsibilities would face formidable challenges.

The Department responded to the deep-seated suspicions with a series of policies targeted at involving the inhabitants of communal areas. As a result of its success, one program – the Communal Areas Management Programme for Indigenous Resources (CAMPFIRE) – came to dominate many of the Department's activities. CAMPFIRE also became the best-known community-based wildlife program in Africa, if not the world.[160]

The cornerstone of CAMPFIRE was the 1982 amendment to the 1975 Wildlife Act, which extended the categories of possible "appropriate authority" over wildlife to include Zimbabwe's district councils. The 1982 amendment made it possible for Zimbabweans living in communal areas to capture some of the benefits of wildlife that private landowners had enjoyed since 1975. Building on this legislation, the Department constructed a purportedly decentralized, community-based policy that widened their bureaucratic mandate, cultivated domestic and international supporters and funds, extended effective enforcement of wildlife laws, and gained the Department great celebrity.

The policy foundations for CAMPFIRE, which had been discussed by Department staff and others in the early 1980s, were laid out in 1986.[161] The overall objective was "to initiate a program for the long term development, management and sustainable utilization of natural resources in the Communal Areas . . . involving forestry, grazing, water, and wildlife."[162] The Department recognized the need to give local communities the opportunity to control their own resources by participating in management and decision making. It also acknowledged that members of local communities must realize benefits if they were to stop their illegal use of natural resources, and that these benefits should be distributed in a manner equating returns with risk.

Although Department officials originally envisioned housing CAMPFIRE in a national level parastatal, the government did not support this idea.[163] Realizing that it had neither the staff nor the resources to initiate the program by itself, the Department chose to "co-opt other organizations to fill in the most glaring gaps."[164] The Centre for Applied Social Sciences at the University of Zambia began to conduct research for CAMPFIRE in 1984. The Zimbabwe Trust (ZimTrust), a nongovernmental organization concerned with improving living conditions in marginal areas, offered its development expertise to the Department in 1987. And the Harare-based Multi-Species Animal Production Systems Project of the World Wide Fund for Nature (WWF) provided technical assistance related to the monitoring of economic and ecological systems in 1988. Together, these three organizations formed the CAMPFIRE Collaborative Group, chaired by the Department. The Department "cultivated" these NGOs, and, rather than immediately seek external funds, it encouraged them to obtain funds only to the level of their CAMPFIRE-related activities.[165]

CAMPFIRE began modestly; the Department granted appropriate Authority status to its first district council because of the high likelihood of success: With an extensive boundary with Lake Kariba, the Nyaminyami District already had relatively well-developed safari and tourist activities, including a four star hotel located nearby.[166] After its first year of Authority status in 1989, the Nyaminyami District Council earned Z$272,000 from safari operation and Z$47,000 from culling.[167] The second district council to be given Authority status, Guruve, allocated monies for its school and clinic, and Z$200 cash to every household in the ward, which contained the most wildlife in the district. Soon thereafter, donors committed modest funds for the extension of CAMPFIRE programs, and the Department began the process of reviewing petitions for appropriate Authority status from nine other districts. By 1993, seventy wards from twelve districts were participating in the program.

Nearly all analyses of CAMPFIRE praise its innovation, especially its decentralization of authority over wildlife. A few observers claim, however, that through the program the Department has actually increased its power over Zimbabwe's wildlife estate.[168] They do not dispute the financial gains from the program or the enthusiasm of the local level officials involved with it. Rather, their claims lie in the way that the Department structured CAMPFIRE.

The source of the Department's power in CAMPFIRE is its ability to grant appropriate authority status. Those with such status are permitted, inter alia, to enter into private contracts for wildlife products and safari hunting, and to receive directly all payments generated from wildlife resources on their lands. In return for these privileges, the appropriate authority must carry out, to the Department's satisfaction, its own problem animal control, law enforcement, and resource protection.[169] The

Wildlife Policy and Structural Choice

Department grants such authority to those district councils that signal "their willingness and preparedness to assume responsibility." Among other specific requirements, the Department also insists that district councils demonstrate an intention to return the benefits to those communities where wildlife is found and provide accountable structures for CAMPFIRE's implementation.

There are powerful reasons for district councils to demonstrate such readiness, intention, and structure. Since independence, Zimbabwe's central government has attempted to foist greater responsibility over local development on district councils while withdrawing financial support (the central government's share of the district councils' budget declined from 100 percent to 85 percent between 1980 and 1991).[170] As a result, district councils search continuously for additional sources of revenue. For those districts with sufficient wildlife populations, CAMPFIRE appears as a gift: The revenue from wildlife represents one of the few nonobligated sources of district council funds.[171] Whereas a council's previous attempts to gain benefits from wildlife were characterized by a lengthy process requiring petitions to both the Department and the Ministry of Local Government and Rural and Urban Development, Authority status eliminates the intermediaries.

CAMPFIRE, however, does not completely decentralize authority to the districts; in fact, the Department's policy can be seen to augment both its power and its reach. The Department retains its authority over setting quotas for hunting and cropping, monitors the appropriate Authority's activities, and requires an annual report from the districts that participate. Ultimate ownership of all wildlife remains with the state: Local uses of wildlife without DN approval remain illegal. Before CAMPFIRE, the Department had no business at the district level besides the control of problem animals or illegal hunting; its smallest administrative unit was the province. Through CAMPFIRE, the Department has constructed a way to extend its influence to the district level. And although the Department does not have the staff to commit to all its appropriate authorities, by assigning communities the responsibility to procure their own wildlife guards, paid for by CAMPFIRE funds and trained by the Department, it increases the level of conservation enforcement in Zimbabwe's rural areas.[172]

Zimbabwe's central government, through the Department, thus remains the ultimate arbiter over wildlife in the country, and "will use the legislation at its disposal to intervene wherever it considers that wildlife is not being adequately preserved or managed."[173] The Department's ability to withdraw appropriate authority status appears a credible threat. Although district councils retained the majority of their CAMPFIRE revenues for their own purposes in the early period of the program, the Department's insistence that the revenues be shared with communities has been heard: The average district council share dropped from 44 percent to around 21 percent between 1989 and 1993.[174]

The Department's strategy appears to support general assertions about the politics of structural choice, especially the model of bureaucrats operating under a parliamentary system.[175] Because legislation generally passes relatively easily under parliamentary systems, bureaucrats seek means other than laws to augment and to insulate their resources. Neither did the Department have to contend with a capricious one-party president sitting atop a patronage pyramid; they did not need to obtain President Mugabe's personal support (as did LIRDP in Zambia and Leakey in Kenya) or to construct elaborate institutions to protect departmental resources from him (as did ADMADE, LIRDP, and the KWS).[176] Instead, the Department used its extant public authority to construct self-enhancing institutions and extralegislative domestic partnerships through CAMPFIRE.

CONCLUSION

During the 1970s and early 1980s, international concern over poaching in Africa reached an all-time high. President Kaunda was as sensitive to international criticism of Zambia's record of protecting wildlife as he was sympathetic to its conservation. He knew how little money his government, still in a downward economic spiral, could afford to allocate to wildlife management. He also knew that few Zambians shared his attitude toward conservation. Of all sectors, international support for domestic public agencies dealing with wildlife conservation would have been most welcomed by Kaunda.

Two groups of conservationists in Zambia capitalized on these circumstances to design new, competing conservation programs. Both sought to expand their control over wildlife; both understood the credible threat a one-party president posed to their plans; and both tried to put their resources out of his reach.

One tactic the programs shared was gaining the backing of an international donor. Agreements with Norway and the United States helped LIRDP and ADMADE secure funding and decision-making structures without which the programs would remain highly vulnerable to President Kaunda and other Zambian politicians.

But given a different share of public authority, ADMADE and LIRDP made dissimilar choices about Kaunda's personal support. NPWS already enjoyed a legislative mandate as protector and administrator of Zambia's wildlife. By keeping ADMADE within their department, NPWS officers believed they did not need political heavyweights to establish or maintain their program. Thus, ADMADE's managers followed a strategy of avoiding conflict with other government agencies while keeping all decision making within the ADMADE Directorate. This allowed the NPWS to enlarge the number of personnel involved with the ADMADE program, replenish the department's financial resources, and expand the area of the country it patrolled. Because of President Kaunda's power and the historical animosity between NPWS and Kaunda, ADMADE's managers purposefully minimized the role of Kaunda in their program, fearing his ability to alter its goals, staff, and institutions.[177] ADMADE was successful at limiting Kaunda to the performance of largely ceremonial functions, such as handing out the "local community share" of ADMADE revenues to chiefs.[178]

LIRDP's codirectors, on the other hand, could not hope to expand and protect their agency's authority through insulation alone. Their goal was to create a new and largely independent government body in the Luangwa Valley; to do this, they knew they would need to expropriate the powers of extant line ministries. To carve out a bureaucratic space for themselves in the short run, LIRDP supporters needed Kaunda's clout, despite the risks posed by the president's involvement. But LIRDP's managers also sought to be free of their dependence on Kaunda in the long run and thus pursued a strategy of gaining an independent power base through legislative means.

The strategies chosen by the managers of both ADMADE and LIRDP had significant consequences for Zambian wildlife policy. In the future, these choices would determine the outcome of the competition between ADMADE and LIRDP for control over Zambian wildlife. In the short term, they generated a particular distribution of benefits to rural residents.

The behavior of agency designers in the cases of Kenya and Zimbabwe adds depth to our understanding of the politics of structural choice. Richard Leakey, operating under a set of incentives similar to those found in Zambia during the same period, followed remarkably similar strategies to those of Zambian bureaucrats. Although Leakey understood the potential for meddling by a one-party president, he also knew that operating in the cutthroat arena of Kenyan patronage politics required Moi's support. While the support lasted, Leakey was able to pursue his insulated policy agenda; when it evaporated, he resigned. Leakey knew that without Moi, his agency was unlikely to be able to protect or to extend its resources.

The officers of Zimbabwe's DNPWM did not confront the same political conditions as their counterparts in Zambia and Kenya. Instead of an all-powerful one-party state, the Department confronted a strong executive that also had to deal with strong domestic groups and coalitions. The Department also enjoyed legislative authority over the country's wildlife estate; in this milieu, they set about attempting to expand their authority and resources without expending a great deal of resources worrying about the country's president. Given the parliamentary nature of government, however, the Department sought extralegislative rather than legislative means to do so. The CAMPFIRE program represented the culmination of the Department's efforts to organize domestic partners.

This chapter has focused on how supporters of public agencies make choices that directly reflect the distribution of power in political systems. Many studies of bureaucracy, while acknowledging how the political arena might undermine public agencies, normally fail to include politics as a fundamental explanation for the structure of bureaucracies. Scholars and practitioners generally criticize the corrupting influence of politics on bureaucratic activity, and, while implicitly hoping for the elimination of politics, forward bureaucratic solutions (more communication, better planning, better training, and so forth) to cure systemic ills.[179] The analysis in this chapter has indicated that politics is more than one of many constraints on effective bureaucratic activity. Politics structures bureaucracy before it has had the chance to design or implement its programmatic goals. Choices about structure cannot be separated from policy mandates. This study supports the conclusions of those scholars who conceptualize bureaucratic design as a reflection of the interests, strategies, and power of those who exercise political power, not as an institutional solution that produces public goods effectively.

This chapter has also established that the politics of structural choice is as important to explanations of political institutions in developing countries with a one-party state as it is in industrial democracies. Political uncertainty stems from a variety of sources, not just democratic elections. The sources in Zambia, Kenya, and Zimbabwe include the powers of one-party and multiparty presidents, the structure of political parties, and the public authority enjoyed by certain bureaucracies. Given the specific pattern of such uncertainty found in each of these three countries, this chapter has been able to anticipate the different and sometimes opposing strategies that groups used to expand their resources and to protect their public agencies from political intervention.

PART III

The Local Politics
of Wildlife Policy

5

The Consequences of Institutional Design:
The Impact of "Community-Based" Wildlife
Management Programs at the
Local Level

We want local people to protect the animals. [Laughter in the National Assembly's chambers.]
The Honorable R. A. Natala, addressing the National
Assembly, 13 August 1982

A growing number of conservationists and development specialists in the 1970s and 1980s, including the administrators of ADMADE and LIRDP, argued that the inclusion of local communities in wildlife management was indispensable for successful conservation. These experts charged that because conventional policies excluded rural residents from the economic benefits of wildlife, they had no incentive to stop illegal hunting. And because the wildlife departments of many African governments were woefully underfunded, locals killed animals with impunity.

To close what had become an open-access wildlife commons in Zambia, ADMADE and LIRDP each offered an array of benefits designed to encourage locals to protect rather than hunt animals. A number of rural residents gained employment as wildlife scouts and general laborers. Certain traditional leaders received control over the revenue that the programs apportioned to local communities. ADMADE and LIRDP revenue built schools, health clinics, roads, bridges, and other community-level projects. And both programs intended to foster cooperation between scouts and residents.

Yet, even with ADMADE and LIRDP in place, rural residents continued to kill, consume, and trade wild animals illegally. Although wildlife scouts made more arrests for poaching-related activities, and although both programs seemed to stem the killing of large mammals, locals kept hunting – at rates comparable to those of the days before ADMADE and LIRDP's operations. ADMADE and LIRDP also failed to defuse the long-standing hostility between scouts and residents.

This chapter examines the implementation of ADMADE and LIRDP at the local level to understand the distributive consequences of particular wildlife policies. Though possessing considerably different structures, ADMADE and LIRDP shared similar assumptions about the rationality and behavior of rural residents and constructed programs with comparable incentive structures. I argue that the administrators of both programs misunderstood the decision problems of chiefs, scouts, and local hunters by focusing on collective, rather than individual, benefits. Consequently, they designed institutions of reward and punishment that prompted locals to continue their hunting, chiefs to monopolize program benefits, and scouts to maintain their adversarial relationship with residents.

The chapter begins by presenting profiles of the three most important actors in wildlife management at the local level in Zambia: rural resident, wildlife scout, and chief. These profiles are then used with noncooperative game theory to explore both the assumptions made by AD-MADE and LIRDP administrators about individuals and their interactions and the actual outcomes of both programs. I argue that the weak performance of the programs is due to the type of costs and benefits they produce: The programs augment conventional enforcement and provide community-level goods. The result of this combination is that individuals continue to hunt but change their prey and hunting method. Rather than convincing individuals to opt for conservation per se, the programs ultimately offer incentives quite similar to those of conventional policy, wherein locals do not own or control their wildlife resources and their use of wildlife remains illegal. Because the essential structure of "community-based" wildlife programs in Kenya and Zimbabwe reflects the Zambian experience, outcomes in these two countries are similar as well.

SCOUT, CHIEF, AND RESIDENT IN RURAL ZAMBIAN SOCIETY

This section examines the three most important actors concerning wildlife in Zambia's rural areas – residents, scouts, and chiefs – to put into context the subsequent analysis of ADMADE and LIRDP's effects at the local level. The section sketches the socioeconomic conditions experienced by each actor living in a typical rural area. It demonstrates how wildlife features in the daily lives of residents, scouts, and chiefs by focusing on the costs and benefits wild animals offer and the control these actors have over them. It also examines how these actors present each other with constraints and opportunities vis-à-vis wildlife resources.

Wildlife Management Programs at the Local Level

Rural Residents

Life in most rural areas of Zambia is difficult.[1] Subsistence farming is the predominant occupation. Families labor on small plots, averaging two hectares, using hand-held hoes. The crops grown depend on local soils and weather; they include maize, cassava, sorghum, and millet.[2] Residents depend on rainfall that, although adequate on average, varies tremendously over space and time, causing frequent droughts and floods.[3] Villagers consume most of what they produce. Occasionally, they may sell small surpluses in order to purchase consumer goods or pay school fees. As in most rural societies, kinship groups are important in the Zambian countryside and can provide needed labor, cash, and food, as well as valuable contacts in the city. Although employment in urban areas is stagnant, most young men and women desire to migrate there, at least for a time, producing a constant flow of individuals moving from one area to the other seeking better opportunities.

Villagers lack many of the conveniences found in the cities or towns. Most rural residents construct their homes from local materials, usually mud and thatch; civil servants and teachers may be allocated a home constructed of concrete blocks and a tin roof. Occasionally, a member of a village will return from an urban area with enough money to build a brick home, an obvious sign of status. Rural communities depend on wells and rivers for their water. Very few villages receive electricity, so women cook with charcoal or wood. Newspapers sometimes circulate to rural villages, but most information passes by word of mouth and battery-operated radio. Almost no one owns a vehicle, but some rural dwellers avoid long walks by pedaling bicycles. If a community is lucky enough to be located near a road, its members stream to trucks and tractors that stop nearby, hoping to hitch rides to urban centers to migrate, visit relatives, or buy what goods they can afford.

Government services in the countryside are substandard. Benefiting from the high revenues from copper in the 1960s, various ministries attempted to build the infrastructure in rural areas that the colonial government had ignored. Many schools and clinics, in fact, were built, but it proved too costly to fulfill all the needs of these widely scattered communities. And the few government inputs that were provided deteriorated rapidly along with the country's economy in the early 1970s. Health clinics in rural areas are few and carry little medicine and few supplies. Education is inferior: The Ministry of Education dispatches novice teachers or disciplinary cases to rural areas, knowing that few desire such remote assignments.[4] Transportation is limited; most "roads" off the country's main north–south and east–west arteries are dirt tracks, making movement difficult at the best of times, and nearly impossible during the rainy season.

The local elites include the chief, headmen, schoolteachers, local party officials, officers of the government stationed in the community, and anyone who might have returned to the village after having received more formal education or accumulated wealth. Decision making at the level of the community rarely includes the active participation of most residents.

In those rural areas near national parks or game management areas, residents confront the additional challenges posed by the presence of wild animals.[5] Wildlife threatens crops. Elephants and buffalo may make dramatic displays of devastating crops, but the daily toll taken by monkeys, baboons, bush pigs, insects, and birds results in greater total losses.[6] Wildlife also prevents animal husbandry. Tsetse fly, harbored by wildlife, kills cattle and goats and sickens humans by passing the parasite trypanosoma. And wildlife endangers lives: Each year buffalos, snakes, elephants, crocodiles, and hippopotami, among others, regularly claim their share of victims.[7]

Wildlife offers advantages, however, in the form of meat and trophies. Game meat helps rural residents survive in difficult circumstances. Residents rarely divulge information about their use or consumption of wildlife, so estimates about the contribution of game meat to an individual's diet are few and range widely.[8] The United Nations' Food and Agriculture Organization found that 13.4 percent of protein in Zambia is consumed in the form of game.[9] Marks estimates that for certain parts of Zambia's Munyamadzi corridor the average adult annually consumed two hundred pounds of game meat in the early 1970s.[10]

Kills also provide rural residents with income and exchange value. Hunters sell meat and trophies to locals and outsiders. They exchange game meat and skins for the cash needed to purchase consumer goods and to pay school fees; they can also receive money and consumer goods for assisting the hunting efforts of others, particularly wealthier outsiders. In addition to economic benefits, some hunters gain social status from providing their kin and fellow villagers with meat and economic goods.[11] According to every conservationist, NPWS officer, NPWS scout, chief, politician, and government bureaucrat I interviewed, hunting and its products remain valuable to the survival of rural residents across Zambia.

The constraints on resident hunting are the local availability of wild animals, ownership of weapons, and the presence of NPWS scouts. Residents prefer to hunt with firearms because they furnish a surer method of killing larger game, which provide greater returns to hunting efforts. Commercially produced weapons are also preferred to locally fashioned firearms, traps, or snares. But manufactured guns are expensive, and permits to import and own them are difficult to obtain. These factors effectively restrict the number of guns, limiting the amount of hunting done with firearms in rural areas. To circumvent these restrictions, villagers often construct their own muzzle loader (the steering column of a Land Rover was for a time the most popular object from which to form a gun's barrel), mix their own gunpowder (fertilizer acts as a base for the homemade mixture), and use various found objects for ammunition (e.g., old screws, nails, bolts, or stones). Such guns frequently misfire, and their use can result in injury or death caused by either the explosion of the muzzle loader or a partially injured – and fully angered – wild animal.

Rural residents also hunt using snares. This method is less easily detectable than using a firearm, whose loud report immediately reveals a hunter's location to those in the area. Snaring usually entails hanging a noose of wire over a well-trodden animal path. An unsuspecting animal will run into the noose headfirst; the noose, normally a slip knot, constricts around the animal's head as it struggles. Snares are usually reserved for smaller animals, but larger species sometimes get wounded or killed by them. The rate of snaring generally correlates with scouts' enforcement efforts – the larger a scout presence in an area, the more locals will resort to setting snares to kill game.[12]

Local hunters easily evade most NPWS scouts.[13] Patrols are infrequent and scouts thinly scattered. Even if caught, hunters can avoid arrest or conviction by hiding their guns and kills, devising elaborate stories to account for their behavior, calling in old debts owed to them by scouts, or using the influence of a prominent relative.[14] Residents may also secure their freedom by providing the scout with part or all of their kill. Despite its wide practice, and the fact that few locals purchase licenses, the probability of arrest and conviction for illegal hunting is low.

Hunting provides another good to rural residents: declining animal populations. Despite the meat and income produced by hunting, villagers consider the costs imposed by wildlife to be extremely burdensome. Hungry animals force villagers to spend extra energy and time driving away garden raiders, building secure storage sheds, and sleeping on observation platforms. Animals jeopardize crops and lives. Thus, the elimination of wildlife in their area would please most rural residents.[15]

Wildlife Scouts

Wildlife scouts endure most of the same difficult living conditions as the local residents.[16] Despite their entitlement to the benefits that flow from a job with a quasi-military branch of the civil service, such as free housing, a salary, protection from arbitrary dismissal, food rations, uniforms, and firearms, scouts frequently lack these goods as a result of the inefficiencies or financial weakness of their department or the central government. Other hardships, ranging from physical danger to social isolation, also confront those who choose to be wildlife scouts.

Individuals from around the country make up the scout force of the Zambian National Parks and Wildlife Service.[17] In order to qualify for the position, one must meet minimum education and physical standards promulgated by the Public Service Commission.[18] Because public sector jobs are scarce and valuable, and because NPWS operates only one training facility, competition is keen for the position; the endorsement of local or regional elites greatly increases an individual's chance of securing a position. If accepted by NPWS, a person receives two years of military-style training at Chunga, the Department's training camp in the Kafue National Park. The subjects covered in the training program include the wildlife code, criminal code, arrest procedures, physical combat skills, and use of weapons.

NPWS posts its Chunga graduates to camps in rural areas or district administrative centers (called "commands"). Most scouts, despite joining a branch of the civil service whose focus is the rural outdoors, would prefer office duties in an urban center, so as to enjoy the amenities and relative safety provided by a town.[19] These positions, however, generally go to more senior scouts or to the favorites of senior officers.[20] The department deploys the majority of scouts to camps in rural areas, usually within or near the country's nineteen national parks and their adjoining thirty-four game management areas (GMAs). Approximately ten scouts and their families occupy each camp.[21] A scout can expect to be transferred between rural camps a number of times throughout his career, for reasons ranging from NPWS operational needs to personal requests.[22] NPWS officers also use transfers to reward scouts (with placement in urban or safari area settings) and to discipline them (with placement in isolated camps).

Scouts face numerous hardships while living in a rural camp. The Zambian government often delays delivering scout salaries, a problem exacerbated by distance. Banks and post offices rarely exist nearby, making it difficult to cash or save their pay. Housing in rural camps is simple and may be substandard. Some scouts live in tin huts, structures that magnify heat to oppressive levels. Others occupy government-built structures. Still others make their own mud and thatch huts. The department sometimes fails to construct or maintain a camp's water wells, forcing the scouts and their family members to seek water from nearby rivers, which always carry the risk of injury or death from territorial hippos or predatory crocodiles.

The scout is poorly equipped. In the best of circumstances, NPWS issues only one weapon for every two scouts.[23] These firearms, moreover, may be antiquated, inoperative, or dangerous.[24] Department officers issue only a few rounds (if any) of ammunition to scouts because of its scarcity and the fear that scouts will use it to hunt illegally.[25] NPWS distributes uniforms and boots only sporadically; often individuals can be seen wearing tattered uniforms or dilapidated boots. Others wear unofficial clothing and go barefoot while on duty.

Despite receiving the pay of a civil servant, scouts often find feeding themselves and their families difficult. NPWS delivers food rations inconsistently, especially during the rainy season. Many scouts attempt to augment their families' diets by planting crops near their camp. Physical and social constraints, however, hamper extensive farming. Many crops need intensive inputs of labor at certain times of the year for planting, weeding, and harvesting. The scout does not have access to the kinship networks or other community groups that can provide the labor inputs required during these periods. A scout's responsibility to patrol (sometimes without notice) also reduces the time he has available to work in his field. Further, because NPWS normally locates camps in areas with considerable wildlife populations, scouts' crops suffer tremendous losses from foraging animals. As a result of these factors, scouts rarely establish large fields. Most of the agriculture around scout camps takes the form of small gardens, usually tended by scouts' wives.

The interaction of scouts and their families with nearby villages generates an uneasy affiliation. Scouts provide the area with some benefits. They spend their income on local foodstuffs, consumer goods, and beer that a village may provide, thus helping the local economy. NPWS vehicles passing through the area can give villagers rides to urban centers or other rural communities. They are also supposed to protect rural residents and their crops from damage done by wild animals.[26]

Local villages provide the scout with benefits as well, especially consumer goods, foodstuffs, and social opportunities. The longer a scout resides in one location, the greater opportunity he has to establish positive associations. Occasionally, a scout will marry a woman from the locality; such a mamage can greatly enhance his ability to secure the advantages of the social networks so important in rural settings.

Yet the law enforcement responsibilities of a wildlife scout often overshadow the positive features of scout–villager interactions, producing a frequently tense – and sometimes overtly hostile – relationship. Wildlife can provide a significant portion of an individual's diet and income in rural areas, and most hunting at this level takes place without licenses. The scout's mandate, meanwhile, is to prevent such illegal uses of wildlife. Given the close proximity of scout camps to surrounding villages, the amount of hunting done at the local level, and a scout's authority as a law enforcement officer, scouts tend to arrest far more locals than outsiders.[27]

In addition to monitoring the local area, scouts' duties include going on patrols in the regions around their camp. These patrols can last from a day to a week, but normally average three days.[28] While on patrol, scouts eat provisions such as beans, maize meal, and dried kapenta (a small fish). Until 1991, NPWS policy allowed patrols to shoot animals for rations, a policy much abused by scout and officer alike, and one of the few benefits of being away from their homes. Scouts still kill animals for food when patrolling, although more discreetly. Aside from the game meat that going on patrol might produce, however, few scouts enjoy the activity; it forces them to endure conditions more uncomfortable than those of camp life (especially in the rainy season). It increases the risks of a hazardous encounter with a wild animal[29] and raises the possibility of encountering hunters from outside the area – who are more likely to shoot because outside hunters are likely to be better armed than scouts and have less chance of avoiding conviction than locals.[30] Nor do scouts need to patrol much to protect their jobs because supervisory visits by senior NPWS officers to scout camps are rare. Consequently, scouts generally avoid going on patrols.[31] When they do go, they often camp near a village, where it is safer, and where food and beer may be purchased.[32]

Some scouts abuse their legal powers, and villagers fear a scout's ability to use his authority capriciously. Rural residents feel excessively harassed and complain that scouts look into cooking pots, ransack huts, and confiscate drums, chairs, or other artifacts in their efforts to recover animal products illegally acquired.[33] Sometimes scouts seize a hunter's illegal kill in order to eat it or sell it themselves. And scouts routinely beat the individuals they arrest.

Scouts, recognizing their partial dependence on the local community, try not to antagonize locals completely. But, generally, locals fear and distrust scouts; children throw stones at them.[34]

Scouts can only advance to the next rank, assistant wildlife ranger, if they possess a secondary school certificate, and few do. The vast majority of scouts, therefore, do not get promoted. As in most bureaucracies, scouts avoid making trouble for fellow scouts or superiors. They enjoy the security and perquisites of a civil service job, while concentrating on procuring life's necessities under difficult conditions.[35]

Village scouts – rural residents hired by ADMADE and LIRDP under the government category of "classified employees" – experience even more difficult conditions of service than their civil servant counterparts. Because they are not protected by the Zambia Civil Service Commission, they can be fired at any time. They receive comparatively lower wages. They must construct their own camps. They undergo greater supervision. And they are given the more dangerous or difficult jobs that regular NPWS scouts do not want to perform. Village scouts also encounter heightened social tension at the local level: They are posted in their home village and expected to know and to ferret out local poachers. Unlike regular NPWS scouts, village scouts cannot afford the luxury of nonperformance.

Chiefs

Chiefs in the rural areas confront the same daily hardships as members of their communities.[36] However, many chiefs still possess considerable influence over social and economic institutions in rural areas, despite the slow erosion of their authority over the past century (see Appendix A for a historical overview of chiefs' powers), allowing them to enhance their own position, as well as the standing of those residents they favor. Most of this authority results from the chiefs' control over access to land.

Because land in most of Zambia's rural areas cannot be privately owned, its distribution is not governed by the economic market. Instead, chiefs retain the right to allocate land as they see fit. In a predominantly agricultural country like Zambia, this prerogative is decisive and generates a substantial amount of deference from local residents to their chief. The chiefs' influence over land maintains his continuing role as the central arbiter of patronage networks and kinship relations. Even urban dwellers offer allegiance to chiefs, because, if they intend to retire to their family's area (which is likely to be in a rural area) they require the chief's permission to secure a plot of land.

Control over access to land also allows chiefs to regulate access to employment opportunities. Because chiefs govern land usufruct in their areas, politicians, government officials, and representatives from nonprofit organizations ask them for advice concerning the location, staffing, and control of development projects and government infrastructure. This position enables chiefs to secure positions for themselves and their family, friends, and supporters. Because formal employment opportunities are scarce in rural areas, a chief's position as a gatekeeper to jobs endows him with continued importance at the local level.

An important aspect of chiefly power stems from allocating land and its associated economic goods; thus chiefs also aim to attract development projects whose benefits they can distribute. The more their area is developed, the greater attraction it has for people to stay or relocate there, and the more a chief's land power is augmented. Consequently, chiefs express great concern about the lack of infrastructure and development projects that inhibit the improvement of the local economy and feel frustrated by the small voice they possess in central and regional government decision making.

Chiefs' power over land allows them to influence other social and economic institutions, including wildlife. Before the arrival of Europeans, most chiefly power resulted from ability to control access to natural resources, especially land and wildlife. Colonial and postindependence governments stripped chiefs of much of this control. Successive laws and wildlife departments essentially usurped the chiefs' de jure control over hunting in their areas.

But some chiefs retain influence over access to wildlife. Some demand that they receive portions of animals killed within their chieftaincy. Outside poachers often ask for the chief's permission to hunt in the area, usually in exchange for a part of the animals or some consumer goods. Other chiefs monopolize local access to wildlife by controlling community-level hunting rings. Still others hunt illegally themselves, secure in the knowledge that few residents or scouts would dare turn them in. Although chiefs cannot control all the illegal hunting in their areas – snaring is difficult to monitor, and some well-armed and/or influential urban dwellers may ignore the chief altogether – they have knowledge of and can influence local residents' use of wildlife.

THE INCENTIVES OF THE "OLD" AND THE "NEW" POLICIES

The rapid escalation of illegal hunting throughout much of Eastern and Central Africa led scholars and practitioners to reevaluate the institutions of conventional wildlife management.[37] ADMADE and LIRDP's administrators explicitly considered many of the limitations faced by the rural resident outlined here.[38] They argued that previous wildlife policies perpetuated a pattern of costs and benefits that significantly disadvantaged rural residents in crucial ways: Tourism and safari enterprises generated significant revenues for their owners, who were generally members of the urban elite, and the government, who taxed the enterprises. They recognized that the very system of hunting quotas and licenses favored wealthy and urban citizens and acknowledged that Zambians living with wildlife in the rural areas experienced significant costs from conventional conservation policy. They admitted that the NPWS lacked the staff and funds to prevent widespread hunting and realized that the cumulative effect of these factors was for rural residents to help themselves to a valuable and de facto open-access resource. The administrators' characterization of the effects of conventional wildlife policy can be presented in game theoretic form. To capture the game between scout and resident under conventional policy, I present a simple model using a noncooperative game with complete information.[39] Noncooperation assumes that communication between the parties is irrelevant, impossible, or forbidden; complete information assumes that all parties know the full structure of the game and the payoffs associated with each outcome.[40] Figure 1 presents the game (in extended form) between scouts and residents under the incentives offered by conventional wildlife policies.

The scout faces two choices in this game, to Enforce or Not Enforce wildlife regulations. The rural resident has three choices, to Hunt Large Game (e.g., elephant, rhino, hippopotamus), Hunt Small Game (e.g., antelope species, warthog), or Not Hunt at all. The game assumes that each player can calculate the payoff of every outcome. The integers 1 through 6 represent each player's ranking of outcomes, with 1 the most preferred.[41] For example, the outcome Not Hunt/Not Enforce yields the next to worst (fifth-highest) outcome for the local hunter, but is the most-preferred outcome for the scout.

Under conventional wildlife conservation policies, the benefits the rural resident receives from hunting are quite high. The meat of wild animals augments their diet, and animal products generate income. Because killing larger species yields more meat – and therefore more income and exchange value – than killing smaller species, local hunters especially prefer to hunt these animals.[42] The low probability of being caught by

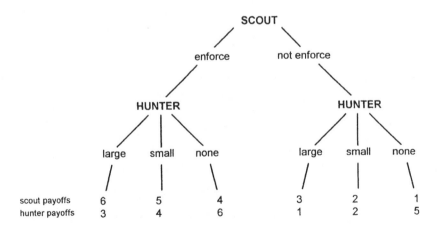

Note: Numbers represent rank order for the players (i.e. 1 is the most preferred outcome).

Figure 1. Extended form game between wildlife scouts and local hunters under conventional wildlife policies.

ill-equipped and scattered scouts has done little to reduce the high pay-offs from these endeavors.[43] Even though scouts can more easily monitor the off take of large rather than small game, the larger species' high returns induce hunters to select the more sizeable species even with the marginal increase in the likelihood of being caught. Given the returns under conventional wildlife policy, the hunter has a dominant strategy to Hunt Large Game.[44]

The scout, meanwhile, confronts significant costs by enforcing wildlife regulations.[45] Enforcement means going on patrols, among other hardships, including risking a confrontation with well-armed poachers. Upholding wildlife law also incites hostility from local communities, on whom scouts depend for social activities and trade. Further, scouts know that because their department has little capacity to monitor their behavior, they will receive their pay whether or not they enforce the law. Scouts prefer that residents do not hunt, because rampant poaching in their areas could get them transferred, thus possibly erasing important social networks they have already constructed. Because the hunting of larger animals, and the failure of scouts to prevent such hunting, are more easily detected by supervisors than the killing of smaller species, scouts also prefer locals to hunt smaller rather than bigger animals.[46] Nevertheless, the cost of any enforcement under conventional management policy is greater than the cost of not enforcing. Thus, Not Enforce is the scout's dominant strategy.

Given the preferences of resident and scout, the game portrayed in Figure 1 results in the equilibrium Hunt Large Game/Not Enforce.[47] This outcome is consistent with the rapid increase in illegal hunting, especially of the larger mammals, in Zambia during the 1970s and 1980s.

ADMADE and LIRDP's administrators suggested various mechanisms to close this wildlife commons.[48] Despite many different organizational features, ADMADE and LIRDP shared a key assumption: Conservation policies would work only if local communities possessed a legal and valuable stake in the resource. Such benefits would encourage rural residents to seek ways to preserve rather than hunt wildlife.

The programs' benefits fell into three broad categories. The first type linked economic rewards directly to wildlife resources: Locals would receive jobs as scouts to protect and monitor the resource, or as wage earners with tourism and safari companies whose activities depend on viewing or consuming it. Local communities would also benefit from the meat of safari-killed game or the sale of meat from culling operations.[49] The second type of benefit was only indirectly linked to wildlife; it consisted of standard goods dispensed by development projects such as health clinics, schools, maize grinding mills, teachers' houses, water wells, famine relief, roads, and bridges. ADMADE and LIRDP financed these development projects from donor monies and taxes on safari operations. The last category of benefit related to the empowerment of rural residents. ADMADE and LIRDP created institutions, explored in more detail later, that supposedly allowed a greater degree of local participation in decision making than conventional wildlife policies.

Because the majority of the programs' revenue and benefits depended on adequate animal populations, ADMADE and LIRDP also increased the enforcement of extant wildlife laws.[50] Escalating enforcement meant expanding the number of scouts in particular areas, delivering adequate equipment and provisions to them, increasing their supervision in the field, and providing incentives for scouts to perform their duties (e.g., cash bonuses for arrests, patrols, and confiscated firearms). Because the Zambian government could not afford to hire additional civil servants, ADMADE and LIRDP employed rural residents as village scouts. As well as constituting an inexpensive way to enlarge the scout force, village scouts offered another distinct advantage to the programs' administrators: They could be dismissed on the spot for failure to perform their duties. ADMADE and LIRDP also valued the detailed knowledge village scouts possessed about their area's wildlife and about those who hunted it. Further, by making an effort to recruit known poachers as scouts and staff, the programs' administrators believed they could terminate these individuals' illegal activities with the income and the status associated with being government employees.

ADMADE and LIRDP's array of development projects, participatory structures, employment opportunities, and increased enforcement intended to change the incentives of the rural hunter and wildlife scout to the pattern depicted by the noncooperative game in Figure 2.

In this game, the incentives linked to the scout's enforcement efforts have changed his ranking of outcomes. Cash bonuses and greater supervision induce the scout to prefer enforcing wildlife law in every case. The scout prefers that residents do not hunt: This maintains animal populations and reduces the danger of enforcement in the field. If locals do hunt, the scout prefers they kill smaller, less valuable species rather than the larger mammals. Regardless of the locals' behavior, if ADMADE and LIRDP work as intended, a scout's new dominant strategy will be Enforce.

ADMADE and LIRDP's packages of benefits intended to change the preferences of the rural resident as well. In this game, the villager prefers that scouts enforce wildlife laws to protect the animals from outside hunters, because the monies that drive the local people's benefits come from safari hunting, which depends on trophy-quality animals. The res-

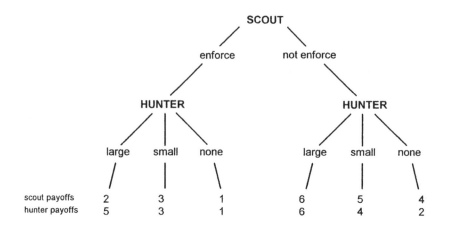

SCOUT

/   \

enforce   not enforce

	scout payoffs	hunter payoffs
HUNTER large	2	5
small	3	3
none	1	1
HUNTER large	6	6
small	5	4
none	4	2

Note: Numbers represent rank order for the players (i.e.1 is the most preferred outcome).

Figure 2. Extended form game between wildlife scouts and local hunters intended by ADMADE and LIRDP.

ident's most preferred alternative is Not Hunt. If circumstances force the individual to hunt, the new programs induce him to hunt smaller, more numerous animals rather than the larger mammals.

The game in Figure 2 results in the equilibrium outcome desired by ADMADE and LIRDP's administrators: Not Hunt/Enforce.[51] If their package of incentives worked as intended, local residents would choose to enjoy the infrastructure, legally culled meat, jobs, income, and decision-making opportunities offered by the new programs, rather than endanger these goods by hunting. Simultaneously, scouts would strictly enforce wildlife laws (presumably against outsiders because the residents have decided to stop hunting) and receive rewards for their efforts. Such a scenario would boast gains for all interested groups: ADMADE and LIRDP would achieve their goal of preserving wild animals, which, through tourism and safari hunting, would continue to fund their efforts; conservationists and donors would see the tide of poaching stemmed; and communities living in these conservation areas would gain revenue for development and take an active part in managing their own resources.

THE IMPACT OF ADMADE AND LIRDP AT THE LOCAL LEVEL

The actual impact of ADMADE and LIRDP, however, differed greatly from the ideal outcome of Figure 2. Of course, some of the programs' weak performance can be attributed to the implementation problems endemic to any policy. The emphasis here, however, is placed on the institutional choices made by ADMADE and LIRDP's administrators. The structures they created resulted in a distribution of goods that did not induce most members of the local community to embrace the new programs.

Chiefs and ADMADE

From its inception, the ADMADE program identified chiefs as the link to the village level.[52] NPWS gave practical and historical reasons for its choice. Because chiefs are "non-political and serve the needs of their subjects and are custodians of the land," NPWS believed the chiefs' administration of ADMADE would be accepted easily at the village level.[53] NPWS also believed that ADMADE would justly reinvest chiefs with the distributive powers they traditionally wielded over wildlife, which had been removed with British rule.[54] So important were the chiefs to ADMADE that in any conflict between a chief and ADMADE staff, NPWS policy was to take the side of the former.[55]

ADMADE gave two powers to the chief. First, he chaired the Wildlife Management Sub-Authority (WMSA). As mentioned in the last chapter, the WMSA duties included submitting suggestions for development projects to be funded from the community's 35 percent share. Second, the chief selected the individuals to be trained and employed as village scouts.

Despite the promise of these powers, NPWS had difficulty convincing the first few chiefs to participate in ADMADE at the program's outset.[56] Deep suspicion surrounded NPWS activities; changes in wildlife policy usually meant greater restrictions on local hunting. As chiefs learned of their colleagues' gains, however, they quickly lined up for inclusion in the program.[57] They became "personally involved in the wildlife management effort in their area" by inspecting wildlife camps and reviewing the work of village scouts. Completely reversing their long-standing opposition to wildlife protected areas, chiefs clamored for their areas to be declared GMAs so they could also participate in ADMADE.[58]

NPWS and consultants regarded the chiefs' enthusiasm for ADMADE as an acceptance of locally oriented conservation principles.[59] Evidence demonstrates, however, that chiefs followed their historical pattern of trying to control the programs' functions and benefits in order to augment their authority. Because ADMADE policy did not define well the composition or operation of the WMSA, chiefs controlled its agenda and membership; their ideas dominated the list of development projects submitted for approval to the Wildlife Management Authority (WMA).[60]

Although chiefs experienced difficulty getting their more flagrantly self-rewarding projects, such as official residences for them (or "palaces"), through the WMA, they did significantly influence the kind and location of ADMADE-funded projects for their area.[61] Chiefs located most new classrooms, houses for teachers, clinics, wells, and maize hammer mills in their own village; in fact, they had many of these projects built close to their own homes.[62] And chiefs hired their closest relatives to staff grinding mills.[63] Villagers complained about the chiefs' monopoly of these community benefits, which led some to believe ADMADE- and LIRDP-funded projects were actually the chiefs' personal property.[64]

As the people responsible for selecting village scouts, the chiefs also managed access to another very valuable commodity: a salaried job with law-enforcement powers. Some consultants and villagers claimed that village scouts felt more loyalty to their patron chief than their actual employer, NPWS.[65] Chiefs sought to augment the enforcement powers of "their" village scouts by providing them with firearms, using headmen to assist the ADMADE unit leader, constructing roadblocks, and cracking down on the illegal ownership of firearms.[66] Predictably, villagers accused chiefs of favoritism in their selections of village scouts and their enforcement of the law.[67]

In questioning policy, chiefs focused on those aspects of ADMADE that limited their authority, protesting the WMA's control over their community's ADMADE bank account, disliking the WMA's ability to veto the WMSA's choices for development projects, and chafing over the cumbersome and time-consuming nature of the approval system.[68] In contrast, they spent little time supporting the conservation and participation goals of ADMADE. In fact, even while belonging to ADMADE some chiefs worked actively against conservation and formed secret hunting rings.[69] In sum, chiefs spent their energies trying to secure more power and resources under ADMADE, relegating local participation and conservation to at best secondary concern.

The Local Leaders Sub-Committee and LIRDP

Like ADMADE, LIRDP used traditional authorities as the "primary avenue" by which local interests could be represented to LIRDP.[70] Rather than create separate committees for each chiefdom it affected, LIRDP created the Local Leaders' Sub-Committee to represent all the rural residents in the project's inhabited area, the Lupande Game Management Area in the Luangwa Valley.[71] The Sub-Committee's membership consisted of the six chiefs of the project area, the four ward chairmen of the ruling party UNIP, and the local member of parliament. LIRDP also allowed each chief to have one assistant and one women's representative as voting members of the Sub-Committee. The nonvoting secretariat of the body included LIRDP directors, their technical staff, and the district executive secretary. Representatives of nongovernmental organizations working in the area were also invited to the meetings.[72] However, chiefs and their assistants comprised the voting majority on the Sub-Committee.

LIRDP sought to transfer control "over the revenues earned in the project area and decisions concerning land and resource use" to the Sub-Committee.[73] LIRDP earmarked 40 percent of the project's earnings for the local community, a sum split into six portions representing the six chieftaincies in the project area. Chiefs on the Sub-Committee also enjoyed the powers of selecting village scouts for training, controlling two culling operations, and issuing district licenses to hunters.[74]

Because the LIRDP codirectors assumed responsibility for setting the agenda and taking minutes for the Sub-Committee meetings, local leaders' preferences did not dominate as they did in ADMADE's Sub-Authorities.[75] Nor could chiefs completely manipulate the program's benefits at the local level, because each was only one of many signatories on LIRDP accounts.[76] But LIRDP's local leaders, like ADMADE's, concerned themselves more with acquisition of power than conservation or participation of community members in decision making.[77] Chiefs told various review missions about their discontent over issues such as the secrecy of LIRDP's financial operations, their share of LIRDP revenues, and the financial accounts of LIRDP projects in their area.[78] Conflicts between the traditional and political leaders involved with the Sub-Committee also emerged over the calculation and distribution of the 40 percent community share.[79] The friction between local leaders prevented some from spending any of their LIRDP 40 percent allocation.[80] Notably, the friction did not prevent the Sub-Committee from allocating "hardship allowances" to its chiefs.[81]

Rural Residents in ADMADE and LIRDP

ADMADE and LIRDP planned to provide two kinds of goods to the GMA resident: economic and political. The programs' largest economic contribution to local communities was employment. Hundreds of residents operated as village scouts. Their salaries, although low when compared to the pay of a regular NPWS scout, did boost the local economy.[82] Additionally, dozens of residents received jobs with grinding mills, culling operations, and road construction. ADMADE and LIRDP revenues also funded community development projects. Under ADMADE from 1989 to 1992, the community's 35 percent share paid for sixty projects, including houses for teachers (twenty-three), classrooms (fourteen), maize grinding mills (nine), and rural health centers (seven).[83] LIRDP funds paid for repair of roads and bridges, establishment of a store and grinding mill in the Luangwa Valley, and extension and credit services to farmers. Finally, some ADMADE and LIRDP areas benefited from culling operations intended to provide local residents a supply of legally acquired and inexpensive game meat.

The programs' administrators also lauded the program's political goals, especially the decentralization of control over wildlife resources.[84] Decision-making powers over wildlife, heretofore preempted by centralized governments, were supposedly given back to the local community.[85]

Most individuals in the programs' areas, however, experienced little direct economic or political benefit from ADMADE or LIRDP. Only about 2 percent of the gross profits from ADMADE-sponsored sport hunting reached rural communities.[86] In some cases, even this small amount never reached the community: One year a WCRF accountant used the area's share to pay village scout salaries.[87] The paucity of ADMADE income received by the WMSA meant that local communities acquired relatively few projects; each Sub-Authority started on average fewer than three projects in ADMADE's first three years. Many of these projects were only partially completed because of a continuing lack of funds and high inflation.[88] ADMADE's own community development officers heard rural residents complaining "over and over again" about the small amount of benefits to locals from ADMADE.[89]

No comparable data exist regarding how much of LIRDP's gross receipts ended up in the 40 percent share targeted for the local community. But the political tension that existed among members of LIRDP Local Leaders' Sub-Committee, especially that between chiefs and members of party and government, prevented much of that revenue from being used. In 1991, only one of the six chieftaincies had spent all of their allocated revenues.[90]

Further, villagers resented the distribution of ADMADE and LIRDP's economic goods. Most of the projects clustered around chiefs' residences. Most jobs went to the chiefs' and ward chairmen's families and friends.[91] Locals indicted culling operations for selling the meat at prices too high for rural residents to afford.[92]

Rural residents also came to doubt ADMADE and LIRDP's promises of local participation. Few villagers were included in the formal bodies of either ADMADE or LIRDP. Local leaders did not receive information about the revenues their area contributed to the programs' revolving funds.[93] And neither ADMADE nor LIRDP developed formal mechanisms for resolving land use conflicts between local communities and safari operators.[94]

Despite the great amount of time and money expended by LIRDP to establish a community-based development institution using and protecting wildlife and other natural resources, many residents living in the program's area did not even know of its existence. Some individuals thought it was a private company.[95] Many residents of ADMADE areas perceived it not as a participatory wildlife management scheme, but as a government-sponsored employment program benefiting some rural residents at the expense of others.[96]

The Role of Scouts in ADMADE and LIRDP

The village scout program was key to the design of both ADMADE and LIRDP.[97] Both programs' managers saw village scouts as the vehicle by which locals could participate in wildlife management as well as gain economic rewards. The scouts were charged with reducing poaching, monitoring wildlife populations, and developing links with the community to foster a more positive attitude toward wildlife conservation.[98] ADMADE and LIRDP's administrators also hoped that local residents would trust village scouts because they had been selected from the area to which they would be deployed.

Despite the intention of the programs to establish a more cooperative relationship between GMA residents and scouts, the village scouts' commitment to enforcement activities made them unpopular in many communities.[99] Village scouts received the greatest benefit from their anti-poaching activities, and consequently, they directed their efforts toward capturing illegal hunters.[100] Where unit leaders monitored scouts, zealous enforcement of wildlife regulations quickly estranged the village scout from his or her community. The invigorated pursuit of poachers led to an increase in villager complaints about harassment by scouts, just as enforcement activities had for decades. In those areas without effective unit leaders, village scouts' commitment waned and residents indicted scouts for their poaching, firewood cutting, and drunkenness.[101]

THE STRATEGIC INTERACTION OF VILLAGER AND SCOUT

The incentives offered by ADMADE and LIRDP did not change the behavior of rural residents and scouts in the intended manner. Figure 3 presents the actual outcome of the noncooperative hunting game under these programs.

Despite ADMADE and LIRDP's benefits, the resident still ranks both hunting options higher than the Not Hunting strategy. Scouts have, however, changed their behavior. The emoluments and supervision instituted by the programs have made enforcement the scout's preferred

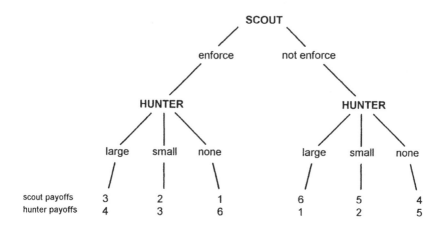

Note: Numbers represent rank order for the players (i.e. 1 is the most preferred outcome).

Figure 3. Extended form game between wildlife scouts and local hunters after ADMADE and LIRDP implementation.

choice. In fact, because the programs linked special rewards to finding the hunters of large animals, the scouts actually preferred that, if locals hunt, they kill the larger species (unlike the intended outcome, in which scouts prefer locals to hunt smaller animals). Given that the resident knows that scouts will now enforce the law, however, he can no longer afford to hunt large game with impunity as he had before implementation of ADMADE. Rather, hunting small game is now the best choice for the resident. Consequently, the result of the game in Figure 3 is the equilibrium Hunt Small Game/Enforce.[102]

If the program's benefits changed behavior of the resident and scout, as indicated by the payoffs in Figure 2, we would hypothesize the following trends in the behavior of residents and scouts: First, as an ever-increasing number of residents choose to enjoy the benefits offered by ADMADE and LIRDP, the rate of illegal hunting should decrease over time. Ultimately, the programs would induce locals to forgo illegal hunting altogether, resulting in an off take of zero. Second, the number of arrests made by scouts should increase during the initial period of enhanced enforcement.[103] Then, as residents accept ADMADE's new distribution of benefits, the level of arrests should decrease.

Evidence suggests the programs are not meeting these expectations. Data from the Munyamadzi GMA in the central Luangwa Valley, where ADMADE had been in effect for five years, reveal that local hunters have not reduced their off takes over time (see Table 1).[104]

Table 1. *Kilograms[a] of meat taken by five local hunters (A–E),*
Munyamadzi Game Management Area, 1988–1993

Year	A	B	C	D	E
1988	1,432	2,586	210	3,996	105
1989	1,362	2,249	225	2,580	315
1990	603	555	155	1,932[b]	60[c]
1991	1,170	1,787	260	[d]	[d]
1992	1,120	613	200	10,395	[d]
1993	1,264[b]	3,930	239	924	[d]

[a] Kilograms (kg) are calculated by using estimated carcass yields for species and sex (around 50–60 percent of live weight). For example, the carcass yield for a bull buffalo is estimated at 366 kg, a female impala at 27 kg, a male warthog at 53 kg.
[b] Results from partial year only.
[c] Hunter E left the area in mid-1990.
[d] No data.
Source: Records of and interviews with local hunters (Stuart Marks, unpublished notes).

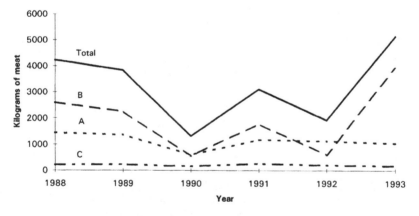

Graph A. Kilograms of meat taken by hunters A, B, and C.

Drought, which killed off animal populations, caused the noticeable drop in off takes during 1990.[105] But by 1993, hunting resumed at much the same levels as in 1988, when ADMADE began. Graph A displays the off takes for hunters A, B, and C, for whom yearly data exist. The graph clearly indicates that both individual and total off takes have rebounded from 1990. Given that the data for hunters A and C represent only a partial year's hunting, the figures presented underestimate their hunting activities in 1993. Further, these hunters operate in the vicinity of a culling station; we would expect off takes on average to be even higher in areas farther from enforcement officials.

Senior NPWS officers indicate that the trend evident in the data is generally observable throughout ADMADE areas. These officers claim that although ADMADE has staved off increases in poaching, the level of illegal hunting has remained relatively stable since the program's inception.

ADMADE and LIRDP were, however, very successful in increasing the number of arrests made by wildlife scouts. NPWS registered a record number of arrests and of firearms confiscated during the programs' first few years.[106] For ADMADE, this trend is reflected both at the local level (in the Munyamadzi GMA, see Table 2) and in the Luangwa area as a whole (see Table 3).[107] For LIRDP's entire project area, the Mambwe District, the results are analogous (Table 4). These numbers represent the commitment to putting more scouts in the field, supervising them, and rewarding them for enforcing wildlife laws, as intended by both programs from the outset.

The number of arrests has not, however, diminished appreciably over time.[108] Although NPWS's record of arrests had not been published regularly, NPWS officers admitted that the numbers have remained fairly stable or increased after their initial surge.[109] If both programs had succeeded in wooing locals away from illegal hunting, this relatively fixed level of arrests could only result from continuous pressure of hunters from outside the ADMADE areas.[110] But Department officials, consultants, and rural residents all claim that outsider hunting has dropped off considerably; locals still make up the vast majority of those arrested.[111] The fact that arrests have not declined over time implies that residents, despite the benefits of ADMADE and LIRDP, continue to hunt. The incentives for killing animals remain so strong that scouts admit that it does little good to put local hunters in jail because they "return to hunting as soon as they are released."[112]

These data suggest ADMADE and LIRDP have not stopped illegal hunting. Rather than cease their poaching, local hunters maintained off take levels by using snares rather than firearms to hunt and by targeting smaller mammals such as warthog, impala, and occasionally buffalo.[113] NPWS officials and conservationists contend that snaring is increasing rapidly in both ADMADE and LIRDP areas. Taken together, these data support the outcome presented in Figure 3: Killing smaller animals by less-detectable methods is the most-preferred choice of the rural resident.[114]

Table 2. *Law enforcement by wildlife scouts, Munyamadzi Wildlife Sub-Authority, 1988–1993*

Year	Arrests	Convictions	Dismissed	Escaped
1988	4	3	0	1
1989	5	5	0	0
1990	8	7	0	1
1991	11	9[a]	0	2
1992	21	10	9	2
1993	19	4[b]	1	2

[a] Includes two punishments handed down by the chief.
[b] Includes three punishments handed down by the chief.
Source: Local records (collected by Stuart Marks).

Table 3. *Law enforcement by the Zambian Wildlife Department, Luangwa Command, 1985–1990*

Year	Arrests	Convictions	Acquittals	Pending
1985	112	97	8	5
1986	149	116	5	28
1987	130	119	4	7
1988	155	137	2	16
1989	165	136	8	21
1990	197	183	7	7

Source: Zambian National Parks and Wildlife Service.

Table 4. *Law enforcement by wildlife scouts, LIRDP Project Area, 1988–1990[a]*

Year	Arrests	Firearms confiscated
1988	188	82
1989	398	244
1990	417	1063

[a] Through October 1990.
Source: LIRDP, *Annual Report 1990*, Chipata, Zambia: LIRDP, 1991.

The Local Politics of Wildlife Policy

THE INCENTIVE PROBLEMS OF ADMADE AND LIRDP

Despite ADMADE and LIRDP's benefits and increased enforcement, the illegal killing of wildlife continued at the local level. Although enhanced enforcement increased the chances for individual hunters to be apprehended, they persisted in taking animals for a number of reasons.

First, case materials clearly demonstrate that the vast majority of residents received only small gains from ADMADE and LIRDP.[115] Community projects and income-generating jobs were relatively few, and little opportunity existed to exert any influence over the legal use of and benefits from wildlife resources. The individual returns from hunting far outweighed a resident's share in the quantity of the goods ADMADE and LIRDP delivered.

Second, the programs failed to acknowledge the different values individuals place on development projects. The logic of economic incentives assumes that individuals will choose that action that provides a more valuable payoff. But people may not secure equal levels of utility from the same project. For example, a new maize grinding mill that requires a cash payment may be irrelevant to most rural residents' daily lives.[116] The location and timing of a development project may also undermine its value.[117] A health clinic, school, well, or grinding mill may provide less benefit to someone who does not live near it, even though the program may consider that individual part of the target community. A delay in the delivery of a project also reduces its value and weakens the cause/effect linkage. Thus, the benefit so critical to motivate people to refrain from hunting may actually have no significant impact if its cost, location, or goal makes it irrelevant to an individual.

Third, and most important, ADMADE and LIRDP did not identify and exclude those persons hunting illegally from enjoying the programs' development projects. As a result, these projects mimicked public goods, whose benefits are nonexcludable.[118] Residents could enjoy the health clinics, schools, grinding mills, and other development projects produced by the new wildlife programs whether they poached or conserved wild animals. ADMADE and LIRDP's benefits encouraged free riding: Rural residents chose to receive the benefits from hunting activities while enjoying the advantages offered by the good. Because ADMADE and LIRDP failed to link most of their benefits to individual behavior, no change could be expected in residents' conduct.

For the wildlife scout, however, ADMADE and LIRDP did join reward with individual action. The programs linked cash, promotions, and jobs with actions such as arrests made, firearms confiscated, and days spent on patrol. In addition, supervisors monitored more closely scout activities. Consequently, ADMADE and LIRDP successfully altered the incentive structure for the scout.[119]

"COMMUNITY-BASED" PROGRAMS AND INCENTIVES IN KENYA AND ZIMBABWE

With a growing sense that local communities need to be a central part of conservation programs, community-based wildlife programs have been established in many African countries. Despite their purported intentions, central governments – through their wildlife departments – generally retain property rights over wildlife. Wildlife departments seem not to devolve significant authority over wildlife resources, but construct programs that extend and augment their own control. Although material benefits do flow to community members in some of these programs, individual villagers face incentives similar to those described in the Zambian case. Given a century of exclusionary laws and the continuance of government ownership of wildlife, villagers are skeptical of government conservation plans. Reductions in poaching appear attributable to increases in enforcement activities, rather than an acceptance by local communities of the goal of conserving wildlife.

Kenya

Like their counterparts in Zambia, Kenyans living in areas with significant wildlife populations bear most of the costs of conservation. Officials of the Kenyan Wildlife Service have become increasingly sensitive to the needs of people living around protected areas, although KWS does not have a nationwide community-based program of wildlife conservation, as do Zambia and Zimbabwe. But wildlife officials in Kenya have had a long history of working with local populations' needs, especially because of the pastoralist Maasai, who live near some of Kenya's most renowned conservation areas. Both the Maasai Mara and Amboseli District Council Game Reserves began with the intent to include communities more than thirty years ago. Importantly, the Maasai do not prefer to eat game and do not hunt for subsistence (except in times of famine). Maasai cattle, however, do compete with wild herbivores for food and water, often creating a conflictual relationship between wildlife officials and local Maasai. A review of this interaction in the Amboseli Reserve helps to illustrate the diverging incentives of bureaucrat and rural dweller: Bureaucrats have long sought to extend their powers over the wildlife estate; Maasai express suspicion at any plans that seek to limit their control over the resources necessary to raising cattle.[120]

The value of Amboseli lies in its water: The six hundred square kilometer Amboseli basin contains large perennial springs in an arid, semi-desert savanna at the northern base of Mt. Kilimanjaro. In the dry season, this water supports grazing for wildlife and cattle. Beginning in the 1930s, government officials began to worry about wildlife's access to Amboseli's water and food and considered making it a national park. The area was designated a national reserve in 1947; locals were still allowed to enter and use the area. Although their strong resistance had prevented Amboseli from being designated as a national park, locals thought the reserve signified an impending land grab by the government. The growth of the Maasai and their herds prompted the Royal National Parks of Kenya to propose a national park for the area again in the late 1950s.[121]

Members of the Kenya Game Department and the wildlife adviser to the government of Kenya disagreed. The large local population of Maasai made creating a national park – which would require the expulsion of all people living in the area – practically and politically difficult, especially in the highly charged times immediately before independence. Instead, the department members chose a novel course: They advocated that if conserving the Amboseli area was to be successful, the Maasai would have to receive some of the benefits of conservation. Thus, in 1961, the government handed over the administration of the Amboseli reserve to the Kajiado County Council.

Although the council negotiated with the Maasai for the establishment of a seventy-eight square kilometer area free of livestock successfully, tensions between the council and the local Maasai quickly grew. The council coveted the revenues from the Amboseli reserve; by 1968, tourist revenues from the reserve generated 75 percent of the council's annual income. The Maasai complained about the mismanagement of the reserve's revenues and the lack of benefits to them. In 1969, the council spent only about one-fortieth of Amboseli's earnings on the reserve itself; the remainder financed development in more densely populated areas of the district.[122] Their exclusion led many Maasai to continue using the basin for their cattle; others began to spear rhinos, lions, and other wildlife to demonstrate their frustration.

The increasing tourism revenues and the conflict between the county council and the Maasai brought the central government into the dispute in the late 1960s. After several studies of wildlife and the practices of the Maasai, a plan was presented to the Kajiado Council to designate the six hundred square kilometer area a national park under the administration of the local council. After Maasai elders overwhelmingly rejected the proposal, the council opposed it as well. As parliamentary elections neared, local candidates fanned Maasai fears that the government was planning another land grab. The council put even less money into the reserve, prompting the minister of tourism to appeal to the president to take action.

In 1971 Kenyatta declared that 200 square kilometers would be taken as government land – something that even the colonial government had feared to do – and Amboseli became a full-fledged national park by presidential decree in 1974. The council erupted in protest; the Maasai speared more wildlife. Because of this backlash, the government agreed to reduce the park area, to construct a permanent water supply for Maasai cattle in the area, to allow the council to receive revenue from tourist lodges and a share of gate receipts, to absorb the costs of maintaining and staffing the park, and to allow the Maasai to obtain title to the rest of the area to be owned cooperatively as group ranches. Over the next three years, the government gave the Maasai additional concessions, including a school, a dispensary, a community center, and a further reduction of the park's total area.

When events occurred that made conservation costly or supported their suspicions of a predatory government, the Maasai responded in their own best interests. When the Wildlife Conservation and Management Department failed to maintain the Maasai's water supply systems, and when gate receipts no longer made their way to group ranch budgets, the Maasai moved their cattle herds back into the park. They expanded their agricultural holdings near the park, so as to be less dependent on either the tourist trade or a government that might attempt to take more nonagricultural land for wildlife. And they continued to kill wildlife that threatened their cattle.[123]

Zimbabwe

Residents of rural Zimbabwe face many of the same daily difficulties that confront individuals in rural Kenya and Zambia.[124] The designers of CAMPFIRE, like the designers of Zambia's ADMADE and LIRDP, recognized at least part of the rural residents' incentives regarding wildlife: Wildlife is a threat offering little, if any, legal benefit to them. CAMPFIRE officials designed their program to add benefits to the costs of living with wildlife, to alter locals' attitudes toward conservation, and to stimulate a sense of ownership among local communities. As it does for ADMADE and LIRDP, the evidence indicates that CAMPFIRE's institutions prevented some hunting, but maintained and even extended the department's powers over Zimbabwe's wildlife estate.

CAMPFIRE officials realized that their attempts to include local communities had been partly stymied by the structure of political institutions in Zimbabwe. Because district councils are the smallest unit to which appropriate authority over wildlife status can be legally assigned, observers locate a great deal of CAMPFIRE's problems concerning the distribution of power and resources at this level.[125] District councils tend to favor using CAMPFIRE-related revenues for their own political purposes. They favor large-scale projects over individual-level benefits and prefer monopolizing decision making to sharing it with ward level institutions.[126] And they prefer to use CAMPFIRE resources for other purposes, such as using wildlife scouts as their own "extension agents."[127] The Department of National Parks and Wildlife Management (the Department) and its CAMPFIRE collaborators continuously battled the district councils' propensity to control resources.

The concentration of power at the district level did not necessarily promote local level participation. For many in Zimbabwe's rural areas, the district council is as far away as the central government. With little authority over CAMPFIRE, individuals at the ward level generally did not feel the sense of proprietorship over wildlife intended by the program.[128]

Other parts of CAMPFIRE also generated incentives that hindered the program from reaching its promulgated goals. CAMPFIRE, like ADMADE and LIRDP, augments the enforcement of conventional laws. The Department recruits locals to become scouts in their area, and pays them with CAMPFIRE funds. (These scouts, in fact, represent the majority of the jobs generated by the program.)[129] Although the scouts get standard enforcement-related training, they receive no instruction in natural resource management; local resource inventories are conspicuous by their absence.[130] The scouts' antipoaching activities are generally directed at local communities. Enforcement is also enhanced by departmental antipoaching campaigns and by the employment of white professional hunters associated with CAMPFIRE to help with patrols and problem animal control.[131] Consequently, CAMPFIRE institutions favor the enforcement of laws by local hires over their management of natural resources.

Although no systematic data exist in published form to support observers' claims that poaching has decreased in CAMPFIRE areas, the evidence suggests that declines have occurred. But, like that for ADMADE and LIRDP in Zambia, the evidence also indicates that increased enforcement activities – and not widespread agreement by rural residents to conserve animals – account for the decrease. For example, three years after receiving its appropriate authority status, the Nyaminyami reported that poaching was growing in its area; in response, local officials proposed bringing in more professional hunters to help.[132] In Guruve District, poaching in two out of three wards remained strong; the remaining Kanyurira ward, which received the first household level cash disbursements from CAMPFIRE, also happens to be the location of a professional hunter's home for most of the season.[133] Peterson (1991) links a distribution of meat from a "proto-CAMPFIRE" cull to a drop in poaching rates in one community, and yet the data for his claim are from a second departmental antipoaching raid in the area. Rural residents are more likely to have reduced their hunting in the face of these continuing raids, not free meat.[134] Even documents designed to promote interest in CAMPFIRE declare that "poaching remains a problem."[135] Such evidence indicates that local hunters in Zimbabwe are making choices similar to those made by their counterparts in Zambia: Not only do they continue to hunt, but they employ a different tool – the snare – to evade arrest.[136]

CAMPFIRE has met some of its goals. The program generates money from wildlife resources, mostly through the selling of hunts to international clients. The program distributes this money to district councils, and it increases the participation of people below the level of the national government in wildlife management.

CAMPFIRE's structure, however, hinders its ability to meet some of its other, more highly touted, goals of decentralization and local control over resources. The program gives appropriate Authority status to district councils, who strive to retain control over the new resources that CAMP-FIRE furnishes. The program does nothing to change the system of property rights over wildlife: The government owns the animals and CAMP-FIRE helps to enforce the government's laws. The program does not change the fact that all direct uses of wildlife by local communities are still illegal. And the program allows little meaningful power to individuals who are not on the district councils or CAMPFIRE's enforcement staff.

Rural residents – even those living in CAMPFIRE areas – still see a resource that benefits others, especially white professional hunters and their clients.[137] They enjoy the benefits of the "supply side" program when they can get them. CAMPFIRE managers seem to assume that some economic benefits and attendance at a couple of meetings held over a few days a year are enough to induce participation in wildlife management.[138] Whether target populations enjoy these benefits or not, and where conventional enforcement activities are lacking, it is clear that Zimbabweans continue to hunt illegally.

CONCLUSION

This chapter has explained why the institutions constructed by AD-MADE and LIRDP's administrators – as well as bureaucrats in Kenya and Zimbabwe – did not create incentive structures sufficient to turn rural residents into conservationists; neither did the programs devolve much authority over wildlife to the local level. The evidence suggests that these "decentralized" programs' ability to curb the illegal hunting of larger animals reflected more an augmentation of conventional wildlife policy – hiring more scouts, providing them with better equipment and support, and improving their supervision in the field – than increased benefits for local people or greater local support for wildlife conservation.[139]

In fact, the new conservation initiatives retain fundamental aspects of their colonial heritage: Ultimate ownership of wildlife remains in the hands of the state, whose agencies control access to the animals using paramilitary scouts. Nearly all of the important decisions about revenues and quotas continue to be made by government personnel. Locals remain disenfranchised from wildlife resources.[140]

Essentially, program administrators misspecify the decision problem faced by the hunters. Data indicate that rural residents do not consider the consumption of benefits such as schools, grinding mills, and health clinics as alternatives to hunting: These goods are not rivalrous. Instead, the programs' structures give residents the benefits of the wildlife programs regardless of their choices over hunting.

Local politicians also attempted to manipulate these programs. In Zambia, chiefs took advantage of the new programs. Following the pattern typical during the last century, chiefs sought to manipulate AD-MADE and LIRDP structures to augment their authority at the local level. They worked to secure their monopoly over the distribution of the programs' benefits at the local level. In Zimbabwe and Kenya, local level political institutions sought to secure power over the distribution of benefits emanating from the programs.

After characterizing illegal hunters as economically rational, why do wildlife bureaucrats fail to construct institutions that reflect these assumptions? And given the importance the programs placed on local participation, why are most rural residents excluded from playing meaningful roles? One explanation for community-based wildlife programs' use of public goods as benefits might be that bureaucrats consider African rural society as communal. Colonial governments in Africa after World War II often advocated collective, tribal property and sought to create "traditional" political controls over the countryside.[141] Bureaucrats in Africa, therefore, may be conditioned to treat agrarian communities differently than urban ones. Social scientists, like those of the moral economy school, have supported this view by characterizing traditional societies as integrative and able to achieve rough equality through patterns of sharing, reciprocity, and mutual obligation.[142] Administrators in Zambia, Kenya, and Zimbabwe may have merely continued the practice of treating rural residents as part of groups, rather than as individuals.[143]

But such an account fails to explain why the programs' administrators originally characterized rural hunters as economically rational in the first place – arguably the most important justification offered by the programs for their existence. Neither does the moral economy position help us to understand why, at certain times, each program explicitly recognized the relationship between incentives and individual behavior; for example, ADMADE and LIRDP hired local hunters as wildlife scouts and gave them inducements to perform well. Finally, an explanation based on "communal bias" does not help explicate why the programs declined to create structures that devolved meaningful powers to these communities.

An alternative explanation for the programs' structures may be found by referring to the previous chapter's discussion of bureaucratic politics. In the highly uncertain world of politics, bureaucrats tend to avoid yielding any authority over wildlife, unless such an action strengthens their control. As explored in Chapter 4, ADMADE and LIRDP's officials made concessions to international donors and domestic politicians only to ensure their programs' existence and authority. A more detailed comparison should, in fact, pursue the idea that the wildlife bureaucrats of the one party states in Zambia and Kenya attempted to retain greater control as a result of facing greater political uncertainty than the wildlife department of Zimbabwe faces.

Most rural residents, unlike donors and politicians, could not threaten the survival of the programs, at least not in the short run. Geographically scattered, politically unorganized, and economically weak, locals did not wield enough clout to demand changes in ADMADE or LIRDP.[144] When locals were organized, as is arguable in certain regions of Kenya and Zimbabwe, they were more able to wrest benefits from the government agencies.

Even if program administrators sincerely hold the belief that local participation was necessary to stem poaching (in order to reap the economic benefits of a future sustainable harvest of animal populations), the political uncertainties surrounding the establishment and maintenance of such institutions create little incentive to relinquish authority to rural residents. ADMADE and LIRDP, for example, supplied locals only the resources necessary to administer the programs: they chose local elite as their agents and hired scouts to secure the areas. By providing benefits through development projects, ADMADE and LIRDP met their mandate of offering local benefits – necessary if only to maintain donor funding – inexpensively and without losing control. Constructing institutions that could monitor and sanction locals individually would have required ADMADE and LIRDP to invest considerable resources. During this period, however, such resources were better spent ensuring their programs' survival. Participatory institutions and individually targeted benefits were too costly.

Although the cases presented from Zambia, Kenya, and Zimbabwe evinced fundamental similarities, the latter two cases differed from Zambia's in one crucial respect: The community-based programs reviewed featured the critical intervention of formal administrative bodies at levels above the community. The district councils in Zimbabwe and county council in Kenya came to depend on the monies generated by wildlife resources and sought to control this important source of revenue. The existence of this additional layer between national-level bureaucracy and community-level institutions further exacerbated the incentive problems of the community-based programs as benefits were channeled to meet other, nonprogram goals.

In significant ways, the community-level programs explored here had negative effects for conservation and local participation. The tactics of excluding locals and distributing collective benefits did not induce conservation behavior. Policies peddled to locals as inclusive were, in some cases, not – thus deepening the suspicion of rural residents toward any wildlife policy. While locals had no formal means by which to press their demands, their continued hunting was a method of protesting the incentive structure offered by these programs.[145]

Political institutions were crucial to the outcomes generated by community-based programs. The array of incentives they offered to members of local communities reveals that their designers had goals in addition to – and sometimes in conflict with – the effective conservation of wildlife.

APPENDIX A

A Short History of Chiefly Authority in Zambia

The position of chief in Zambia's rural areas has varied tremendously over the past century. Colonial and postindependence governments have curbed many of the means by which chiefs maintained their position. But chiefs have also managed to retain some level of authority in the countryside by controlling and distributing valuable benefits, and by manipulating local government institutions.

Before the arrival of European administrators, the authority of Zambian leaders ranged from the hierarchically arranged chieftaincy of the Lozis in the west,[146] to the loosely affiliated kinship groups of the Tonga in the south.[147] Those communities with a chief would choose him or her by following certain descent and selection rules. The individual chosen often emerged as a compromise choice of the most powerful kinship groups. The chief's subsequent authority depended on an ability to manage a complex web of patron–client relationships and to enforce decisions through the support of kinship groups, the local system of justice, weapons, warriors, and lesser leaders.

Crucial to a chief's powers was control over natural resources. Chiefs allocated land for settlement and farming, declared open and closed seasons for fishing and hunting, and determined which species could be killed and by whom. Certain chiefs also claimed exclusive rights to hunt specific species. In exchange for the privilege of hunting, individuals gave chiefs a share of the kill; this "tribute" usually entailed hunting the more valuable animals, for instance, presenting ivory from elephants. A person's failure to provide such tribute could be taken as a sign of rebellion.[148] Chiefs generally left the hunting of smaller and less valuable species unregulated.[149] In some cases these restrictions affected the conservation of some plants and animals; in others, a chief's plundering of "his" animals led to certain species' near extinction in particular areas.[150]

The administrators of the British South Africa Company undermined the authority of chiefs by removing some of their ability to make and enforce rules. Under the BSAC Administration of Natives Protectorate No. 8 of 1916, chiefs became "minor constables" who enforced Europeans' regulations: apprehending criminals, collecting taxes, mobilizing labor, and suppressing witchcraft.[151] While chiefs retained some powers of adjudication at the village level, their decisions remained subject to BSAC oversight. The position of the chiefs within the BSAC structure decreased their popularity among Zambians, who had already witnessed the chiefs' impotence to stop white colonization.[152]

The BSAC administration also struck at the heart of chiefs' control over wildlife. Regulations curtailed the ability of Africans to own guns and powder, designated a few game reserves, and published some hunting restrictions. These measures, though generally unenforced, at least demonstrated that chiefs no longer acted as de jure gatekeepers to wildlife resources.[153]

After the BSAC relinquished Northern Rhodesia to the British government, some chiefs' powers increased under the policy of indirect rule. The Native Authorities Ordinance and Native Courts Ordinance of 1929 sought to "preserve and maintain all that is good in native custom" while depending on chiefs to provide an inexpensive means to administer the protectorate.[154] The ordinances allowed chiefs once again to control land for settlements[155] as well as supervise the brewing and consumption of beer, regulate the movement of women, and adjudicate a wider range of civil and criminal cases.[156] In return for these new powers, chiefs enforced colonial edicts, cleared paths, constructed sanitary facilities, reported illnesses, and facilitated the recruitment of labor within their area.[157] The "Native Authorities" also could declare their own minor rules and orders, subject to the approval of the British district officer in the area.[158] Many chiefs used their new powers – now actively supported by the British colonial government – to extend their own authority.[159] They sentenced people to extended periods of labor in their fields,[160] used their court messengers (*kapasu*) to arrest people,[161] and meted out high fines to those found guilty of breaking the law. Much of the money ended up in the chiefs' pockets.[162]

Despite the powers generated from affiliation with colonial authorities, chiefs' influence continued to decline. Chiefs no longer held a monopoly over rural residents' social and economic choices. Industrialization and urban migration allowed villagers to secure other sources of wealth, status, and justice, severing the patron–client linkages with chiefs.[163] This subverted the authority the chiefs had realized from distributing benefits at the local level.[164]

The chiefs' control over natural resources – especially wildlife – dwindled as well. The colonial government assumed complete jurisdiction over all natural resources and retained supreme authority over questions of land use. Increasingly detailed legislation regarding wildlife emerged, along with government agencies to enforce it. Colonial administrators refined and extended a system of hunting quotas, licenses, and game reserves.[165] As a result, Game Department staff supplanted the chief in rural areas: Scouts were now responsible for local access to animals and game reserves, control of marauding animals, and collection of ivory.

The postindependence UNIP government further stripped the chiefs of their already meager powers.[166] The newly elected President Kaunda lost no time punishing chiefs for their support of the British during pre-independence struggles. The Chiefs Act of 1965 allowed chiefs to perform only those "customary duties" that did not contravene the Zambian Constitution and required them to preserve the public peace; the act also made the position of the chief overtly political by giving the president the power to confirm or dismiss chiefs.[167] For small tasks, chiefs received a small salary and the services of a kapasu. Additional measures by the UNIP government further weakened the chiefs. A reorganization of government institutions allowed only one chief – elected by chiefs in the area – to sit on the district council, the most important government body at the local level. In contrast, all the districts' party ward chairmen were members.[168]

Chiefs did what they could to capture the powers of the state for their own use at the local level. Some manipulated the institutions of local-level development schemes to reclaim their previous powers of arrest and punishment.[169] Others tried to exert influence through traditional courts, to which residents still brought cases concerning witchcraft and intra-community disputes.[170]

6

Conclusion: Exploring the Political Economy of African Wildlife Policy

> When I shot game to feed myself and my Zande servants, who had at last arrived, they [the Nuer] took the animals and ate them in the bush, answering my remonstrances with the rejoinder that since the beasts had been killed on their land they had a right to them.
>
> E. E. Evans-Pritchard, *The Nuer*, 1940

Evans-Pritchard's experiences with wildlife in the Sudan encapsulate many of this book's central issues: wildlife's value, the different actors who seek its benefits, their contestation over access to wildlife, and the particular strategies they choose to advantage themselves. Evans-Pritchard lost control over the wildlife he killed – he had few institutions to back his claims while in the field and, as an anthropologist, chose not to use force of arms. In contrast, the history of wildlife policy in Zambia, Kenya, and Zimbabwe includes both institutions and force. This study has explored how and why individuals and groups competed to shape the content, continuity, and change of wildlife policy in Zambia from 1964 to 1991. It has compared the detailed analysis of Zambia with more preliminary investigations of events in Kenya and Zimbabwe. Throughout, the investigation of policy is grounded in the study of political institutions.

THE CONTRIBUTIONS OF THE CHAPTERS

Four empirical questions have framed this examination of wildlife policy. First, why did the initial independent governments of Zambia, Kenya, and Zimbabwe keep colonial wildlife laws intact, despite prior promises by nationalists to reverse such exclusionary measures? Second, why did these powerful African presidents respond in different ways to the rise of poaching? Third, why did the administrators of these countries' wildlife programs in the 1980s create bureaucratic structures that frustrated certain conservation goals? And fourth, why did these same programs, designed to offer incentives to conserve animals, fail to stop illegal hunting?

In the exploration of these empirical puzzles, I have not followed the theoretical tack of prevailing analyses of African wildlife policy, which generally ignore politics and political institutions, focus on the impediments to either the policy process or policy implementation, and assume that wildlife conservation is an uncontested public good. Rather, I have argued that policy processes and policy implementation are only parts of a larger political conflict between individuals and groups seeking to construct wildlife policy to suit their preferences (Chapter 1). My approach also diverges from those accounts of African politics that assume either the omnipotence of African rulers or the impotence of African governments. I have assumed neither but placed the influence of political institutions at the center of the analysis. Each chapter demonstrates the ways in which political institutions influenced the choices of individuals and groups in their pursuit of advantageous wildlife policies.

The book's first empirical chapter (Chapter 2) examined the role of wildlife in the periods immediately before and after the independence of Zambia, Kenya, and Zimbabwe. Despite efforts by successive British colonial and settler governments to remove most Africans' access to wildlife, it remained central to the livelihoods of many. So valuable was wildlife to Africans – and so irritated were they by these colonial restrictions – that African nationalists were able to use these exclusionary wildlife laws as propaganda in their campaigns against white rule. When we control our own country, the activists promised, the restrictions on hunting will be removed. Such strong statements fueled the fears of many international conservation organizations, which envisioned the wholesale slaughter of wildlife with African independence.

But the old laws were not overturned under the independent governments of Zambia, Kenya, and Zimbabwe. Instead, the new governments maintained and augmented measures that limited the hunting of wildlife and the trading of its products, regulated the ownership of firearms, and established an extensive network of protected areas. In Zambia, the strong support of Zambia's first president, Kenneth Kaunda, was one reason that the 1968 wildlife conservation bill became law. Why didn't opposition parties use Kaunda's wildlife policy, clearly unpopular with most of the electorate, against him? Why didn't his own party members force him to change his conservationist stance? As Chapter 2 indicated, the structure of political institutions during the First Republic allowed Kaunda to establish such disliked measures at relatively low political cost. The multiparty electoral and political rules promoted party discipline, giving parliamentarians strong incentives to follow their leader's policy position on wildlife, despite its lack of popularity with the vast majority of Zambians. At this time, national executives controlled political parties from the center by selecting candidates and providing funding. Further, parties were regionally oriented, so that most elections were a contest between party labels rather than specific issues. Thus, opposing Kaunda's preferences for wildlife conservation policy both threatened the political careers of United National Independence Party (UNIP) candidates and produced few discernible benefits for them at the polls.

And yet the 1968 wildlife bill did more than just please Kaunda at the expense of the public. Chapter 2 also demonstrated how the restrictive wildlife laws enabled the incumbent UNIP to use wildlife as a resource for patronage politics. The party dispensed hundreds of valuable jobs, controlled the allocation of licenses (which were sometimes distributed in direct violation of official conservation policy), and selectively enforced wildlife regulations. As in the colonial era, wildlife remained a valuable resource that politicians could use to reward friends and punish enemies. Thus, Chapter 2 presented several factors to explain why Zambian government officials retained the old, colonial conservation policy: Kaunda preferred conservation, the political institutions of the First Republic enabled him to establish this policy with the support of parliamentarians, and the incumbent party benefited from the distribution of patronage resources.

The experiences of Kenya and Zimbabwe share some fascinating similarities with the Zambian case. The new governments of these countries also enjoyed the discretionary power that the status quo policy offered. Prevailing electoral and governmental institutions did not facilitate a powerful anticonservation lobby, even though widespread antipathy toward wildlife policy existed. Although neither Kenya nor Zimbabwe boasted a leader who strongly supported wildlife conservation as Kaunda did, their countries did derive important benefits from wildlife-related businesses, whose owners would support the inherited policies. Consequently, the only relatively organized groups related to wildlife policy would be those advocating the strengthening of the status quo, not radically changing it.

The second important puzzle this study has considered is why the governments of Zambia, Kenya, and Zimbabwe followed different approaches to the poaching crisis of the 1970s and 1980s (Chapter 3). A related question is why the conservationist President Kaunda, empowered by the new institutions of a one-party state during the Second Republic, failed in his efforts to stem the poaching crisis of the 1970s.

Two important shocks changed Zambia's de facto conservation policies during this period. First, the value of wildlife increased as a result of the rapid decline of Zambian incomes and the concomitant rise of an international wildlife market. That increase stimulated a massive expansion of illegal hunting in Zambia. Second, Kaunda succeeded in instituting a one-party state, which centralized party and government power in his person. However, although he enjoyed newly augmented powers of decision making to create policies he most preferred, Kaunda was ineffective in his efforts to stem or even curtail the increasing rate of poaching in his country.

Chapter 3 indicated that although some of the political institutions of the one-party state did indeed significantly empower Kaunda, other new structures simultaneously motivated parliamentarians (MPs) to oppose the president's desire to stiffen wildlife laws. New electoral and party rules gave local party officials greater authority over the selection and campaigns of parliamentary candidates. The lack of opposition parties meant that candidates had to distinguish themselves along dimensions other than party label. These new rules made MPs more accountable to their constituents, who had never wavered in their antipathy for wildlife regulation. Not all issues salient to locals created incentives for MPs to risk Kaunda's wrath by challenging his preferred policy positions; neither did all MPs respond to their constituents' demands on the wildlife issue. The analysis in Chapter 3 indicates that those parliamentarians running in close elections and representing citizens living near wildlife populations were more likely to express hostility toward Kaunda's legislative attempts to end the poaching crises; these MPs succeeded in delaying and diluting Kaunda's proposals.

President Kenyatta did not respond as Kaunda did to the poaching that was also raging in Kenya. At the time, allowing poaching and illegal trade in wildlife constituted political equilibrium for Kenyatta. Politicians at every level needed new sources of patronage during the country's economic downturn and gladly turned to wildlife when its value increased internationally. As usual, most rural communities also enjoyed a lack of wildlife law enforcement. International and domestic conservationists put pressure on Kenyatta's government for a change in wildlife policy, but the political benefits of the status quo policy outweighed external concerns and little significant change ensued. Only under the threat of a severely damaged tourism industry – a pivotal source of Kenya's foreign exchange – did President Moi act to augment wildlife policy.

Chapter 3 also investigated how the political institutions of independent Zimbabwe helped to prevent an overall increase in the country's poaching rate. Robert Mugabe and his ruling party had not constructed a centralized patronage system to the extent found in Zambia and Kenya; in fact, the country remained a de jure multiparty state with several different centers of domestic political power. One result of these factors was a higher level of bureaucratic oversight, which prevented widespread corruption among wildlife department staff. Additionally, because Zimbabwe's economy did not falter as did Zambia's and Kenya's, there was less pressure on wildlife resources as economic options and wildlife department officials were allowed to continue their enforcement activities. Contrary to the generalizations about "the poaching epidemic in Africa," Chapter 3's analysis of the policy responses in Zambia, Kenya, and Zimbabwe showed variation in the extent of illegal wildlife use and explores its causes.

The analysis of the legislative and electoral battles in Chapter 3 presented important lessons for the study of African politics, as well as the politics of one-party rule more generally.[1] Unlike much of the literature that examines the African one-party state, this chapter indicated that one-party electoral and political institutions could, in some circumstances, lead politicians to challenge a one-party ruler. In the Zambian case, a one-party legislature was not merely a "rubber-stamp" institution, but an important obstacle to Kaunda's policy goals. Further, the specific electoral rules of Zambia's one-party Second Republic led to greater constituency service, despite the lack of opposition parties. In Zimbabwe, too, parliamentarians voiced and voted their opposition to the Mugabe government's policy. By showing the influence of party and electoral rules, these findings also challenged the "strongman" approach's assertion that African rulers are constrained only by informal institutions. Chapter 3's results, therefore, should caution those who only apply categories of government systems to drive their analyses of politics. Instead, researchers should pay close attention to how patterns of incentives embedded within particular sets of political institutions influence individual decisions and thus political outcomes.[2]

Chapter 4 shifted this study of wildlife policy to the bureaucratic level as it probed a third important question: Why did conservation bureaucrats in the 1980s design institutions that ignored important conservation goals? In the early 1980s, international funds and ideas became available to conservationists for use in their efforts to close what had become an open access wildlife commons in many African countries, including Zambia and Kenya. In Zambia, European conservationists worried that small efforts targeted only at wildlife resources would not overcome the incentives for locals to hunt. These conservationists thus preferred a multiresource conservation project. Zambian bureaucrats, especially the members of the National Parks and Wildlife Service (NPWS), feared that the Europeans' plans would supplant them as managers of Zambia's wildlife estate. The officers of the NPWS responded to this challenge by creating their own conservation program.

Chapter 4 offered evidence that both groups sought to expand their control over wildlife resources. But within this general response each created strategies to protect its programs from the specific kind of political uncertainty generated by the institutions of Zambia's one-party state. Although certain groups and institutions did constrain Kaunda's actions, he remained the most important political actor in the country. His ability to intervene in policy making made him a dangerous enemy and a powerful ally. The two groups were forced to deal with the unpredictability of Kaunda's actions as they pursued their own policy agendas. One strategy that both the European conservationists and NPWS officers followed was to collaborate with international donor agencies in order to secure independent sources of revenue and oversight.

But, because of their different shares of public authority, NPWS officers and European conservationists also followed strikingly divergent strategies in their relationship with Kaunda. NPWS officers, already backed by a legislative mandate to manage Zambia's wildlife, did not need to ally themselves with Kaunda – who distrusted NPWS and had consistently intervened in their affairs. NPWS officers sought protection from Kaunda by constructing the Administrative Design for Game Management Areas (ADMADE), a program they hoped would insulate their activities from Kaunda's interference. The European conservationists, on the other hand, had no legal foundation upon which to construct their program. In fact, their plans for a multisectoral quasi-independent agency required that they usurp existing Zambian bureaucracies. Without a legislative mandate, and with the real possibility of political conflicts with other bureaucrats, this group constructed the Luangwa Integrated Resource Development Project (LIRDP), a program that depended heavily on the patronage of Kaunda. In the short term, LIRDP's administrators hoped to use his support to carve out a bureaucratic space for themselves, in the long run, they also sought structures to limit potential presidential interference.

The institutions of the one-party state prevented both programs' managers from choosing the most effective conservation structures. Their decisions regarding budgets, personnel, and expansion had less to do with promoting conservation than with protecting themselves from the political uncertainty caused by Kaunda's dominant policy making position.

This trend continued even after the programs had been established. ADMADE's managers focused their activities on isolating their decisions and securing more resources, trying to prevent any involvement with Kaunda and simultaneously seeking to avoid his displeasure. LIRDP's administrators intensified their pursuit of a legal foundation, both to reduce dependence on Kaunda and to gain additional state resources. Chapter 4 demonstrated that the political uncertainty generated by Kaunda's one-party state critically influenced the choices of LIRDP and

ADMADE bureaucrats and, consequently, the content and change of Zambian wildlife policy.

Chapter 4's extension of structural choice concepts to the cases of Kenya and Zimbabwe yielded interesting comparisons. In Kenya, Richard Leakey used both the political support of the one-party president and the public authority of the Kenyan Wildlife Service to augment and insulate his agency from the high levels of political uncertainty generated by Kenyan political institutions. As did the strategy of LIRDP in Zambia, the decision to ally himself closely with a one-party president was costly to Leakey, who lost his job when Moi withdrew his political support. In Zimbabwe, DNPWM officials did not confront the same political environment as did their colleagues in Zambia and Kenya. Zimbabwe's de jure multiparty institutions did not centralize as much power in the president, and thus political uncertainty stemmed less from the capricious nature of an individual and more from a political system with multiple important actors. DNPWM also possessed public authority over wildlife in Zimbabwe. Thus, officials could expend less effort allying with and insulating themselves from Mugabe, and more time cultivating a broad alliance of domestic support that ranged from the black residents in communal areas to white farmers on large private farms.

Chapter 4's analysis of wildlife policy at the bureaucratic level contributes to our understanding of the bureaucratic politics in the developing world: employing the insights of the structural choice approach – heretofore reserved for the study of industrialized countries – to an African setting and extending these insights to include less democratic systems. Thus, the examination of the choices made by wildlife bureaucrats not only helps to explain the direction and content of Zambian, Kenyan, and Zimbabwean wildlife policy in the 1980s, but also deepens our knowledge of bureaucrats and their choices in developing countries.

Chapter 5 shifted focus to the local level in order to address the final question considered in this study: Why did rural residents not respond to the incentives offered by community-based wildlife programs? Despite the politics of structural choice examined in Chapter 4, wildlife managers still faced sets of choices that included effective, decentralized, and participatory conservation programs. Most of these programs started with the assumption that illegal hunting produced economic benefits to local hunters. To reduce illegal hunting, therefore, the programs provided an array of costs and benefits to induce locals to cease hunting and to support the new conservation programs. In addition to offering material incentives, the programs created structures that allowed residents to participate in certain decisions regarding the programs' funds and personnel.

The Local Politics of Wildlife Policy

Chapter 5 presented evidence indicating that rural residents did not respond to the incentives of these programs in the manner intended by the creators. Rather than stop hunting, many became "free riders," continuing to hunt while accepting the programs' benefits. Part of the programs' poor outcomes was due to the type of goods they offered the rural residents; because administrators made no attempt to identify hunters and exclude them from program benefits, these goods (schools, roads, grinding mills, clinics, game meat, and so on) became open access resources to hunters and nonhunters alike. Neither did the managers devolve much authority over the most important aspects of their programs. As a consequence, many locals "defected" by enjoying the benefits without paying the costs of not hunting.

Evidence demonstrates that the programs did, however, curtail the hunting of larger animals, as a result of stepped-up enforcement activities. In Chapter 5, game theory indicated that the best strategy for locals was to switch from hunting large animals to hunting smaller ones. Thus, some of the claims made by the programs' supporters have validity – especially for the protection of larger mammals such as the elephant. But these conservation gains appear to have resulted from increased enforcement, and not from local acceptance of conservation. Locals continued to hunt, to avoid (and despise) government enforcement officers, and to demand greater access to wildlife resources.

Chapter 5 presents an important case for those interested in the human dimensions of natural resource management and for studies of participatory development policy more generally. The cases demonstrated that although rural residents respond to incentives, bureaucrats do not appear interested in creating policies that undercut their own authority. Thus, even at the grass-roots level, the structure of political institutions matters to policy content and outcomes. Chapter 5 also underscored how deeply the politics of wildlife extend: Those rural residents who may remain untouched by other development schemes, as well as national development plans, continue to be intensely concerned about securing access to wild animals.

THE CONTRIBUTIONS OF THE STUDY

In addition to its particular contribution to the study of wildlife policy, each chapter has provided theoretical and empirical grist for two more general themes: First, wildlife is politically important in Zambia. Second, political institutions critically shape the content and change of wildlife policy.

The Political Economy of African Wildlife Policy

The Politics of Wildlife

Wildlife was and is important in many, if not most, African countries. Before colonization, it was a crucial component of the economic, political, and cultural lives of Africans. In many areas, it helped determine the pattern of European advance on the continent.[3] Wildlife still provides a significant part of individuals' diets, and extensive markets – both legal and illegal – exist to manage the trade of its products.[4] A few countries continue to rely on wildlife as an important source of foreign exchange,[5] and wildlife remains central to a wide variety of cultural practices.[6]

Despite the many facets of wildlife's value, relatively few social scientists have explored how individuals, groups, and governments in Africa seek to exploit it. This is even more striking when one considers that much of Western popular culture in developed countries sees the continent *only* through the lens of its wildlife: Television and films in industrialized countries deal almost exclusively with "wild" Africa.[7] For all this popularization of Africa's wild animals, they remain underanalyzed: A recently published text addressing the environmental and economic dilemmas facing Africa did not include wildlife at all.[8]

This lacuna probably has multiple origins. Wildlife is not central to the daily experiences of most people in developed countries, and thus may not be an obvious topic for research; researchers who do study wildlife tend to be natural scientists. Social scientists studying Africa may deliberately choose to avoid those topics that seem to buttress stereotypes about the continent and its people. Until recently, government officials in Africa seemed to dodge discussions about wildlife, preferring to address subjects that they, as well as donors, found more salient to their country's economic development. Nevertheless, as this analysis has shown, wildlife offers significant benefits to a wide variety of individuals and groups in Africa. The struggle to control its value, in which many people continue to risk their lives, makes wildlife an appropriate object of inquiry for the social scientist.

This examination of African wildlife policy is grounded in politics and highlights how individuals and groups have struggled to define the debate over wildlife in a way that advantages their private interests. The political significance of wildlife appears at every stage of Zambia's, Kenya's, and Zimbabwe's history.

In the precolonial period, wildlife occupied a central place in lineage and governance systems. In the preindependence era, Europeans sought control over wildlife, both to glean its benefits – meat, ivory, sport – and to limit its threat to crops and cattle. The regulations imposed by colonial and settler governments, and the importance of wildlife resources to

Africans, made it a valuable tool to black African political activists in their fight for independence.

The politics of wildlife persisted after independence. At the national level, African politicians retained and extended the inherited wildlife policies for their distributive goods, even though the vast majority of citizens preferred fewer, not more, rules limiting their access to wildlife. Conflict over access to wild animals erupted during the financial crises of the 1970s and 1980s, when members of the Zambian and Kenyan governments could not prevent the growth of (and, in fact, actively participated in) a flourishing market for wildlife products, whereas Zimbabwe's political institutions supported a more successful response to poaching. Contestation over wildlife policy was also evident at the bureaucratic level. In Zambia, ADMADE and LIRDP administrators battled for nearly a decade over who would be the preeminent custodian of Zambia's wildlife estate. In Kenya, Richard Leakey fought to create and retain control over the Kenyan Wildlife Service. In Zimbabwe, DNPWM officials contested district councils' rights to wildlife benefits. And, at the local level in all three countries, citizens challenged and evaded attempts to incorporate them into state- and donor-sponsored schemes.[9]

This book has demonstrated that the politics of wildlife in Africa do not conform to the explanations provided by typical conservation policy analyses or approaches to African politics. Wildlife politics includes more than configuring policies to meet the conservation goals of wildlife biologists: It includes more actors than one-party rulers, formal as well as informal institutions. By conceptualizing wildlife politics as a struggle over access to valuable natural resources, this study has explored wildlife policy's multiple layers, multiple actors, and multiple issues.

Wildlife Politics and Institutions

The political struggles over wildlife are central to explanations of Zambian wildlife policy, but they did not occur in an institutional vacuum. The second theme of this book is that political institutions shape the strategies of individuals seeking their preferred wildlife policy; thus, these institutions significantly influence policy outcomes.

A variety of institutions critically affected individuals' strategies during each period examined by this study. The incentives generated by electoral and party systems in Zambia, Kenya, and Zimbabwe's first republics did not reward constituency service, and little political activism related to the wildlife issue emerged. President Kaunda's desire to retain the colonial-style policy of exclusion and centralized control was relatively unchallenged. This quiescence changed with the structures of party and electoral systems during Zambia's one-party Second Republic, as examined in Chapter 3. New institutions provided new incentives to parliamentarians. Tied to their electorate in new ways, MPs championed rural and urban dwellers' desire for greater access to wild animals. The incentives of bureaucrats also changed with the alteration in the political institutional environment. Unlike NPWS officers in the 1960s, the administrators of ADMADE and LIRDP had to contend with the political uncertainty caused by a powerful one-party president. As a result, they built public agencies far different from those needed to implement conservation policy effectively.

Institutions affected the behavior of those Zambians who lived with wildlife as well. The incentives generated by ADMADE and LIRDP greatly influenced the strategies of rural residents, producing both intended and unintended effects on the actions of local hunters, wildlife scouts, and chiefs. Rural hunters responded to the costs and benefits engendered by ADMADE and LIRDP by changing their prey from larger to smaller animals, and by altering their weapons from firearms to snares. Chiefs helped cover up poaching activities while enjoying their enhanced power as money and wildlife scouts augmented their social position within their community. Scouts reacted to greater supervision and material incentives by increasing their enforcement of wildlife laws.

Unlike those of new institutionalists who emphasize institutions as solutions to social dilemmas, this study has demonstrated that individuals create or change institutions to attain their private goals. Such a perspective does not preclude the existence of socially minded individuals; nor does it mean that such people never create institutions that produce social goods. What it does indicate is that socially benevolent institutions must be explained with reference to the incentives, opportunities, and constraints of the individuals who construct them. And it suggests that in contests over resources that are considered valuable, beneficent individuals may be in relatively short supply.

FUTURE DIRECTIONS IN THE STUDY OF WILDLIFE POLICY

Increasing numbers of studies about conservation now include human beings. A central task of these studies is to account for the changes induced by humans on Earth's biophysical systems. Good data are being accumulated at a remarkable pace, and many individuals and groups are using these data in efforts to influence government policy.

This study indicates that such a strategy is not adequate to create sound conservation policy. In the rush to utilize hard-won and important biophysical data, we risk oversimplifying the nature of human systems, especially political institutions that affect the production, protection, and distribution of natural resources. Political institutions can thwart or augment natural resource conservation, while disregarding biophysical data. We have also seen examples of wildlife policies that have little relevance or legitimacy in the eyes of those individuals who can make or break conservation initiatives – politicians, rural residents, hunters, and business owners. These actors can occupy various levels of society and government. They possess different sets of preferences about what they consider to be the "appropriate" rules governing wildlife resources. And they act under different sets of institutional constraints. Creating wildlife policy that can work, consequently, means more than establishing the trends and performance of biological systems and passing laws to protect them. It demands an understanding of the most important political actors and the institutions that affect their behavior. The study of wildlife policy – and indeed all conservation policy – thus requires an understanding of politics.

Notes

1. POLITICS, INSTITUTIONS, AND ANIMALS: EXPLAINING THE CONTENT, CONTINUITY, AND CHANGE OF AFRICAN WILDLIFE POLICY

1. T. G. C. Vaughan-Jones, *A Short Survey of the Aims and Functions of the Department of Game and Tsetse Control* (Lusaka: Government Printer, 1948), p. 5.

2. I use North's definition: Institutions are "the rules of the game in a society or, more formally, are the humanly derived constraints that shape human interaction." Douglass North, *Institutions, Institutional Change, and Economic Performance* (Cambridge: Cambridge University Press, 1990), p. 3.

3. For example, see William Beinart and Peter Coates, *Environment and History: The Taming of Nature in the USA and South Africa* (London: Routledge, 1995); K. M. Homewood and W. A. Rogers, *Maasailand Ecology* (Cambridge: Cambridge University Press, 1991); John M. MacKenzie, *The Empire of Nature: Hunting, Conservation and British Imperialism* (Manchester: Manchester University Press, 1988); Marvin P. Miracle, *Maize in Tropical Africa* (Madison: University of Wisconsin Press, 1966); Robin Palmer and Neil Parsons, eds., *The Roots of Rural Poverty in Central and Southern Africa* (Berkeley: University of California Press, 1977); Harold K. Schneider, "Traditional African Economies," in Phyllis Martin and Patrick O'Meara, eds., *Africa* (Bloomington: Indiana University Press, 1986), pp. 181–98; Thayer Scudder, *Gathering among African Woodland Savannah Cultivators*, Zambian Papers, no. 5 (Lusaka: Institute for African Studies, 1971); E. I. Steinhart, "Hunters, Poachers and Gamekeepers: Towards a Social History of Hunting in Colonial Kenya," *Journal of African History* 30 (1989): 247–64. The few estimates of human consumption of wildlife in Africa show its persistence. For example, Mayers estimates the annual sale of wild meat in Liberia in 1990 was around $40 million; J. Mayers, "Getting Back to Bushmeat," *BBC Wildlife* (January 1991): 16. A more recent survey in Southern Ghana reveals that 95 percent of respondents eat wildlife on occasion; J. Falconer, *Non-Timber Forest Products in Southern Ghana*, Overseas Development Administration Forestry Series, no. 2 (London: Natural Resources Institute, 1992). An older estimate from Zaire states that 75 percent of animal protein consumed in Zaire came from wild animals; see J. C. Heymans and J. S. Maurice, "Introduction a l'Exploitation de la Faune comme Resource Alimentaire en Republique du Zaire," *Forum Universitaire* (1973): 6–12.

4. Stuart A. Marks, *Large Mammals and a Brave People: Subsistence Hunters in Zambia* (Seattle: University of Washington Press, 1976); John M. MacKenzie, "Chivalry, Social Darwinism and Ritualised Killing: The Hunting Ethos in Central

165

Africa up to 1914," in David Anderson and Richard Groves, eds., *Conservation in Africa: People, Policies and Practice* (Cambridge: Cambridge University Press, 1987).

5. Palmer and Parsons, *Roots*; MacKenzie, "Ethos," pp. 41–61.

6. E. A. Alpers, *The East African Slave Trade* (Nairobi: East African Publishing House, 1967); Alpers, *Ivory and Slaves: Changing Pattern of International Trade in East Central Africa to the Later Nineteenth Century* (Berkeley: University of California Press, 1975); Suzanne Miers and Igor Kopytoff, eds., *Slavery in Africa: Historical and Anthropological Perspectives* (Madison: University of Wisconsin Press, 1977); James Walvin, *Black Ivory: A History of British Slavery* (London: Fontana Press, 1992).

7. Anderson and Grove, *Conservation in Africa*; Steinhart, "Hunters"; Jane Carruthers, *The Kruger National Park: A Social and Political History* (Pietermaritzburg: University of Natal Press, 1995), pp. 247–64. John M. MacKenzie, *The Empire of Nature: Hunting, Conservation and British Imperialism* (Manchester: Manchester University Press, 1988).

8. Marks, *Large Mammals*; Stuart A. Marks, *The Imperial Lion: Human Dimensions of Wildlife Management in Central Africa* (Boulder: Westview Press, 1984); Carruthers, *The Kruger National Park*; Richard Hasler, *Agriculture, Foraging and Wildlife Resource Use in Africa* (London: Kegan Paul, 1996).

9. Marks, *Large Mammals*; Urs P. Kreuter and Randy P. Simmons, "Who Owns the Elephant? The Political Economy of Saving the African Elephant," in Terry L. Anderson and Peter J. Hill, eds., *Wildlife in the Marketplace* (Tatowa, N.J.: Rowman & Littlefield, 1995), pp. 147–65; Graham Child, *Wildlife and People: The Zimbabwean Success* (Harare: Wisdom Foundation, 1995).

10. John Ford, *The Role of Trypanosomiases in African Ecology: A Study of the Tsetse Fly Problem* (London: Oxford University Press, 1971); John J. McKelvey, *Man against Tsetse: Struggle for Africa* (Ithaca: Cornell University Press, 1973); John M. MacKenzie, "Experts and Amateurs: Tsetse, Nagana and Sleeping Sickness in East and Central Africa," in John M. MacKenzie, ed., *Imperialism and the Natural World* (Manchester: Manchester University Press, 1990), pp. 187–211; J. Desmond Clark and Steven A. Brandt, *From Hunters to Farmers: The Cause and Consequences of Food Production in Africa* (Berkeley: University of California Press, 1984).

11. Leroy Vail, "Ecology and History: The Example of Eastern Zambia," *Journal of Southern African Studies* 3 (1977): 129–55; Marks, *Imperial Lion*; Hasler, *Agriculture*.

12. Jonathan McShane and Thomas Adams, *The Myth of Wild Africa* (New York: Norton, 1992); Raymond Bonner, *At the Hand of Man: Peril and Hope for Africa's Wildlife* (New York: Alfred A. Knopf, 1993); Hasler, *Agriculture*.

13. For example, see E. E. Evans-Pritchard, *The Nuer* (London: Oxford University Press, 1947). For areas near and in Zambia, see the following chapters in Elizabeth Colson and Max Gluckman, eds., *Seven Tribes of British Central Africa* (Manchester: Manchester University Press, 1961): Max Gluckman, "The Lozi of Barotseland in North-Western Rhodesia," pp. 1–93; Elizabeth Colson, "The Plateau Tonga of Northern Rhodesia," pp. 94–162; Audrey I. Richards, "The Bemba of North-Eastern Rhodesia," pp. 164–93; J. A. Barnes, "The Fort Jameson Ngoni," pp. 194–252; and J. C. Mitchell, "The Yao of Southern Nyasaland," pp. 292–353. Also see Elizabeth Colson, *The Social Organization of the Gwembe Tonga* (Manchester: Manchester University Press, 1960).

14. Carruthers, *The Kruger National Park*, p. 16.

15. One of the earliest exceptions was the work of Stuart Marks, *Large Mammals*.

16. See, for example, R. H. V. Bell and E. McShane-Caluzi, eds., *Conservation and*

Wildlife Management in Africa (Washington, D.C.: U.S. Peace Corps, 1984); Daniel Henning, *Environmental Policy and Administration* (Elsevier, N.Y.: American Press, 1974); Owen-Smith and R. Norman, eds., *Management of Large Mammals in African Conservation Areas* (Pretoria: Haum Educational Publishers, 1983).

17. See Richard H. V. Bell, "Conservation with a Human Face," in Grove and Anderson, *Conservation in Africa*, pp. 79–102; David Western and R. Michael Wright, eds., *Natural Connections: Perspectives in Community-Based Conservation* (New York: Island Press, 1994); Jeffrey McNeely and David Pitt, eds., *Culture and Conservation: The Human Dimension in Wildlife Planning* (London: Croon Helm, 1985); Dale Lewis and Nick Carter, eds., *Voices from Africa* (Washington, D.C.: World Wildlife Fund, 1993); Gary Gray, *Wildlife and People: The Human Dimensions of Wildlife Ecology* (Urbana and Chicago: University of Illinois Press, 1993); Bonner, *At the Hand of Man*; McShane and Adams, *Myth of Wild Africa.*

18. Owen-Smith and Norman, *Management of Large Mammals*; Henning, *Environmental Policy*; William Ascher and Robert Healy, *Natural Resource Policymaking in Developing Countries* (Durham and London: Duke University Press, 1990); Anderson and Grove, *Conservation in Africa*; Bell and McShane-Caluzi, *Conservation and Wildlife Management*; P. Jewell and S. Holt, eds., *Problems in Management of Locally Abundant Wild Animals* (New York: Academic Press, 1981); Fred Gilbert and Donald Dodds, *The Philosophy and Practice of Wildlife Management* (Melbourne, Fla.: Krieger Publishing, 1992).

19. For example, see Rodger Yeager and Norman N. Miller, *Wildlife, Wild Death: Land Use and Survival in Eastern Africa* (Albany: State University of New York Press, 1986). Natural scientists generally adopt this view in their examination of policy.

20. J. Z. Z. Matowanyika, "Cast Out of Eden: Peasants versus Wildlife Policy in Savanna Africa," *Alternatives* 16(1) (1989): 30–39; Marks, *Imperial Lion*; Grove and Anderson, *Conservation in Africa*; Bonner, *At the Hand of Man.*

21. Lloyd Timberlake, *Africa in Crisis* (Philadelphia: New Society Publishers, 1986); Iain Douglas-Hamilton and Oria Douglas-Hamilton, *Battle for the Elephants* (New York: Viking Press, 1992); Bonner, *Hand of Man*; McShane and Adams, *Myth of Wild Africa*; Marks, *Imperial Lion*. The theoretical foundation for predatory states comes from Anne O. Krueger, "The Political Economy of Rent-Seeking," *American Economic Review* 3 (1974): 291–303.

22. This general policy process approach is used by both the "preservationist" and "consumptive utilization" schools of conservation in Africa. It is also employed by economists whose analyses tend to focus on economic gain rather than conservation. Economists assert that governments should choose the most economically efficient alternatives when they design policies regarding natural resources. For an example of this argument in a non-Western country, see Robert Repetto and Malcolm Gillis, eds., *Public Policy and the Misuse of Forest Resources* (Cambridge: Cambridge University Press, 1988); Clement A. Tisdell, *Economics of Environmental Conservation* (New York: Elsevier, 1991). The same argument has been put forward many times in reference to the United States; see, for example, Richard Stroup and John A. Baden, *Natural Resources: Bureaucratic Myths and Environmental Management* (Cambridge: Ballinger Publishing/Harper & Row, 1983); William J. Baumol and Wallace E. Oates, *The Theory of Environmental Policy* (Cambridge: Cambridge University Press, 1988). It is pertinent to note, however, that with the exception of those of Kenya and possibly South Africa, most wildlife managers admit that animals are a losing financial proposition to most central governments, including Zambia's. See Bell and McShane-Caluzi, *Conservation and Wildlife Management in Africa*; N.

Leader-Williams and S. D. Albon, "Allocation of Resources for Conservation," *Nature* 336 (1988): 533–35.

23. This emphasis on the collective good of conservation likely results from the "crisis mentality" that characterizes early inquiry into environmental policy in the 1960s and 1970s. See, for example, Stuart S. Nagel, ed., *Environmental Politics* (New York: Praeger, 1974); Lynton Keith Caldwell, *Environment: A Challenge to Modern Society* (Garden City, N.Y.: Doubleday, 1971); James Ridgeway, *The Politics of Ecology* (New York: E. P. Dutton, 1970); Phillip O. Foss, *Politics and Ecology* (Belmont, Calif.: Duxbury Press, 1972); Clarence J. Davies, *The Politics of Pollution* (New York: Pegasus, 1970); George Laycock, *Diligent Destroyers* (Garden City, N.Y.: Doubleday, 1970).

24. An important contribution to the analysis of divergent preferences over wildlife can be found in N. Abel and P. Blaikie, "Elephants, Parks, People and Development: The Case of the Luangwa Valley, Zambia," *Environmental Management*, 10 (1986): 735–51. An explicit focus on the disjuncture between the distributive and collective aspects of environmental policy in the United States is taken by the contributors to Michael S. Greve and Fred L. Smith, Jr., eds., *Environmental Politics: Public Costs, Private Benefits* (New York: Praeger, 1992).

25. Robert H. Jackson and Carl G. Rosberg, *Personal Rule in Black Africa: Prince, Autocrat, Prophet, Tyrant* (Berkeley: University of California Press, 1982). See also idem, "The Political Economy of African Personal Rule," in David E. Apter and Carl G. Rosberg, eds., *Political Development and the New Realism in Sub-Saharan Africa* (Charlottesville and London: University Press of Virginia, 1994), pp. 291–322; David E. Apter and Carl G. Rosberg, "Changing African Perspectives," in Apter and Rosberg, *Political Development*, pp. 1–60.

26. See the sources cited in n. 25. See also Richard A. Joseph, *Democracy and Prebendal Politics in Nigeria: The Rise and Fall of the Second Republic* (Cambridge: Cambridge University Press, 1987); Jean-François Medard, "The Underdeveloped State in Tropical Africa: Political Clientelism or Neopatrimonialism," in Christopher Clapham, ed., *Private Patronage and Public Power: Political Clientelism in the Modern State* (London: Francis Pinter, 1982), pp. 180–203.

27. The failure of personal rulers in Africa to "develop" or even maintain effective control within their countries led many scholars of Africa to move their focus away from the politics of the "state." See Edmund J. Keller, "The State in Contemporary Africa: A Critical Assessment of Theory and Practice," in Dankwart A. Rustow and Kenneth P. Erickson, eds., *Comparative Political Dynamics: Global Research Perspectives* (New York: HarperCollins, 1991), pp. 134–59.

28. M. Bratton, "Beyond the State: Civil and Associational Life in Africa," *World Politics* 41(3) (1989): 407–30; Patrick Chabal, ed., *Political Domination in Africa* (Cambridge: Cambridge University Press, 1986). The influence of the state/society approach mushroomed with the advent of multiparty elections in Africa. "Civil society" – rather than formal institutions such as elections – is seen as the most critical variable to sustaining stable democracies. See the many contributions using this theme in the issues of *The Journal of Democracy*. Naomi Chazan and Donald Rothchild, eds., *The Precarious Balance: State and Society in Africa* (Boulder: Westview Press, 1988).

29. Indeed, one of its strongest proponents admitted that some phenomena could be considered both disengagement and incorporation simultaneously. See Victor Azarya, "Reordering State–Society Relations: Incorporation and Disengagement," in Rothchild and Chazan, *Precarious Balance*, pp. 10–11.

30. These trends have different labels as they occur in different literatures. For example, some work is called *environment history* (see Richard White, "American Environmental History," *Pacific Historical Review* 54 [3]: 297–335; Daniel Worster, ed., *The Ends of the Earth: Perspectives on Modern Environmental*

History [Cambridge: Cambridge University Press, 1988]); others offer the label *political ecology*. Some well-known work that specifically addresses Africa includes MacKenzie, *Empire of Nature*; Carruthers, *The Kruger National Park; Journal of Southern African Studies* (Special Issue) 15 (1989); Richard Grove, *Green Imperialism: Colonial Expansion Tropical Island Edens and the Origins of Environmentalism 1600–1860* (New York: Cambridge University Press, 1995); William Beinart and Peter Coates, *Environment and History: The Taming of Nature in the U.S.A. and South Africa* (London: Routledge, 1995); Hasler, *Agriculture.*

31. The work of Kevin A. Hill is a valuable exception; see "Interest Groups and the Politics of the Environment: Wildlife Conservation Policy, the State, and Organized Interests in Zimbabwe" (Ph.D. dissertation, University of Florida, 1993).

32. This section focuses on what is labeled *rational choice institutionalism* and the *new institutionalism* in economics. Many names have been applied to the analysis of institutions using a rational choice approach, including *neoinstitutional economics*, the *new institutional economics*, the *economics of institutions*, the *new economics of organization*, and the *new institutionalism*. Hall and Taylor identify four schools of the new institutionalism: historical institutionalism, rational choice institutionalism, economic institutionalism, and sociological institutionalism. Peter A. Hall and Rosemary C. R. Taylor, "Political Science and the Four New Institutionalisms," paper presented to the 1994 Annual Meeting of the American Political Science Association, Toronto, 1994. See also Geoffrey M. Hodgson, "Institutional Economics: Surveying the Old and New," *Metroeconomica* 44 (1993): 1–28; Kathleen Thelen and Sven Steinmo, "Historical Institutionalism in Comparative Politics," in Sven Steinmo, Kathleen Thelen, and Frank Longstreth, eds., *Structuring Politics: Historical Institutionalism in Comparative Analysis* (Cambridge: Cambridge University Press, 1992), pp. 1–32.

33. Garrett Hardin, "The Tragedy of the Commons," *Science* 162 (December 1968): 1243–48.

34. Kreps provides a lucid account of simple games, including the prisoner's dilemma, in David M. Kreps, *A Course in Microeconomic Theory* (Princeton, N.J.: Princeton University Press, 1990).

35. Douglass C. North, *Institutions, Institutional Change and Economic Performance* (Cambridge: Cambridge University Press, 1990), pp. 1–50.

36. The seminal works include Frank H. Knight, *Risk, Uncertainty and Profit* (Boston: Houghton Mifflin, 1921); Ronald H. Coase, "The Economic Nature of the Firm," *Econometrica* 4 (November 1937): 386–405.

37. Oliver Williamson, *Markets and Hierarchies: Analysis and Antitrust Implications* (New York: Free Press, 1975); Williamson, *The Economic Institutions of Capitalism: Firms, Markets and Relational Contracting* (New York: Free Press, 1985); North, *Institutions*; Douglass C. North and Paul Thomas, *The Rise of the Western World* (Cambridge: Cambridge University Press, 1973); Margaret Levi, *Of Rule and Revenue* (Berkeley: University of California Press, 1988); Yoram Barzel, "An Economic Analysis of Slavery," *Journal of Law and Economics* 20 (1977): 87–110; Barzel, "Measurement Cost and the Organization of Markets," *Journal of Law and Economics* 25 (1985): 27–48; Barzel, *Economic Analysis of Property Rights* (Cambridge: Cambridge University Press, 1989); Steven N. S. Cheung, "A Theory of Price Control," *Journal of Law and Economics* 12 (1974): 23–45; Cheung, "The Contractual Nature of the Firm,"*Journal of Law and Economics* 17 (1983): 53–71. For a short review see Thrainn Eggertsson, *Economic Behavior and Institutions* (Cambridge: Cambridge University Press, 1990), pp. 9–13, 28–32.

38. Michael C. Jensen and William H. Meckling, "Theory of the Firm: Managerial Behavior, Agency Costs and Capital Structure,"*Journal of Financial Economics*

3 (October 1976): 305–60; Eugene F. Fama and Michael C. Jensen, "Agency Problems and Residual Claims," *Journal of Law and Economics* 26 (June 1983): 327–49; idem, "Separation of Ownership and Control," *Journal of Financial Economics* 14 (1985): 101–19.

39. Some leading examples of this approach are Elinor Ostrom, *Governing the Commons: The Evolution of Institutions for Collective Action* (Cambridge: Cambridge University Press, 1990); Douglass C. North and Barry R. Weingast, "Constitutions and Commitment: The Evolution of Institutions Governing Public Choice in Seventeenth Century England," *Journal of Economic History* 49 (1989): 803–32; Margaret Levi, *Of Rule and Revenue* (Berkeley: University of California Press, 1988); Robert H. Bates, *Beyond the Miracle of the Market: The Political Economy of Agrarian Development in Kenya* (Cambridge: Cambridge University Press, 1989).

40. For critiques of using Pareto optimality or stability in explanations of institutions, see Russell Hardin, "Difficulties in the Notion of Economic Rationality," *Social Science Information* 19 (1984): 453–67; see also Jack Knight, *Institutions and Social Conflict* (Cambridge: Cambridge University Press, 1992), pp. 30–115; Knight and Itai Sened, eds., *Explaining Social Institutions* (Ann Arbor: University of Michigan Press, 1995). Eggertsson asserts that it is misleading for scholars to use a dynamic model when criticizing the Pareto criterion, because individuals would make choices based on all information, present and future. Thrainn Eggertsson, interview by author, Bloomington, Indiana, 20 February 1995.

41. Mancur Olson, *The Logic of Collective Action* (Cambridge, Mass.: Harvard University Press, 1965). The provision of an institution to solve a collective action problem is itself a collective action problem. Bates calls this a "second-order" dilemma. See Robert H. Bates, "Contra Contractarianism: Some Reflections on the New Institutionalism," *Politics and Society* 16 (1988): 387–401. See also Ostrom, *Governing*, pp. 42–43.

42. The focus on the distributional character of institutions found in this section follows Knight's approach; see Knight, *Institutions and Social Conflict*. Whereas most new institutionalists outside economics would deny that social actors enjoy relatively equal access to resources, some scholars have chosen empirical puzzles that allow them to retain this view (for example, see Ostrom, *Governing*). Such foci may help explain why some new institutionalists disregard the political dimension of institutional explanations. Moe mentions some of these apolitical tendencies in his review of positive political theory in Terry M. Moe, "Political Institutions: The Neglected Side of the Story," *Journal of Law, Economics, and Organization* 6 (1990): 213–35.

43. Marx and Weber are the most well-known contributors to our understanding of extractive and redistributive institutions. For an account of why their theories fail to specify the mechanism of institutional change, see Knight, *Institutions and Social Conflict*, pp. 8–9.

44. Scholars evoking collective benefits to explain institutions deny institutional change that produces inefficient, Pareto-inferior, or unstable outcomes. Bates suggests that these theoretical problems also push scholars to the study of the "softer" explanations offered by anthropology, such as reputation, symbolic action, and custom. Robert H. Bates, *Social Dilemmas and Rational Individuals: An Essay on the New Institutionalism*, Duke University Program in Political Economy Working Papers (Durham: Duke University Press, 1992). Indeed, a growing body of work uses "soft phenomena" to explain the origin and maintenance of institutions. Joseph Kalt, *Where's the Glue? Institutional Bases of American Indian Economic Development*, John F. Kennedy School of Government, Harvard University, Working Paper series (Cambridge, Mass.: Harvard University Press, 1991); Barry R. Weingast, "A Rational Choice Perspective on the Role

of Ideas: Shared Belief Systems and State Sovereignty in International Cooperation," *Politics and Society* 23 (4) (1995): 449–64; Gary Miller, *Managerial Dilemmas: The Political Economy of Hierarchy* (New York: Cambridge University
Press, 1992); David Kreps and R. Wilson, "Reputation and Imperfect Information," *Journal of Economic Theory* 27 (1982): 253–79; Randall Calvert, "Coordination and Power: The Foundation of Leadership among Rational Legislators,"
American Political Science Association Annual Meeting, Chicago, 1991; Margaret Levi, *Of Rule and Revenue,* pp. 10–40; idem, "Death, Taxes and Bureaucrats," University of Maryland, Baltimore, 1994 (mimeo.); idem, "A Logic of
Institutional Change," in Karen Schweers Cook and M. Levi, eds., *The Limits of
Rationality* (Chicago and London: University of Chicago Press, 1990), pp. 408–
09. Results emerging from the work on noncooperative games also stimulated
the search for phenomena that could overcome individuals' incentives to defect
from cooperative behavior. See especially the work of Michael Taylor: *Anarchy
and Cooperation* (London: John Wiley, 1976); idem, *The Possibility of Cooperation* (Cambridge: Cambridge University Press, 1987).

45. Knight and Sened refer to these scholars as bargaining theorists. See Knight and
Sened, "Introduction," in Knight and Sened, *Explaining Social Institutions,*
pp. 1–13. See also the various contributions in the special issue of *Politics and
Society* No. 2–3 (1988).

46. See North, *Institutions,* p. 48; Margaret Levi, "A Logic of Institutional Change,"
in Cook and Levi, *Limits of Rationality,* p. 406. Interestingly, even Pareto indicates the possibility of predatory government leaders. Vilfredo Pareto, *Sociological Writings,* edited by S. E. Finer, translated by Derrick Mirfin (New York:
Praeger, 1966), pp. 114–20.

47. Tsebelis, *Nested Games,* pp. 96–100; Robert H. Bates, *Institutions as Investments,* Duke University Program in Political Economy Working Papers (Durham:
Duke University Press, 1990).

48. See Levi, "A Logic," p. 406. Buchanan, Tollison, and Tullock presented the view
that governments would seek to augment their own power regardless of economic efficiency. For example, see James D. Buchanan, Robert D. Tollison, and
Gordon Tullock, eds., *Toward a Theory of a Rent-Seeking Society* (College
Station: Texas A&M Press, 1980). Tsebelis points out that Marx strongly believed that economic and political institutions entrenched the power of the capi-
talist class. Tsebelis, *Nested Games,* p. 114.

49. Miller and Cook provide a fascinating account of cycling that begins with a
discussion of hierarchy among primates before proceeding to human institutions.
Gary Miller and Kathleen Cook, "Leveling and Leadership in States and Firms,"
University of Maryland, Baltimore, 1994 (mimeo.).

50. While admitting to the theoretical possibility of payments, as used in Posner's
theory of primitive society, Knight argues that the empirical evidence supporting
the use of side payments to construct a social institution is weak. See Knight,
Institutions, p. 115.

51. Levi, "A Logic," p. 407.

52. Ibid., p. 415.

53. North, *Institutions,* p. 100. The distributive nature of institutions does not preclude institutions that produce socially desirable outcomes: If institutional change
is incremental and path dependent, entrepreneurs operating under the constraints
of previous growth-promoting institutions will likely push for institutional
change along similar growth-producing lines. Nevertheless, individuals face opportunities that "overwhelmingly favor activities that promote redistributive
rather than productive activity." North, *Institutions,* p. 9; see also pp. 16–17,
110. North takes a similar position in chapter 3 of his earlier work, *Structure
and Change in Economic History* (New York: Norton, 1981).

54. North, *Institutions*, p. 112. Armen Alchian, on the other hand, argues that the market selects only the more efficient institutions; consequently, institutional change proceeds along an ever more efficient path. See Alchian, "Uncertainty, Evolution and Economic Theory," *Journal of Political Economy* 58 (1950): 211–21. Tsebelis points out, however, that most social science explanations involving an evolutionary explanation fail because they do not account for the maintenance of the enforcement mechanism. See Tsebelis, *Nested Games*, pp. 100–103.
55. North, *Institutions*, p. 8; Tsebelis, *Nested Games*, 110–15. Asserting that it takes more than "hard" incentives to create institutions, Levi argues that institutional change may result from a breakdown in the shared norm of fairness, reducing people's "contingent consent" for an institutional arrangement. Such people may withdraw their consent, leading to institutional breakdown. Levi, "A Logic," p. 410. "Historical institutionalists" offer reasons for institutional change that are similar to the ones presented here; however, they often fail to link explicitly their explanations with individual actors. See Thelen and Steinmo, "Historical Institutionalism," pp. 3–27.
56. This is the cost of institutional supply, the "second-order" collective action problem mentioned by Bates. See Robert H. Bates, "Contra Contractarianism," pp. 397–99; see also Ostrom, *Governing*, pp. 42–43.
57. See, for example, Alice Amsden, "The State and Taiwan's Economic Development," in Robert H. Bates, ed., *Toward a Political Economy of Development* (Berkeley and Los Angeles: University of California Press, 1988); Bates, *Beyond the Miracle of the Market* (Cambridge: Cambridge University Press, 1989); Peter B. Evans, Dietrich Rueschemeyer, and Theda Skocpol, eds., *Bringing the State Back In* (Cambridge: Cambridge University Press, 1985); Peter Katzenstein, *Small States and World Markets* (Ithaca, N.Y.: Cornell University Press, 1985).
58. Moe, "Political Institutions," p. 221.
59. New institutionalists are well aware of the lack of a well-developed theory. Tsebelis, for example, states, "I do not know how far theorizing about redistributive institutions can go," because such institutions are a "matter of political choice and coalition building." Tsebelis, *Nested Games*, p. 110. See the related statements by Eggertsson, *Economic Behavior*, p. 310; and North, *Institutions*, p. 416.
60. North, *Institutions*, p. 416.

2. UNKEPT PROMISES AND PARTY LARGESSE: THE POLITICS OF WILDLIFE IN THE INDEPENDENCE PERIOD

1. Department of Games and Fisheries, *Annual Report, 1964* (Lusaka: Government Printer, 1965); Stuart A. Marks, *The Imperial Lion: Human Dimensions of Wildlife Management in Central Africa* (Boulder: Westview Press, 1984), p. 106.
2. See Republic of Zambia, *Statutory Instruments*, nos. 1–5, 80, 88, of 1971 (amendments to the National Parks and Wildlife Act of 1971).
3. The text of Minister Kalulu's speech to the National Assembly may be found in Appendix A of the National Parks and Wildlife Department, *Annual Report for the Year 1971* (Lusaka: Government Printer, 1972).
4. D. Hywel Davies, ed., *Zambia in Maps* (London: University of London Press, 1971).
5. R. C. Bigalke, "Mammals," in M. J. A. Werger, ed., *Biogeography and Ecology of Southern Africa* (The Hague: Junk, 1978), pp. 981–1048; C. W. Benson et al., *The Birds of Zambia* (London: Collins, 1971); B. L. Mitchell and W. F. H. Ansell, *Wildlife of Kafue and Luangwa: A Tourist Field Guide* (Lusaka: National Tourist Bureau, 1971), p. 1965; J. Hanks, *Mammals of Zambia* (Lusaka: National Tourist Bureau, 1972); United States Agency for International Development, "Environ-

mental Profile of Zambia," 1982 (draft), National Park Service Contract CX-001-0-0003.

6. Thayer Scudder, *Gathering among African Woodland Savannah Cultivators* (Lusaka: Institute for African Studies, 1971), Zambian Papers, no. 5; Marks, *Imperial Lion*; Samuel N. Chipungu, *The State, Technology and Peasant Differentiation in Zambia: A Case Study of the Southern Province, 1930–1986* (Lusaka: Historical Association of Zambia, 1988).

7. E. A. Alpers, *The East African Slave Trade* (Nairobi: East African Publishing House, 1967), p. 124.

8. Ibid. Establishing control over African ownership of guns and powder also reduced the possibility of armed uprisings.

9. The earliest European attempts to conserve natural resources in Africa were stimulated by fears of ecological disaster, and certain conservation laws regarding flora were established as early as the 1820s in the Cape Colony. In the 1840s, reports received from India and the Cape Colony underlined growing problems in soil erosion and deforestation. Restrictions on hunting followed soon after, the result of a massive increase in the killing of the larger mammals for food and profit. In 1858, the Cape Colony initiated the protection of elephant and buffalo in certain areas. It was not until the 1886 Cape Act for the Preservation of Game that a more systematic approach to game legislation was undertaken in Africa. See Richard Grove, "Early Themes in African Conservation: The Cape in the Nineteenth Century," in David Anderson and Richard Grove, eds., *Conservation in Africa: People, Policies and Practice* (Cambridge: Cambridge University Press, 1987), pp. 21–34. As a result of the rapid decrease in wildlife populations from the pressures of hunting and a rinderpest epidemic, and the growing lobbying efforts by conservation groups in London, the commissioner of British Central Africa extended the act to include all the other areas operated by the British South Africa Company, including Northern Rhodesia, in 1891. The BSAC issued modifications to the act later in the decade, then consolidated and amended the regulations in 1899 and 1906. In 1899 the Mweru Marsh Game Reserve was created in Northern Rhodesia, and a reserve for giraffe was founded in the Luangwa Valley in 1902. See John Ford, *The Role of Trypanosomiasis in African Ecology* (London: Oxford University Press, 1971); Marks, *Imperial Lion*, pp. 66, 106; John M. MacKenzie, "Chivalry, Social Darwinism and Ritualised Killing: The Hunting Ethos in Central Africa up to 1914," in Anderson and Grove, *Conservation in Africa*, pp. 41–61.

10. See the debate of the Legislative Council concerning this ordinance in *Legislative Council Debates: Second Session of the First Council, May 15th–May 30th, 1925* (Livingstone, Northern Rhodesia: Government Printer, 1925), pp. 154–58.

11. T. G. C. Vaughan-Jones, *A Short Survey of the Aims and Functions of the Department of Game and Tsetse Control* (Lusaka: Government Printer, 1948), p. 4. But Vaughan-Jones elsewhere states the department was "constituted with effect from 1st January, 1940." See his "*Game and Tsetse Control Department: Progress Report to 31st December, 1943*," n.d. (mimeo.): p. 1.

12. Vaughan-Jones, *Short Survey*, p. 4.

13. Game conservation was also part of two other ordinances: The Game Ordinance (Capital Law 106) provided separate legislation for national parks; the Victoria Falls Ordinance (Capital Law 252) provided for conservation in the Victoria Falls Trust Area.

14. Northern Rhodesia, *Fauna Conservation, Chapter 241 of the Laws* (Lusaka: Government Printer, 1964).

15. The crucial difference between national parks and game management areas is that the latter could be gazetted or degazetted by the governor alone; national parks needed action by a legislature.

16. Mwelwa C. Musambachime, "Colonialism and the Environment in Zambia, 1890–1964," in Samuel N. Chipungu, ed., *Guardians in Their Time: Experiences of Zambians under Colonial Rule, 1890–1964* (London: Macmillan, 1992); Leroy Vail, "Ecology and History: The Example of Eastern Africa," *Journal of Southern African Studies* 3 (1977): 129–55.

17. See the letter regarding fishing rights in the Luangwa Valley Game Reserve from Senior Ranger W. E. Poles to the Provincial Game Officer, Northern Province, 10 January 1955; also the exchange of letters between the Provincial Commissioner (Northern Province), Director of Game and Tsetse Control, Senior Agricultural Officer and District Commissioner (Mpika) regarding locals' concern about the Luangwa Valley Game Reserve boundaries in 1943, dated 7 January, 15 January, 23 January, 12 July, 29 September, 13 October, 16 October, 23 October, 31 October, and 24 November (all in National Archives of Zambia).

18. See W. E. Poles, *A Report on a Tour in the Luangwa (Southern) Game Reserve and the Areas of Native Settlement Closely Adjacent Thereto* (Mpika, Northern Rhodesia: Game and Tsetse Control Department, 1947), p. 20.

19. Interview with Norman Carr, former officer of the Department of Game and Tsetse Control, Kapani Lodge, Mfuwe, Zambia, 10 August 1991.

20. Some chiefs during this period did attempt to get their lands designated as controlled areas. See Northern Rhodesia Game and Tsetse Control Department, *Annual Report* (Livingstone: Government Printer, 1944). Later, Game Department officials would realize that the chiefs were more interested in the share of revenues they received from the sale of hunting licenses than in conversation when their chiefdoms were designated as controlled areas. "That even Native Authorities have little conscience in these matters was well instanced" by the situation disclosed by the district commissioner, Lundazi, and the police in that district. An illicit ivory and gun-running trade had been built up, in which nine of the local chiefs "were personally responsible." Idem, 1947, p. 9.

    An intense debate in the early to mid-1950s between the provincial commissioners (Northern and Eastern Provinces) and officers in the Game Department regarding the boundaries of African fishing rights in the Luangwa Game Reserve reveals the politically sensitive nature of the size of protected areas and, especially, the issue of relocating villages out of these lands. The provincial commissioners tended to be sympathetic to Africans' land and fishing needs; the Game Department officers tended to see Africans as poachers of game. See the following correspondence: District Commissioner (Mpika District) to Provincial Commissioner (Northern) (12 May 1952); Provincial Commissioner (Northern) to the District Commissioner (Mpika) (19 May 1952); Provincial Game Officer (Northern) to Game Ranger (Mpika) (25 January 1954); Game Ranger to Provincial Game Officer (15 March 1954); Provincial Game Officer to Provincial Commissioner (Northern) (22 December 1954); Director to Provincial Commissioner (Eastern) (5 January 1955); Senior Ranger to Provincial Commissioner (Northern) (10 January 1955); Provincial Commissioner (Northern) to Provincial Commissioner (Eastern) (14 January 1955); Provincial Commissioner (Eastern) to Director (29 January 1955); Director of Game to Provincial Commissioner (14 February 1955); Provincial Commissioner (Northern) to Director of Game and Tse Tse Control Department (4 May 1955) (all in National Archives of Zambia).

21. See the Game Department's *Annual Reports* for descriptions of how its staff died over the course of the years.

22. See the Game Department's *Annual Reports* from 1950 to 1970 for the many schemes used to "educate" rural Africans about conservation. See also the recommendations of Dr. Frasier Darling in Darling, *Wildlife in an African Territory:*

A Study Made for the Game and Tsetse Control Department of Northern Rhodesia (London: Oxford University Press, 1960), p. 34.

23. See, for example, the letter from Senior Ranger W. E. Poles to the Provincial Game Officer, 10 January 1955 (National Archives of Zambia).

24. Department of Game and Tsetse Control, *Annual Report* (Lusaka: Government Printer, 1947), p. 9.

25. Department of Game and Tsetse Control, *Annual Report* (Lusaka: Government Printer, 1946), p. 7.

26. Other regulatory policies used by African nationalists included agriculture and soil measures. See Thomas Rasmussen, "The Popular Basis of Anti-Colonial Protest," in William Tordoff, ed., *Politics in Zambia* (Manchester: Manchester University Press, 1974), pp. 40–61.

27. Government of Northern Rhodesia, *Annual Report of African Affairs: Fort Jameson District* (Lusaka: Government Printer, 1960).

28. Robert H. Bates, *Rural Responses to Industrialization* (New Haven and London: Yale University Press, 1976), p. 87.

29. Interview with Richard Bell, codirector, Luangwa Integrated Rural Development Programme, Chipata, Zambia, 28 May 1991.

30. Government of Northern Rhodesia, *Annual Report on African Affairs: Namwala District* (Lusaka: Government Printer, 1957); see also idem, *Annual Report – Southern Province* (Lusaka: Government Printer, 1957), p. 80.

31. See, for example, Rasmussen, "Popular Basis," pp. 51–53; L. H. Gann, *A History of Northern Rhodesia: Early Days to 1953* (London: Chatto and Windus, 1964), pp. 306–7. For an example of how local politicians even transformed land surveys into political issues, see also *Annual Report – Southern Province* (1957), p. 76.

32. Marks, *Imperial Lion*, p. 105.

33. Interview with President Kenneth Kaunda, Lusaka, Zambia, 18 August 1992.

34. Ibid. Also interview with W. Astle, former officer, Department of Game and Fisheries, Lusaka, Zambia, 24 July 1992; interview with P. S. M. Berry, former officer, Department of Game and Fisheries, Mfuwe, Zambia, 2 August 1992.

35. Members were elected in single-district, plurality voting. The 1964 elections also included ten reserve roll seats for Europeans in the new seventy-five-member postindependence National Assembly. The National Progress Party won all these seats in 1964. The reserve roll seats were eliminated before the 1968 general elections. See Robert Molteno and Ian Scott, "The 1968 General Election and the Political System," in Tordoff, *Politics in Zambia*, pp. 155–96.

36. William Tordoff and Ian Scott, "Political Parties: Structure and Policies," in Tordoff, *Politics in Zambia*, p. 112.

37. United National Independence Party, "1967 Constitution," Lusaka, p. 168 (mimeo.).

38. Molteno and Scott, "1968 General Election," pp. 171–75.

39. Tordoff and Scott, "Political Parties," p. 134.

40. Molteno and Scott, "1968 General Election," p. 164.

41. Ibid., p. 176; see also William Tordoff and Robert Molteno, "Parliament," in Tordoff, *Politics in Zambia*, pp. 204–5.

42. Molteno and Scott, "1968 General Election," p. 177.

43. Constitution Act No. 2 of 1966. This paralleled a law passed earlier in Kenya. See Molteno and Scott, "Parliament," p. 205.

44. Ibid.

45. The ANC's strength came from the Southern Province, and from the western part of Central Province; UNIP was popular in most other areas. Some members of UNIP, believing that the interest of the Lozis in the Western Province were not being adequately met by UNIP, broke away to form the United Party (UP) in

1966. The UP was banned after its followers clashed with UNIP supporters in August 1968. Thereafter, the UP threw its weight behind the ANC and delivered eight of the eleven Western Province seats to the opposition. This result, defying as it did the efforts of UNIP to create a one-party state through the ballot box, precipitated Kaunda's declaration of the one-party Second Republic in 1972. See Molteno and Scott, "1968 General Election," pp. 160–80.

46. Tordoff and Scott, "Political Parties," pp. 141–54.
47. Ibid., p. 193.
48. Sometimes local chiefs mediated conflict and helped to represent individuals before government agencies. Constituents did not generally write to or visit their MPs. Ibid., p. 214.
49. Tordoff and Molteno, "Government and Administration," pp. 244–52.
50. Tordoff and Molteno, "Parliament," pp. 236–7.
51. Ibid., p. 211.
52. Ibid.
53. Ibid., p. 238.
54. Molteno and Scott, "1968 General Election," p. 176.
55. Tordoff and Scott, "Political Parties," pp. 135–48.
56. Tordoff and Molteno, "Parliament," p. 234.
57. Marks, *Imperial Lion*, pp. 113–17.
58. Republic of Zambia, *Debates of the First Session of the National Assembly, 30 October 1968*, pp. 571–94.
59. The economic viability of wildlife conservation had been promoted by the colonial Game Department since the early 1940s. See Department of Game and Tsetse Control, *Annual Reports* (Lusaka: Government Printer, various years).
60. The 1962 Game Ordinance provided for three types of protected areas, game reserves (which could be declared by the governor), controlled hunting areas, and private hunting areas. Essentially, the new bill changed the name of reserves to national parks, and required the approval of both the president and the National Assembly to create or change them. The new bill also combined private and controlled areas into game management areas. Hunting was only permitted in the game management areas, not in national parks.
61. Republic of Zambia, *Debates of the First Session*, pp. 573–75.
62. Ibid., p. 575. Under the old game ordinances, the maximum penalty for an infraction was 600 kwacha (K), nine months in jail, or both. The new bill proposed a maximum sentence of 2,500K and/or five years in prison: Killing a protected species could reap a 3,000K and/or seven year sentence.
63. Ibid., p. 573.
64. Ibid., p. 576.
65. The Europeans were Mitchley, Farmer, Burney, and Burnside.
66. Republic of Zambia, *Debates of the First Session*, p. 586.
67. Ibid., p. 580.
68. Ibid., p. 584.
69. Ibid., p. 583.
70. Ibid., pp. 586–87.
71. Republic of Zambia, *Debates of the Second Session of the Second National Assembly, 7th January–25th March 1970*, pp. 550–51.
72. Molteno and Scott, "1968 General Election," pp. 187, 193.
73. William Tordoff and Robert Molteno, "Government and Administration," in Tordoff, *Politics in Zambia*, p. 243.
74. Republic of Zambia, *First National Development Plan, 1966–70* (Lusaka: Government Printer, 1966).
75. Republic of Zambia, *Annual Estimates of Revenue and Expenditure* (Lusaka: Government Printer, various years).

76. Republic of Zambia, *Manpower Report: A Report and Statistical Handbook on Manpower, Education, Training and Zambianization, 1965–66* (Lusaka: Government Printer, 1967).
77. William Tordoff and Robert Molteno, "Introduction," in Tordoff, *Politics in Zambia*, p. 11.
78. Department of Game and Fisheries, *Annual Report, 1965* (Lusaka: Government Printer, 1966), 26. By 1966, the department felt "most gratified" by its place in the First National Development Plan, whose provisions outlined "ambitious development throughout the game estate." Idem, *Annual Report, 1966*, p. 25.
79. The figures presented in this section can be found in the Department of Game and Fisheries, *Annual Reports* (Lusaka: Government Printer, various years). The numbers presented refer only to the staff employed in the game division of the department and do not include fisheries personnel.
80. The department also felt the competition between different government agencies over skilled candidates, particularly for senior posts. Lack of fluency in English was one major obstacle to its hiring plans. Department of Game and Fisheries, *Annual Report, 1966* (Lusaka: Government Printer, 1967).
81. The department also became consumed with the building of houses for these junior level appointments. See Department of Game and Fisheries, *Annual Reports* (Lusaka: Government Printer, 1965–1970).
82. Interview with W. Astle, former officer of the Department of Game and Fisheries, 12 August 1992.
83. Department of Game and Fisheries, *Annual Report, 1966* (Lusaka: Government Printer, 1967).
84. Interview with Francis X. Nkhoma, 17 July 1992, Lusaka. The wildlife department admits to helping in this endeavor. See Department of Game and Fisheries, *Annual Report, 1967* (Lusaka: Government Printer, 1968). Ministers of the colonial administration had very similar powers and also used them for political and personal reasons. See Northern Rhodesia, *Fauna Conservation, Chapter 241 of the Laws, 1964 Edition* (Lusaka: Government Printer, 1964), sec. 4 and 18.
85. Although passed in 1968, the National Parks and Wildlife Act did not become law until 1 January 1971 because of these amendments.
86. Republic of Zambia, *Parliamentary Debates of the National Assembly, 9 December 1970* (Lusaka: Government Printer, 1971), pp. 75–76.
87. Interview with P. S. M. Berry, former officer of the Department of Game and Fisheries, Chinzombo Safari Lodge, Mfuwe, Zambia, 22 June 1991.
88. The value of the minister's extensive control over wildlife resources would grow with the value of wildlife products and the safari hunting business. Over the next three decades observers would note how individuals would lobby the minister for special licenses, trophy export permits, and rights to hunting areas. Ministers' offices were often seen stuffed with crates of alcoholic beverages and foodstuffs, inciting rumors about illegal deals between ministers and business owners interested in wildlife. Ministers themselves were sometimes at the center of investigations regarding the export of ivory and rhino horn.
89. Tordoff and Molteno, "Introduction," p. 15.
90. Rasmussen, "Popular Basis," p. 58.
91. Department of Wildlife, Fisheries and National Parks, *Annual Report, 1970* (Lusaka: Government Printer, 1972), p. 13.
92. Department of Game and Fisheries, *Annual Report* (Lusaka: Government Printer, 1966), pp. 9, 41. See the similar comments made in subsequent *Annual Reports*.
93. Department of Game and Fisheries, *Annual Report, 1968* (Lusaka: Government Printer, 1970), p. 43.
94. Interview with Norman Carr, 10 August 1991, Mfuwe, Zambia.
95. See Michael Jensen and William Meckling, "The Theory of the Firm: Managerial

Behavior, Agency Costs and Ownership Structure," in Louis Putterman, ed., *The Economic Nature of the Firm* (New York: Cambridge University Press, 1986), pp. 305–60. See also Terry Moe, "The New Economics of Organization," *American Journal of Political Science* 28 (1984): pp. 739–77.

96. Armen Alchian and Harold Demsetz, "Production, Information Costs and Economic Organization," in Putterman, *Economic Nature of the Firm*, pp. 111–34.

97. Gary Miller, *Managerial Dilemmas: The Political Economy of Hierarchy* (New York: Cambridge University Press, 1992).

98. Bengt Holstrom, "Moral Hazard in Teams," *Bell Journal of Economics* 13 (1982): 324–40.

99. Mathew McCubbins and Talbot Page, "A Theory of Congressional Delegation," in Mathew McCubbins and Terry Sullivan, eds., *Congress: Structure and Policy* (Cambridge: Cambridge University Press, 1987), pp. 409–25. See also Randall Calvert, Mark Moran, and Barry Weingast, "Congressional Influence over Policy Making," pp. 493–522, and Mathew McCubbins and Thomas Schwartz, "Congressional Oversight Overlooked: Police Patrols Versus Fire Alarms," 426–40, in the same volume.

100. Interview with President Kaunda, 14 August 1992, Lusaka, Zambia.

101. Wildlife also entered the realm of international relations under the BEAC. The company was very concerned that the hunting by Europeans in Kenya's interior might initiate a conflict with Africans that would require a punitive mission by BEAC staff. See Thomas Ofcansky, "A History of Game Preservation in British East Africa, 1895–1963" (Ph.D. dissertation, West Virginia University, 1981), pp. 5–10.

102. Raymond Bonner, *At the Hand of Man: Peril and Hope for Africa's Wildlife* (New York: Knopf, 1993), p. 42.

103. Noel Simon, *Between the Sunlight and the Thunder* (Boston: Houghton Mifflin, 1963), p. 124; John M. MacKenzie, *The Empire of Nature: Hunting, Conservation and British Imperialism* (Manchester: Manchester University Press, 1988), p. 215.

104. MacKenzie, *Empire*, pp. 220–21; Ofcansky, *History*, pp. 33–37.

105. Ofcansky, *History*, p. 37.

106. Bonner, *At the Hand of Man*, p. 50.

107. M. Cowie, *Walk with Lions* (New York: Macmillan, 1961), p. 80.

108. Ofcansky, *History*, pp. 219–20.

109. Ibid., p. 230; see also MacKenzie, *Empire*, p. 220.

110. See Jennifer A. Widner, "Single Party States and Agricultural Policies: The Cases of Ivory Coast and Kenya," *Comparative Politics* 26 (1984): 127–47; Peter Anyang' Nyong'o, "State and Society in Kenya: The Disintegration of the Nationalist Coalitions and the Rise of Presidential Authoritarianism, 1963–78," *African Affairs* 88 (1989): 229–51; Robert H. Jackson and Carl G. Rosberg, "The States of East Africa: Tanzania, Uganda, and Kenya," in Peter Duignan and Robert H. Jackson, eds., *Politics and Government in African States* (Stanford, Calif.: Hoover Institution Press, 1986), pp. 202–52.

111. Robert H. Bates, *Beyond the Miracle of the Market: The Political Economy of Agrarian Development in Kenya* (Cambridge: Cambridge University Press, 1989), p. 48.

112. Ibid., pp. 47–48.

113. Rodger Yeager and Norman Miller, *Wildlife, Wild Death: Land Use and Survival in Eastern Africa* (Albany: State University of New York Press, 1986), p. 15. For example, tourism at Amboseli National Park grew 22 percent annually from 1965 to 1969. See F. Mitchell, *Forecasts of Returns to Kajiado County Council from the Maasai Amboseli Game Reserve*, Nairobi

Institute for Development Studies Discussion Paper no. 87 (Nairobi: University of Nairobi, 1969). MacKenzie puts the value of the tourist industry at eight million pounds at the time of Kenya's independence (Mackenzie, *Empire*, p. 277).

114. John J. Okumu and Frank Holmquist, "Party and Party–State Relations," in Joel Barkan, ed., *Politics and Public Policy in Kenya and Tanzania*, pp. 45–69; Jackson and Rosberg, "The States of East Africa," p. 230.

115. This follows from Olson's analysis of collective action. Those affected by exclusionary wildlife policy confront the greatest obstacles to initiating successful collective action (Mancur Olson, *The Logic of Collective Action* [Cambridge, Mass.: Harvard University Press, 1971]). Bates as well as others note this in their work on African rural populations and state policy, see, for example, Robert H. Bates, *Essays on the Political Economy of Rural Africa* (Cambridge: Cambridge University Press, 1983).

116. Graham Child, *Wildlife and People: The Zimbabwean Success* (Harare and New York: Wisdom, 1996), p. 50. Although Masona argues that early colonial administrators did allow the Africans the hunting of crop raiders and the distribution of game meat during times of famine, he would contest this neutral reading of the game laws. See Tafirenyika Masona, "Colonial Game Policy: A Study of the Origin and Administration of Game Policy in Southern Rhodesia – 1890–1945" (Master's thesis, University of Zimbabwe, 1987).

117. Kay Muir, Jan Bojo, and Robert Cunliffe, "Economic Policy, Wildlife, and Land Use in Zimbabwe," in *The Economics of Wildlife: Case Studies from Ghana, Kenya, Namibia, and Zimbabwe* (Washington, D.C.: World Bank, 1966), p. 123.

118. Child, *Wildlife and People*, p. 51.

119. Ibid.

120. Ibid., pp. 59–60; see also John McCraken, "Colonialism, Capitalism and the Ecological Crisis in Malawi: A Reassessment," in David Anderson and Richard Grove, *Conservation in Africa* (Cambridge: Cambridge University Press, 1987), p. 72.

121. Masona, "Colonial Game Policy," p. 25.

122. Ibid., p. 74.

123. Colin Stoneman and Lionel Cliffe, *Zimbabwe: Politics, Economics and Society* (London and New York: Pinter Publishers, 1989).

124. Masona, "Colonial Game Policy," p. 95.

125. Child, *Wildlife and People*, pp. 51–52.

126. Felix Murindagomo, "Zimbabwe: WINDFALL and CAMPFIRE," in Agnes Kiss, ed., *Living with Wildlife: Wildlife Resource Management and Local Participation in Africa*, World Bank Technical Paper no. 130 (Washington, D.C.: World Bank, 1990), p. 12.

127. Muir et al., "Economic Policy," pp. 117–19.

128. Kevin A. Hill, "*Interest Groups and the Politics of the Environment*" (Ph.D. dissertation, University of Florida, 1993).

129. D. Martin and B. Johnson, *The Struggle for Zimbabwe: The Chimurenga War* (London: P. Faber and Faber, 1981); D. Lan, *Guns and Rain: Guerrilla and Spirit Mediums in Zimbabwe* (Berkeley and Los Angeles: University of California Press, 1985); T. Ranger, *Peasant Consciousness and Guerrilla War in Zimbabwe* (Harare: Zimbabwe Publishing House, 1985); M. Drinkwater, *The State and Agrarian Change in Zimbabwe's Communal Areas* (London: Macmillan, 1991).

130. B. Derman, "Environmental NGOs, Dispossession, and the State: The Ideology and Praxis of African Nature and Development," *Human Ecology* 23(2) (1995): 190–215.

131. The two leading parties were the Zimbabwe African National Union (Patriotic Front) (ZANU[PF]) and Patriotic Front – Zimbabwe Active People's Union (PF – ZAPU).
132. Hill, *Interest Groups*, pp. 81–82.
133. Lloyd Timberlake, *Africa in Crisis* (Philadelphia: New Society Publishers, 1986).
134. Hill, *Interest Groups*, pp. 81–82.
135. Such differentiation probably would not have mattered much anyway because Mugabe's Zimbabwean African National Union–Patriotic Front controlled an overwhelming majority of legislative seats.
136. Ibid., p. 200.
137. See Derman, "Environmental NGOs," p. 205.
138. Some observers claim that expatriates in Zambia's game department influenced the president's volte-face on wildlife policy; see Marks, *Imperial Lion*, p. 106. Supposedly, Kaunda went to the Luangwa Valley soon after becoming the country's new president. While he was in the valley, a game officer, Johnny Ace, took Kaunda on personal tours of the wildlife areas, convincing him that protection was indeed necessary. Kaunda claims that although he had a "great deal of respect of Mr. Ace," he did not need to be persuaded to continue a policy of wildlife conservation because he had always been a conservationist at heart. Kaunda himself claims that his original call for open hunting was strategic: He had used the British wildlife conservation policy as a "weapon" against the colonial regime. But, having always understood the importance of wildlife conservation, Kaunda told his followers immediately after independence to "undo what they had done" and reverse their opposition to wildlife conservation policy. Interview with President Kaunda.
139. Ibid.
140. Bonner, *At the Hand of Man*, p. 65.

3. THE POLITICAL LOGIC OF POACHING IN ONE-PARTY STATES

1. Eugenia West, "The Politics of Hope" (Ph.D. dissertation, Yale University, 1989), p. 51.
2. See Cherry Gertzel, Carolyn Baylies, and Morris Szeftel, "The Making of a One-Party State," in Gertzel, Baylies, and Szeftel, eds., *The Dynamics of the One-Party State in Zambia* (Manchester: Manchester University Press, 1984), pp. 1–28.
3. See, for example, Republic of Zambia, *Report of the National Commission on the Establishment of a One-Party Participatory Democracy in Zambia: Summary of Recommendations Accepted by Government* (Lusaka: Government Printer, 1972), pp. 24–25.
4. A diagram of the structure of government and party bodies in the Second Republic can be found in P. E. Ollawa, *Participatory Democracy in Zambia* (Elms Court, Great Britain: Arthur H. Stockwell, 1979), p. 263.
5. Nsolo Mijere, "The State and Development," *Africa Today* (Second Quarter 1980): 21–25.
6. Constitution of Zambia, Article 53(2).
7. Republic of Zambia, *The Electoral Act of 1973* (Lusaka: Government Printer, 1973). See also idem, *Constitution of Zambia Act 1973, 75 (3)*.
8. The Central Committee enjoyed the power to reject any individual whose candidacy was considered "inimical to the interests of the state." See *UNIP Manual of Rules and Regulations Governing the 1973 General Elections* (Lusaka: Issued by the Central Committee, n.d.).
9. See Ollawa, *Participatory Democracy in Zambia*, p. 284; Marcia M. Burdette,

Zambia: Between Two Worlds (Boulder: Westview Press, 1988), p. 75; West, "Politics of Hope," p. 108.

10. West, "Politics of Hope," p. 108.
11. Robert H. Bates and Paul Collier, "The Politics and Economics of Policy Reform in Zambia," in Robert H. Bates and Anne O. Krueger, eds., *Political and Economic Interactions in Economic Policy Reform* (Cambridge, Mass.: Blackwell Publishers, 1993), pp. 391–406.
12. William Tordoff, "Residual Legislatures in African One-Party States," *Journal of Comparative and Commonwealth Studies* 15 (1977): 235–49.
13. Ibid.
14. Marcia Burdette, *Zambia: Between Two Worlds*, p. 102.
15. Ibid. See also Doris Jansen, *Trade, Exchange Rate and Agricultural Pricing Policies in Zambia* (Washington, D.C.: World Bank, 1988), p. 4.
16. By 1984 Zambia was the most indebted country in the world relative to its GDP. See Bates and Collier, "Politics and Economics of Policy Reform in Zambia," pp. 388–89.
17. In contrast, the inflation rate averaged only 6 percent over the period 1964 to 1974.
18. West, "Politics of Hope," p. 51. Accurate data for total agricultural output before 1982 do not exist. Although the total amount of agricultural production marketed through government fell considerably, this does not take into account the large degree of smuggling that occurred: Border prices for maize from the early 1970s through the 1980s generally exceeded government's guaranteed producer prices. See also Jansen, *Trade, Exchange Rate and Agricultural Pricing Policies in Zambia*, p. 87. The United Nations International Labor Office (ILO) estimated 60 percent of marketed agriculture was smuggled out of the country. See United Nations International Labor Office (hereafter ILO), *Zambia: Basic Needs in an Economy under Pressure* (Addis Ababa: United Printers, 1981), p. 127.
19. Jansen, *Trade, Exchange Rate*, p. 88. This figure takes into account the effects of both direct and indirect intervention.
20. Ibid., p. 191.
21. ILO, *Zambia: Basic Needs*, p. 23.
22. Cherry Gertzel, "Dissent and Authority in the One-Party State," in Gertzel et al., *Dynamics of the One-Party State*, p. 82.
23. Jansen, *Trade, Exchange Rate*, p. 195. See also Government of Zambia Prices and Incomes Commission, *Pilot Household Budget Survey, 1982: Some Preliminary Findings* (Lusaka: Government Printer, 1986).
24. ILO, *Zambia: Basic Needs*, p. 130.
25. The influx of foreign truckers carrying goods from East African ports after the closure of Zambia's border with Rhodesia also facilitated a market for illegal animal products. Mike Faddy, Save the Rhino Trust, personal communication, 26 May 1994.
26. Estimates for the actual world price of raw ivory vary tremendously and are based on different data and assumptions. Prices also varied across exporting African countries as the wave of poaching swept through Africa at different rates. On the basis of legal import and export documents, Edward B. Barbier, Joanne C. Burgess, Timothy M. Swanson, and David W. Pearce assert that the world ivory price hovered around $60 per kilogram, from 1979–1985, then exploded to $120 in 1987 and $300 in 1989. See Edward Barbier et al., *Elephants, Economics and Ivory* (London: Earthscan Publications, 1990), p. 4. Ian Parker claims that some ivory had passed $120 a kilo in 1978. See Iain and Oria Douglas-Hamilton, *Battle for the Elephants* (New York: Viking, 1992), p. 127. The price for a kilogram of ivory probably increased sixfold from the mid-1970s to the late 1980s.

27. Calculated from Barbier et al., *Elephants, Economics and Ivory*, pp. 3–6, and the UNEP/IUCN/WWF study. See also G. Caughly and J. Goddard, "Abundance and Distribution of Elephants in the Luangwa Valley, Zambia," *East African Wildlife Journal* 13 (1975): 39–48. It is important to note that estimates of elephant populations are notoriously inexact and hotly contested, and NPWS collected few data during this period.

28. Douglas-Hamilton and Douglas-Hamilton, *Battle for the Elephants*, p. 175.

29. G. B. Kaweche, F. Munyenyembe, H. Mwima, F. B. Lungu, and R. H. V. Bell, *Aerial Census of Elephant in the Luangwa Valley* (LIRDP Report No. 1, 9 March 1987), p. 1.

30. I base my calculations on an ivory price of seventy-five dollars per kilogram, and an average pair of tusks weighing nine kilograms. See Barbier et al., *Elephants, Economics and Ivory*, p. 5.

31. Demand for rhino horn stems from its use in Yemeni dagger handles and Asian medicines. Tim Inskipp and Sue Wells, *International Trade in Wildlife* (London: International Institute for Environment and Development [IIED], 1979) estimate that rhino horn sold for $27 a kilogram in 1975, and $675 in 1978. In China, a kilogram of African rhino horn cost $16,304 in 1989. Asian rhino horn, which is smaller and therefore considered more potent, sold for $54,000 per kilogram in Taiwan in 1990 – more than the price of cocaine in Miami at the time (World Wide Fund for Nature, *Campaign Report* [Washington, D.C.: WWF, April 1991]).

32. Heavy rhino poaching began in the 1970s, and, over the next twenty years, hunters killed 85 percent of all rhinos in Africa and Asia. Some one hundred tons of rhino horn have been traded in international markets from 1970 to 1987, equivalent to forty thousand animals. Over 95 percent of the African black rhino population has been slain since 1970.

33. S. Robinson, "Saving the Rhino: Zambia's Fight against Big-Time Poaching," *Black Lechwe* 1 (1981): 7–9. Mike Faddy of Save the Rhino Trust, and Stuart Marks, among others, consider this estimate extremely high. Mike Faddy, personal communication, 26 May 1994; interview with Stuart Marks, 7 April 1993, Durham, North Carolina.

34. Robinson, "Saving the Rhino," pp. 8–9.

35. Faddy, personal communication. NPWS officers believe that a few were alive in 1992, but that those did not compose a viable breeding population. Interview with Edwin Matokwani, wildlife ranger, Nyamaluma Training Center, Mfuwe, Zambia, July 1991.

36. Faddy asserts that most of the large-scale meat poaching took place in the western half of the country and the Bangweulu swamp areas. Less illegal hunting occurred in the Luangwa Valley because it was so difficult to transport meat out of the valley. Faddy, personal communication.

The United Nations Food and Agriculture Organization (FAO) reported that game meat costs considerably less than beef in Africa and claimed that 13.4 percent of the annual amount of protein consumed in Zambia (around 3.7 kilogram per person) was in the form of game from 1974 to 1977. See Robert Prescott-Allen and Christine Prescott-Allen, *What's Wildlife Worth?* (London: IIED, 1982), p. 15. Marks calculates that in certain parts of Zambia's Muny-amadzi corridor, where domesticated animals cannot live because of tsetse fly infestation, the average adult annually consumed 91 kilograms of game meat in the early 1970s, or about 5–10 percent of the weight of all food consumed. See Stuart Marks, *Large Mammals and a Brave People* (Seattle: University of Washington Press, 1976), p. 204. Abel and Blaikie estimate that residents of game management areas around the South Luangwa National Park hunt enough to supply every resident with 20 kilograms of game meat annually. See Nick Abel and Piers Blaikie, "Elephants, People Parks and Development: The Case of the Luangwa Valley, Zambia," *Environmental Management* 10(6) (1986): 735–51.

37. Interview with Gilson Kaweche, deputy director – NPWS, Chipata, Zambia, 14 July 1992.

Little research exists regarding the returns to meat poaching in Zambia, a trade uninterrupted during this century. One small survey, however, does illustrate its potential returns. In 1972 NPWS sponsored a project carried out by the Zambian National Food and Nutrition Program to study the behavior of subsistence hunters in three game management areas of the Luangwa Valley. The project found that hunters obtained an average of 440 kilograms of meat per year, worth between 135 and 200 kwacha (in comparison, a cook for a safari company could expect to earn 35 kwacha per month). Because licenses cost only 75 ngwee (1 kwacha = 100 ngwee), the economic barrier to hunting would be the cost of securing the use of a firearm and ammunition. Even with these additional costs, incentives to hunt remained strong. And many rural residents used the inexpensive tactic of snaring to procure game meat. The NFNP estimated the total number of animals killed exceeded that hunted legally by 55 percent. It is also instructive to note that NFNP completed this survey *before* Zambia's economic decline. Hunting pressure on animal populations probably increased in subsequent years.

38. As discussed in the last chapter, the operative wildlife law was contained in Capital Law 316 of the Laws of Zambia, passed as the National Parks and Wildlife Act of 1971.

39. Only the Ministry of Education's departments experienced greater financial reductions. See Republic of Zambia, *Financial Reports* (Lusaka: Government Printer, 1975–1980).

40. The Department of Fisheries was removed from the NPWS budget in 1975, no doubt accounting for some of the decline in spending on wildlife in that year. However, a pattern of deep cuts continued even after the Fisheries split off as a separate entity: The NPWS budget was cut 9.2 percent in 1976, 39 percent in 1977, and 19 percent in 1978. See Republic of Zambia, *Financial Report* (Lusaka: Government Printer, various years).

41. National Parks and Wildlife Service, *1967 Annual Report* (Lusaka: Government Printer, 1968), pp. 12–13.

42. Idem, *1973 Annual Report*, p. 6.

43. Idem, *1977 Annual Report*, pp. 1–4.

44. Idem, *1978 Annual Report*, p. 3. As if to underscore the budget difficulties of the department at this time, this report appears to be written on a typewriter rather than professionally typeset as previous reports were.

45. Interview with Norman Carr, Kapani Safari Lodge, Zambia, 10 August 1991.

46. National Parks and Wildlife Service, *1979 Annual Report*, p. 2.

47. Idem, *1984 Annual Report*, p. 1.

48. Idem, *1979 Annual Report*, pp. 2–5.

49. The government strictly controlled imports after the copper shock. Most of the commodities needed for antipoaching operations were imports that other politically important groups, such as industry and the security forces, also wanted.

50. Interview with Richard Bell, Chipata, Zambia, 15 June 1991.

51. Game meat is a substitute for domesticated meat in urban Zambians' diet. In their 1976 *Annual Report*, NPWS blames some of the increase of the poaching of game animals on the rise of domestic beef prices.

52. According to the 1991 Anti-Corruption Commission, "Govt. Quasi-Govt. Persons Arrested by SPD for Poaching Related Offenses" (mimeo. prepared for the author), two of the eleven are chiefs. NPWS officers have also blamed chiefs for running illegal hunting rings.

53. I conducted an informal survey of approximately twenty-five township residents representing five different sections of greater Lusaka. Each respondent asserted that game meat was plentiful in the townships and was easily purchased. Residents considered prices for game meat to be high.

   A typical commercial meat operation would include a sponsor contracting with a hunter(s) to kill buffalo. The sponsor would pay for the weapons, ammunition, and porters (carrying the sections of a single buffalo requires four people). The meat, usually dried in situ, would be transported and sold in urban areas. The profit on the meat of a single buffalo equaled a university professor's monthly salary.

54. Interview with Richard Bell, Chipata, Zambia, 15 June 1991. Chitambala, the former minister of tourism, accused business "big shots" of supporting most poaching and using villagers as mere "tools." See *The Times of Zambia*, 7 February 1989.

55. The military and police still use their influence and equipment to poach. Zambia's Anti-Corruption Commission arrested a number of policemen for poaching-related offenses. See Anti-Corruption Commission, "Govt./Quasi-Govt. Persons Arrested."

56. Zambian newspapers regularly include stories of police and soldiers slaughtering game in protected areas. See, for example, *The Times of Zambia*, 8 January 1991.

57. Information was provided by NPWS officers, conservationists, ministers, ministers of state, and law enforcement officers. But see also *The Times of Zambia*, 22 May 1991. NPWS openly supplied political rallies with game meat; see NPWS, *Annual Reports*, 1968–1973.

58. Zambia, National Assembly, *Parliamentary Debates*, no. 61 (13 August 1982), p. 4112.

59. *The Times of Zambia*, 28 November 1986.

60. Ibid. Also Faddy, personal communication, 29 October 1993.

61. Faddy asserts that civil servants accused of poaching would retain the services of a private solicitor, who, by virtue of superior training, could easily defeat the state's prosecutors. Faddy, personal communication.

62. The wildlife artist David Shepherd also lobbied President Kaunda for stronger conservation policy. He created his own foundation in the mid-1980s in Zambia.

63. Interviews with Norman Carr, Kapani Safari Lodge, Mfuwe, Zambia, 10 August 1991; Mike Faddy; and David Frost, former president Professional Hunters Association of Zambia, Lusaka, 23 March 1991.

64. Interview with former President Kenneth Kaunda, Lusaka, 14 August 1992.

65. Republic of Zambia, Cap. 316 of the laws of Zambia, sec. 8 (Lusaka: Government Printer, 1971).

66. Faddy believes that little was achieved by these military operations besides the harassment of local villagers. He characterized the military's involvement as "using a sledge hammer to crack a nut." Faddy, personal communication, 26 May 1994.

67. Ibid.

68. I exclude the school-aged African membership.

69. Bates and Collier, "Politics and Economics of Policy Reform in Zambia," pp. 391–406.

70. Jansen, *Trade, Exchange Rate*, p. 16.

71. Interviews with Akim Mwenya, director – NPWS, Chilanga, Zambia, 6 November 1991; G. Kaweche; Mike Faddy, 21 March 1991.

72. Interview with Francis Nkhoma, former governor of the Bank of Zambia, Lusaka, Zambia, 10 August 1992.

73. See the opening address of Fitzpatrick Chuula, minister of lands and natural

resources, in D. B. Dalal-Clayton, ed., *Proceedings of the Lupande Development Workshop* (Lusaka: Government Printer, 1984), pp. 3–4.

74. Ibid. Also interview with Richard Bell, Chipata, Zambia, 15 June 1991.
75. See, for example, the address by Chief G. Malama, p. 8, and the contribution of S. L. Atkins, "Socio-Economic Aspects of the Lupande Game Management Area," in Dalal-Clayton, ed., *Proceedings of the Lupande Development Workshop*, pp. 49–55.
76. Interview with Nkhoma, Lusaka, 10 August 1992.
77. It is difficult to identify by observation whether certain principal–agent problems are motivated by shirking or slippage. An individual can claim that his shirking is really an example of institutional slippage. As motivations are impossible to determine from actions alone, no attempt is made here to distinguish between the two forms.
78. Bates and Collier, "Politics and Economics of Policy Reform in Zambia," pp. 392–429.
79. Interview with Mwenya, 14 July 1992, Chilanga, Zambia. See also West, "Politics of Hope," p. 102.
80. Interviews with Faddy, 21 March 1991, 29 October 1993, Lusaka, Zambia; Akim Mwenya, Chilanga, Zambia, 14 July 1992.
81. Interview with P. S. M. Berry, Chinzombo Safari Lodge, Mfuwe, Zambia, 22 June 1991.
82. *Economist Intelligence Unit* 2 (1979): 6.
83. Marcia M. Burdette, "The Dynamics of Nationalization between Multinational Companies and Peripheral States: Negotiations between AMAX, Inc., and the Anglo-American Corporation of South Africa, Ltd., and the Government of the Republic of Zambia" (Ph.D. dissertation, Columbia University, 1979), pp. 450, 404–7, 427–34. See the similarities in Key's analysis of politics in the American south in V. O. Key, *Southern Politics in State and Nation* (New York: Alfred Knopf, 1949).
84. See Republic of Zambia, Office of Elections, *Report on the Results of the 1968 Presidential and Parliamentary Elections* (Lusaka: Government Printer, 1968), and the 1973 and 1978 reports. The 1968 elections had thirty uncontested seats. In 1973 this number dropped to fourteen. In the 1978 elections, only six constituencies were uncontested.
85. Ibid. From 1973 to 1978, 43 percent more people ran for the National Assembly, an average increase of one more candidate for every constituency.
86. *Election Special* (Lusaka: Government Printers), 10 November 1978.
87. Baylies and Szeftel, "Elections in a One-Party State," pp. 46–51, in Gertzel, Baylies, and Szeftel, *The Dynamics of the One-Party State*. See also Bornwell Chikulo, "The Impact of Elections in Zambia's One Party Second Republic," *Africa Today* (Second Quarter 1988): 43.
88. Baylies and Szeftel, "Elections in a One-Party State," p. 46.
89. Bornwell Chikulo, "The 1978 Zambian Elections," in *The Evolving Structure of Zambian Society* (Edinburgh: Centre of African Studies, May 1980), pp. 96–119.
90. See Republic of Zambia, *Report of the National Commission on the Establishment of a One-Party Participatory Democracy in Zambia (The Chona Commission)* (Lusaka: Government Printer, October 1972). The government rejected many of the suggestions that dealt with term limitations for presidents, curtailment executive power, and limits on party control over elections. See Republic of Zambia, *Report of the National Commission on the Establishment of a One-Party Participatory Democracy in Zambia, Summary of Recommendations Accepted by Government* (Lusaka: Government Printer, 1972).
91. Cherry Gertzel, "Dissent and Authority in the Zambian One-Party State," in Gertzel and Szeftel, *Dynamics of the One-Party State*, pp. 79–85.

92. For example, see the biting testimony of Mrs. Muyunda, minister of state for decentralization, against the 1982 Amendment to the National Parks and Wildlife Act in Zambia, National Assembly, *Daily Parliamentary Debates*, No. 60th (13 August 1982), p. 4140.
93. Interview with Wezi Kaunda, member of Parliament–Malambo constituency, Lusaka, Zambia, 6 August 1992.
94. From the results of interviews with 125 villagers living in five different chiefdoms in the Luangwa Valley, July–August 1991.
95. See, for example, the address by Chief G. Malama in Dalal-Clayton, ed., *Proceedings of the Lupande Development Workshop*, p. 8.
96. The question of Zambians' inability to pay the price of licenses is debatable. District licenses were available at very low cost to rural dwellers. Faddy, personal communication. The calculations of the villager may, however, include the transactions of acquiring the licenses (transport and time) and the license's negligible benefit.
97. Interview with Rabbison Chongo, former minister of finance, Lusaka, Zambia, 10 August 1992. Stuart Marks notes the same behavior in 1953. See Marks, *Imperial Lion*, pp. 108–12.
98. Interview with General Kingsley Chinkuli, member of UNIP Central Committee, Lusaka, Zambia, 11 August 1992. He stated, "MPs, especially rural MPs, were afraid of losing popularity in their constituencies."
99. Ibid. The minister of lands and natural resources and the director of NPWS held the best positions for granting favors over wildlife. By law, each could alter quotas and distribute hunting licenses. Parliamentarians, on the other hand, could only intervene for individuals on an ad hoc basis. Predictably, great numbers of individuals seeking hunting-related favors visited the offices of the minister and director after 1975.
100. Interview with G. Kaweche, 14 July 1992, Chilanga, Zambia.
101. See Cap. 316 of the Laws of Zambia. Cap. 316 remained in force until 1991.
102. Called the minister of lands, natural resources and tourism from 1974 to 1976.
103. Zambia, National Assembly, *Parliamentary Debates*, No. 60th (10 August 1982).
104. Cap. 316 of the Laws of Zambia gave the magistrate the right to offer the convicted poacher the option of paying fines.
105. Ibid., pp. 4118–40.
106. Ibid., p. 4140.
107. Of the 128 parliamentarians, 49 were ministers, 6 were nominated members, and 10 were district governors, giving the front bench a majority. Of course, there were other back benchers who could be counted on to be strongly pro-government, such as the 7 MPs who had run unopposed in the last election.
108. Ibid., p. 4128.
109. Ibid., pp. 4118–19.
110. Interview with Wezi Kaunda, 6 August 1992, Lusaka, Zambia. W. Kaunda felt particularly pressured because his father was the most important conservationist in Zambia, yet W. Kaunda represented a constituency that not only was rural but whose area was dominated by national parks.

    Even a government-owned newspaper criticized the move by President Kaunda to appoint sixteen members of parliament as district governors: In the Zambia *Daily Mail* 29 January 1982, the action was seen as a way to make parliamentarians quieter by drawing them onto the executive's side of the issues.
111. Ibid., p. 4128.
112. Ibid., p. 3990.
113. Ibid., pp. 3990–97.
114. Ibid., p. 4119.

115. Ibid., p. 4130.
116. Ibid., pp. 4132–35, and idem, *Parliamentary Debates*, No. 60 (10 December 1982), p. 4886.
117. Ibid., p. 4880.
118. Ibid., p. 4129.
119. Ibid., p. 4912.
120. Ibid., p. 4910.
121. Ibid., pp. 4799–4916.
122. Faddy, personal communication.
123. Because only six government officials spoke for the bill, those members who spoke in support of it are combined with those who remained silent.
124. Gertzel et al., *Dynamics of the One-Party State*; Robert Molteno, "Cleavage and Conflict in Zambian Politics: A Study in Sectionalism," in William Tordoff, ed., *Politics in Zambia* (Manchester: Manchester University Press, 1974), pp. 62–106.
125. Several provinces contain both towns and rural areas. For the purposes of this study, urban provinces are those along the line of rail that extend from the city of Livingstone on Zambia's border with Zimbabwe to the Copperbelt region next to Zaire and include Southern, Lusaka, Copperbelt, and Central; rural provinces are Western, Northwestern, Northern, Lualpula, and Eastern.
126. John H. Aldrich and Forrest D. Nelson, *Linear Probability, Logit and Probit Models* (Beverly Hills: Sage Publications, 1984).
127. Ibid.
128. These probabilities were calculated by holding all other independent variables at their mean values. I then calculated the probability of speaking out when the frontbencher variable equaled 1. I made a similar calculation with the frontbencher variable equal to 0. The difference between these two probabilities was .19. The probabilities reported in the rest of this chapter were calculated in a similar fashion. For additional information on calculating probabilities with logit, see Aldrich and Nelson, *Linear Probability*, pp. 40–65.
129. For insights into the behavior of these individuals, I am indebted to Douglas Anglin, Robert Bates, Michael Bratton, Sheridan Johns, Ilse Mwanza, Jacob Mwanza, and James R. Scarritt.
130. Fleefort Chirwa, Joshua Lumina, Rupiah Banda, and F. X. Nkhoma.
131. John Kalenga, representing Mwinilungu West constituency.
132. Lupunga represented the predominantly urban Masaiti constituency.
133. Unlike that of Zambia, the ruling party Kenyan Africa National Union (KANU) never had strong control over local party matters. See, for example, John J. Okumu and Frank Holmquist, "Party and Party–State Relations," in Joel Barkan, ed., *Politics and Public Policy in Kenya and Tanzania*, pp. 45–69. Many works examine the structures of Kenya's one-party state. Some of the most useful to this analysis include Barkan, *Politics and Public Policy*; Barkan, "The Rise and Fall of a Governance Realm in Kenya," in Goran Hyden and Michael Bratton, *Governance and Politics in Africa* (Boulder and London: Lynne Rienner, 1992), pp. 167–92; Barkan, "The Electoral Process and Peasant–State Relations in Kenya," in Fred M. Hayward, ed., *Elections in Independent Africa* (Boulder: Westview Press, 1987), pp. 213–37; Cherry Gertzel, *The Politics of Independent Kenya, 1963–1968* (Evanston: Northwestern University Press, 1970); Robert H. Bates, *Beyond the Miracle of the Market* (Cambridge: Cambridge University Press, 1989); Charles Hornsby, "The Social Structure of the National Assembly in Kenya, 1963–83," *Journal of Modern African Studies* 27 (2) (1989): 275–96.
134. Joel Barkan, "Legislators, Elections, and Political Linkage," in Barkan, *Politics and Public Policy*, pp. 71–101.

135. P. Anyang' Nyong'o, "State and Society in Kenya: The Disintegration of the Nationalists' Coalitions and the Rise of Presidential Authoritarianism, 1963–78," *African Affairs* 88 (351): 229–51.

136. Malcolm Wallis, "District Planning and Local Government in Kenya," *Public Administration and Development* 10 (1990): 437–52; James Kariuki, " 'Paramoia': Anatomy of a Dictatorship in Kenya," *Journal of Contemporary African Studies* 14 (1) (1996): 70–86.

137. Barkan, "Legislators," pp. 71–101.

138. John J. Okumu and Frank Holmquist, "Party and Party–State Relations," in Barkan, *Politics and Public Policy*, pp. 45–69; David K. Leonard, *Reaching the Peasant Farmer: Organization Theory and Practice in Kenya* (Chicago: University of Chicago Press, 1977), pp. 193–94.

139. Rodger Yeager and Norman N. Miller, *Wildlife Wild Death: Land Use and Survival in Eastern Africa* (Albany: State University of New York Press, 1986), pp. 88–89.

140. Raymond Bonner, *At the Hand of Man: Peril and Hope for Africa's Wildlife* (New York: Knopf, 1993), p. 51.

141. Ibid., p. 131.

142. Kariuki, " 'Paramoia,' " p. 74; Barkan, "Rise and Fall," p. 172.

143. Jane Perlez, "Kenya's Government Fights for Control in a War That Endangers Tourism," *The New York Times*, August 27, 1989, p. 2, sec. 4; Bonner, *At the Hand of Man*, p. 131.

144. Yeager and Miller, *Wildlife*, p. 121; Michael A. Hiltzik, "Public Backs Noted Paleontologist Leakey," *The Los Angeles Times*, May 8, 1989, pt. 1, p. 6.

145. Bonner, *At the Hand of Man*, p. 132.

146. L. H. Gann, "Malawi, Zambia, and Zimbabwe," in Peter Duignan and Robert H. Jackson, eds., *Politics and Government in African State, 1960–1985* (London: Croom Helm, 1986), pp. 162–201.

147. The lower house comprised one hundred seats, twenty of which were reserved for whites. In the independence elections, ZANU received fifty-seven of the eighty black seats: a slim majority to the combined seats held by whites and the opposition Zimbabwe African People's Union.

148. Bratton discusses the institutions that helped promote the professionalism of Zimbabwean bureaucracy. Michael Bratton, "The Comrades in the Countryside: The Politics of Agricultural Policy in Zimbabwe," *World Politics* 39 (2) (1987): 174–202.

149. See, for example, Jeffrey Herbst, *State Politics in Zimbabwe* (Berkeley: University of California Press, 1990); Christine Sylvester, *Zimbabwe: The Terrain of Contradictory Development* (Boulder: Westview Press, 1991); and Jonothan N. Moyo, *Voting for Democracy: Electoral Politics in Zimbabwe* (Harare: University of Zimbabwe Publications, 1992). Skalnes notes that the government was largely unsuccessful in its attempt to place interest groups more firmly under political control. See Tor Skalnes, *The Politics of Economic Reform in Zimbabwe: Continuity and Change in Development* (New York: St. Martin's Press, 1995), pp. 97–115.

150. Bonner, *At the Hand of Man*, p. 138.

151. J. H. Peterson, *A Proto-CAMPFIRE Initiative in Mahenye Ward, Chipinge District*, Occasional Paper no. 3 (Harare: Centre for Applied Social Sciences, University of Zimbabwe, 1992), pp. 6–7.

152. Kay Muir and Jan Bojo, "Economic Policy, Wildlife, and Land Use in Zimbabwe," in Jan Bojo, ed., *The Economic of Wildlife: Case Studies from Ghana, Kenya, Namibia, and Zimbabwe* (Washington, D.C.: World Bank, 1996), pp. 117–37.

153. Kevin A. Hill, "Interest Groups and the Politics of the Environment" (Ph.D. dissertation, University of Florida, 1993), p. 166.

154. Ibid., p. 165.

155. Muir and Bojo, "Economic Policy," pp. 117–37.

156. Faddy, personal communication.

157. Gwendolyn Carter, *African One-Party States* (Ithaca: Cornell University Press, 1962); Aristide Zolberg, *Creating Political Order: The Party-States of West Africa* (Chicago: Rand McNally, 1966); James Wunsch and Dele Olowu, *The Failure of the Centralized State* (Boulder: Westview Press, 1990); Robert Jackson and Carl Rosberg, *Personal Rule in Black Africa* (Berkeley: University of California Press, 1982); Peter Meyns and Dani Wadada Nabudere, eds., *Democracy and the One-Party State in Africa* (Hamburg: Institut Fur Afrika-Kunde, 1989); Tordoff, "Residual Legislatures," pp. 235–49.

158. Richard Sandbrook recognizes that fairly open intraparty elections can link national leaders to the grass roots. See Richard Sandbrook, *The Politics of Africa's Economic Stagnation* (Cambridge: Cambridge University Press, 1988), p. 93.

159. Peter Meyns, "The Road to One-Party Rule in Zambia and Zimbabwe," in Meyns and Nabudere, eds., *Democracy and the One-Party State in Africa*, pp. 179–202. William Tordoff, "Residual Legislatures," pp. 235–49.

4. THE CONSERVATIONISTS STRIKE BACK: "COMMUNITY-BASED" WILDLIFE POLICY AND THE POLITICS OF STRUCTURAL CHOICE, 1983–1991

1. In many documents LIRDP is referred to as a project, and ADMADE as a policy. However, both LIRDP and ADMADE promoted policies and incorporated new organizational structures with which to carry out these policies.

2. In contrast, R. Michael Wright writes, "No goal of ADMADE is more important than community development." See his "Alleviating Poverty and Conserving Wildlife in Africa: An 'Inefficient' Model from Africa," *The Nature Conservancy*, n.d., p. 20.

3. Woodrow Wilson, "The Study of Administration," *Political Science Quarterly* 2 (1887): 197–222; Leonard D. White, *The Civil Service in the Modern State* (Chicago: University of Chicago Press, 1930).

4. Paul H. Appleby, *Policy and Administration* (Tuscaloosa: University of Alabama Press, 1949), pp. 197–222.

5. The literature is large. For a review of some of this work see Walter A. Rosenbaum, "The Bureaucracy and Environmental Policy," in James P. Lester, ed., *Environmental Politics and Policy* (Durham: Duke University Press, 1995), pp. 206–41.

6. See, for example, Daniel Henning, *Environmental Policy and Administration* (Elsevier, N.Y.: American Press, 1974); William Ascher and Robert Healy, *Natural Resource Policymaking in Developing Countries* (Durham: Duke University Press, 1990). For wildlife policy more specifically, see R. H. V. Bell and E. McShane-Caluzi, eds., *Conservation and Wildlife Management in Africa* (Washington, D.C.: U.S. Peace Corps, 1984); A. Owen-Smith and R. Norman, eds., *Management of Large Mammals in African Conservation Areas* (Pretoria: Haum Educational Publishers, 1983); P. Jewell and S. Holt, eds., *Problems in Management of Locally Abundant Wild Animals* (New York: Academic Press, 1981); Fred Gilbert and Donald Dodds, *The Philosophy and Practice of Wildlife Management* (Melbourne, Fla.: Krieger Publishing, 1992).

7. Paul A. Sabatier, John Loomis, and Catherine McCarthy, "Hierarchical Con-

trols, Professional Norms, Local Constituencies, and Budget Maximization: An Analysis of the U.S. Forest Service Planning Decisions," *American Journal of Political Science* 39 (1995): 204–42; Ferrel Heady, *Public Administration: A Comparative Perspective* (New York: Dekker, 1984). One good exception is Merilee Grindle's *Bureaucrats, Politicians, and Peasants in Mexico: A Case Study in Public Policy* (Berkeley: University of California Press, 1977).

8. William Niskanen, *Bureaucracy and Representative Government* (Chicago: Aldine-Atherton, 1971); Eugene Bardach, *The Implementation Game* (Cambridge, Mass.: MIT Press, 1977); Gary Miller and Terry M. Moe, "Bureaucrats, Legislators, and Size of Governments," *American Political Science Review* 77 (1983): 297–323.

9. Randall Calvert, Mathew McCubbins, and Barry Weingast, "A Theory of Political Control of Agency Discretion," *American Journal of Political Science* 33 (1989): 588–610; Daniel Spulber and David Besanko, "Delegation, Commitment, and the Regulatory Mandate," *Journal of Law, Economics, and Organization* 8 (1992): 126–54; Terry M. Moe, "Regulatory Performance and Presidential Administration," *American Journal of Political Science* 26 (1992): 197–224; Terry M. Moe, "Control and Feedback in Economic Regulation," *American Political Science Review* 79 (1985): 1094–116; John E. Chubb, "The Political Economy of Federalism," *American Political Science Review* 79 (1985): 994–1015; Marc A. Eisner and Kenneth J. Meier, "Presidential Control versus Bureaucratic Power: Explaining the Reagan Revolution in Antitrust," *American Journal of Political Science* 34 (1990): 269–87; Dan B. Wood, "Federalism and Policy Responsiveness: The Clean Air Case," *Journal of Politics* 53 (1991): 851–59; Dan B. Wood, "Modeling Federal Implementation as a System," *American Journal of Political Science* 36 (1992): 40–67.

10. Barry R. Weingast and Mark Moran, "Bureaucratic Discretion or Congressional Control: Regulatory Policymaking by the Federal Trade Commission," *Journal of Political Economy* 91 (1983): 765–800; John T. Scholz and Feng Hang Wei, "Regulatory Enforcement in a Federalist System," *American Political Science Review* 80 (1986): 1249–70; Mathew McCubbins and Thomas Schwartz, "Congressional Oversight Overlooked: Police Patrols versus Fire Alarms," *American Journal of Political Science* 28 (1984): 165–79; Arthur Lupia and Mathew McCubbins, "Learning from Oversight: Fire Alarms and Police Patrols Reconstructed," *Journal of Law, Economics and Organization* 10(1) (1994): 96; David Epstein and Sharyn O'Halloran, "Administrative Procedures, Information, and Agency," *American Journal of Political Science* 38 (1994): 697–722.

11. Jerry Mashaw, "Explaining Administrative Process: Normative, Positive, and Critical Stories of Legal Development," *Journal of Law, Economics, and Organization* 6 (1990): 267–98.

12. Terry M. Moe, "Political Institutions: The Neglected Side of the Story," *Journal of Law, Economics, and Organization* 6 (1990): 213–66.

13. Terry M. Moe, "The Politics of Structural Choice: Toward a Theory of Public Bureaucracy," in Oliver Williamson, ed., *Organizational Theory from Chester Bernard to the Present* (Oxford: Oxford University Press, 1990b), pp. 116–53.

14. Ibid.

15. James Q. Wilson, *Bureaucracy: What Government Agencies Do and Why They Do It* (New York: Basic Books, 1989).

16. Terry M. Moe, "Political Institutions," pp. 213–20.

17. The following section draws from more detailed analyses of the behavior of and constraints on single-party leaders. See especially Robert H. Jackson and Carl G. Rosberg, *Personal Rule in Black Africa* (Berkeley and Los Angeles: University of California Press, 1982), pp. 14–80 and passim.; Patrick Chabal, ed., *Political Domination in Africa* (Cambridge: Cambridge University Press, 1986); Rene

Lemarchand, "The State, the Parallel Economy, and the Changing Structure of Patronage Systems," in Donald Rothchild and Naomi Chazan, eds., *The Precarious Balance* (Boulder: Westview Press, 1988), pp. 149–70; Richard Sandbrook, *The Politics of Africa's Economic Stagnation* (Cambridge: Cambridge University Press, 1985), pp. 83–110; Gwendolyn M. Carter, ed., *African One-Party States* (Ithaca: Cornell University Press, 1962); and James S. Wunsch and Dele Olowu, eds., *The Failure of the Centralized State* (Boulder: Westview Press, 1990).

The political strength of the military, labor unions, regional organizations, ethnic groups, or civil servant association may prevent their complete co-optation or annihilation, but one-party presidents generally possess the ability to alter significantly their membership and activities. In the case of Zambia, see Cherry Gertzel, "Dissent and Authority in the Zambian One-Party State," in Gertzel, Carolyn Baylies, and Morris Szeftel, eds., *The Dynamics of the One-Party State* (Manchester: Manchester University Press, 1984), pp. 100–101.

18. The ruler of a one-party state is hereafter referred to as a *president*.

19. One-party presidents use their control over job appointments to co-opt elites into the one-party state. Employment within the government links individuals with state sources of goods and services. Given the dominant economic position of the state under a one-party system and the generally underdeveloped private sector, government jobs are extremely valuable. For examples from Zambia, see Eugenia West, "The Politics of Hope" (Ph.D. dissertation, Yale University, 1989), p. 96; James A. Scarritt, "The Analysis of Social Class, Political Participation and Public Policy in Zambia," *Africa Today* 30 (1983): 16–17; for an example from Zaire, see D. J. Gould, "The Administration of Underdevelopment," in Guy Gran, ed., *Zaire: The Political Economy of Underdevelopment* (New York: Praeger, 1979), pp. 87–107.

President Kaunda used his control over the state's resources to keep rival politicians or groups off-balance and incapable of establishing independent bases of economic wealth or political power. Kaunda often employed the "prodigal son" routine, dismissing promising political elites only to welcome them back later with high positions within the government or party. This strategy helped to sanction the more independent activities of individuals while keeping them tied to the patronage system. See West, "Politics of Hope," pp. 95–98, and Marcia Burdette, *Zambia: Between Two Worlds* (Boulder: Westview Press, 1988), p. 108.

20. This analysis resonates with work regarding the problem of eliciting credible commitments from sovereigns. See, for example, Hilton L. Root. "Tying the King's Hands: Credible Commitments and Royal Fiscal Policy during the Old Regime," *Rationality and Society* 1 (October 1989): 240–58; Douglass C. North, *Structure and Change in Economic History* (New York: W. W. Norton, 1971); idem, *Institutions, Institutional Change and Economic Performance* (Cambridge: Cambridge University Press, 1990), pp. 54–60; North and Barry R. Weingast, "Constitutions and Credible Commitments: The Evolution of Institutions of Public Choice in 17th Century England," *Journal of Economic History* 49 (1989): 803–32; Margaret Levi, *Of Rule and Revenue* (Berkeley: University of California Press, 1988); and Barry R. Weingast, "The Economic Role of Political Institutions: Market Preserving Federalism and Economic Development," *Journal of Law, Economics, and Organization* 11(1) (1995): 1–31.

21. Parliamentarians, bureaucrats, and interest groups complain about one-party presidents' proclivity to announce new projects or goals without consulting either the affected public agencies or interested groups. In almost every interview I conducted for this study, public and private officials complained about President Kaunda's penchant for declaring policy independently without consultation. Similar trends occur in other one-party states. See, for example, William Tordoff,

"Residual Legislatures in African One-Party States," *Journal of Comparative and Commonwealth Politics* 15(3) (1977): 241.

Without countervailing political institutions, policy direction under a one-party system is vulnerable to frequent policy shifts for two reasons. First, one-party presidents use policy change as a strategy to neutralize the political or economic power of individuals and groups. See West, "Politics of Hope," p. 51; Robert H. Bates and Paul Collier, "The Politics and Economics of Policy Reform in Zambia," in Robert H. Bates and Anne O. Krueger, eds., *Political and Economic Interactions in Economic Policy Reform* (Cambridge, Mass.: Blackwell Publishers, 1993). Second, such unrivaled public authority allows one-party presidents to implement their own possibly shifting ideas (and those of their trusted advisers), contributing to apparently erratic policy trajectories. For example, it is well known that many of the tenets of President Kaunda's philosophies are contradictory. See Carolyn Baylies, "The State and Class Formation in Zambia" (Ph.D. dissertation, University of Wisconsin-Madison, 1978), pp. 873–74.

22. Zambia had a long history of involvement with ideas and funding from the international arena. The degree of international interest reached new heights in the 1980s; the public outcry at the slaughter of African wildlife in the 1970s led to the creation of a number of new international conservation organizations and increased revenues for those already established. Additionally, bilateral foreign aid began to target conservation projects. Consequently, both public and private conservationists in the 1980s could tap into more money from more sources than in the previous two decades. NORAD, USAID, and the WWF would provide decisive revenue to the cause of Zambian conservationists. See John McCormick, *Reclaiming Paradise* (Bloomington: Indiana University Press, 1989); John C. Pierce, Mary Ann E. Steger, Brent S. Steel, and Nicholas P. Lovrich, *Citizens, Political Communication, and Interest Groups* (Westport, Conn.: Praeger, 1992); and David Adamson, *Defending the World* (London: I. B. Tauris & Co., 1990).

23. The South Lupande Game Management Area is part of the Luangwa catchment region, containing the most varied and dense populations of wildlife in Zambia. It lies to the east of the Luangwa River and is sparsely populated. Besides the few local residents employed by safari hunters and the NPWS, most residents engage in subsistence farming, hunting, and fishing. Most of Zambia's wildlife tourism business occurs in the Luangwa Valley, and specifically in the vicinity of the Lupande Game Management Area. It is also considered one of the best areas for safari hunting. This region is also the best protected wildlife sanctuary, as a result of its distance from city centers, the efforts of NPWS, and the prevalence of tourists and safari hunters.

24. In Lewis's research zone, less than 1 percent of family income resulted from legal forms of wildlife utilization. See, for example, S. L. Atkins, "The Socio-Economic Aspects of the Lupande Game Management Area," in D. B. Dalal-Clayton, ed., *Proceedings of the Lupande Development Workshop* (Lusaka: Government Printer, 1984), p. 52.

Others in the international conservation community had come to similar conclusions. Many wildlife managers found that preservationism, the style of conservation that excluded the use of any of the natural resources within a protected area, was not an effective policy. Locals who did not perceive gains from conservation programs flouted laws by gathering firewood, fishing, or hunting in protected areas. Additionally, wildlife departments in developing countries, like Zambia, found the management costs of preservation strategies unmanageably burdensome. To mitigate local residents' illegal activities and to augment the finances of wildlife departments, wildlife managers had begun to espouse theories of wildlife management grounded on local participation. This concept held that locals should be included in the decision making related to and benefits of wildlife resources. By providing some degree of property rights over wildlife to local residents, conservationists thought that they could induce individuals to stop unsustainable resource use and help wildlife departments to monitor illegal activities. Interview with Richard Bell, Chipata, Zambia, 15 June 1991. See also David Anderson and Richard Grove, eds., *Conservation in Africa: People, Policies and Practice* (Cambridge: Cambridge University Press, 1987), pp. 1–12; Marks, *The Imperial Lion*; and David Western, "Amboseli National Park: Human Values and the Conservation of a Savanna Ecosystem," in J. A. McNeely and K. R. Miller, eds., *National Parks, Conservation and Development: The Role of Protected Areas in Sustaining Society, Proceedings of the World Congress on National Parks (Bali, Indonesia)* (Washington, D.C.: Smithsonian Institution Press, 1984), pp. 93–100.

25. Of the thirty-eight individuals on the official participants list, nine were officers of the NPWS and another twenty belonged to government departments most concerned with conservation and whose budgets had also deteriorated tremendously after the 1973 copper shock, such as the Department of Agriculture and the Department of Forestry. Seven members of various private conservation groups attended the workshop. Despite the intended goal of including the voice of local villagers in the proceedings, Chief Malama was the only local Zambian at the proceedings. Fifteen participants were European. See Dalal-Clayton, ed., *Proceedings*, pp. vii–viii.

26. The Luangwa catchment covers almost 20 percent of Zambia's land surface and includes five national parks and seven game management areas.

27. "Resolutions Passed at the Lupande Development Workshop," in Dalal-Clayton, ed., *Proceedings*, p. 99. Participants also agreed to the formation of an Interim Planning Group to prepare programs and budgets to support the project, and the need for an independent review to explore the feasibility of a policy that featured an integrated resource approach and to ensure that no single department or ministry dominated the design-making stage.

28. Lewis chose to work closely with the National Parks and Wildlife Service from the start of his research efforts in Zambia. He befriended many of the junior officers (and became an officer himself). He collaborated with them to publish academic papers. He worked actively to secure grants for research activities that included NPWS. He brought the latest concepts of the international wildlife management community to the attention of NPWS. And he publicly supported NPWS's constitutional mandate as the protector and manager of wildlife resources in Zambia.

It is difficult to distinguish between the ideas of Lewis and those of others of the NPWS Directorate. NPWS officers and Lewis purposefully give each other credit to enhance the perception of the NPWS as a unified, Zambian agency. Although Lewis clearly did not dictate decisions, most NPWS officers interviewed agree that he was crucial to many NPWS policy changes, especially ADMADE. Although I often use "NPWS" in the text, Lewis's instrumental role in NPWS decision making should not be underestimated.

29. President Kaunda said he "doubted some of the cheaters at NPWS." Interview with President Kenneth Kaunda, Lusaka, 14 August 1992.

30. NPWS asserted that the pilot project, called the Lupande Development Project, was designed to solve the land use conflicts between humans and wildlife, to develop greater responsibility for the local management of natural resources, and to demonstrate the sustainable use of natural resources. See *Lupande News and Views* No. 1 (September 1985), pp. 1–5.

31. Interview with Dale Lewis, ADMADE technical adviser, Nyamaluma Camp, Zambia, 28 June 1991.

32. Safari-hunting clients themselves paid several types of fees: fees for the various

animals hunted, a basic safari license fee, a standard fee for exporting trophies, and a tax on each trophy exported.

33. Significantly, NPWS did not have to rely on Kaunda or other public agencies for these changes, so neither the transfer of the concession area nor the new tax required NPWS to fight other government officials. The Minister of Tourism had the authority to declare these actions unilaterally.

34. Under Republic of Zambia, Cap. 600 of the laws of Zambia, government agencies capable of supporting themselves had been able to apply for their own "working funds" since 1969. The government wanted such funds to allow agencies, especially those related to the mining industry, quickly to procure needed inputs from their own revenues without having to go through the Ministry of Finance. Interview with B. Nair, director of internal accounts, Ministry of Finance, Lusaka, 1 April 1991.

35. Ibid. Mr. Nair believes that because of a lack of oversight, many of these revolving fund administrators became wealthier.

36. Ibid. Also see Wright, "Alleviating Poverty," p. 14; A. N. Mwenya, D. M. Lewis, and G. B. Kaweche, *ADMADE: Policy, Background and Future* (Lusaka, Zambia: National Parks and Wildlife Service, 1990), p. 4, also interview with B. Nair, Lusaka, 1 April 1991. The government seeded the Wildlife Conservation Revolving Fund with a grant of 418,618 kwacha in 1984. LIRDP would use the WCRF to deposit its earnings until it gained its own revolving fund in 1987.

37. Wright, "Alleviating Poverty," p. 14.

38. Ibid., p. 15.

39. Interview with D. Lewis, Nyamaluma Camp, Zambia, 22 July 1991.

40. Although the local Kunda ethnic group do not prefer to eat hippo meat, it was still cropped because its products could be sold elsewhere, and the number of hippo in the area could well withstand a significant amount of off take.

41. In 1986, NPWS collected 134,444.41 Zambian kwacha (ZK) in safari concession fees, of which the community's share was ZK 53,777.76. Using a nominal exchange rate of 7.5 kwacha to the U.S. dollar, the amounts represent approximately $18,000 and $7,200, respectively. See A. N. Mwenya, G. B. Kaweche, and D. M. Lewis, *Administrative Design for Game Management Areas (ADMADE)* (Chilanga, Zambia: National Parks and Wildlife Service, January 1988), p. 6. The exchange rate used here is the average of the nominal figures presented for the four quarters of 1986. See Doris Jansen, *Trade Exchange Rate, and Agricultural Pricing Policies in Zambia* (Washington, D.C.: World Bank, 1988), table 6, p. 21. Because these are nominal figures, and the kwacha was overvalued by the Zambian government, the amounts given overestimate the value of the ADMADE revenues.

42. NPWS claims the pilot project produced over $35,000 in gross revenues and provided twenty-one full-time and thirty-seven part-time jobs. See National Parks and Wildlife Service/Lupande Development Project (NPWSI-LDP), *Zambian Wildlands and Human Needs Newsletter* 1 (Nyamaluma Camp, May 1988), pp. 1–3; Mwenya et al., "Administrative Management," pp. 5–6.

43. Mwenya, Kaweche, and Lewis, *ADMADE: Policy*, p. 4.

44. For example, other ADMADE documents are less certain about the significance of the project to local attitudes. "Overwhelming evidence supported the conclusion that the more positive attitudes toward wildlife conservation found among residents in the Lupande Project area was [sic] at least *partially* due to the significant economic benefits from wildlife available to the local community" (emphasis added). See NPWS/LDP, *Zambian Wildlands and Human Needs Newsletter*, p. 2.

Some individuals disputed the validity of the pilot project's claims to have significantly reduced poaching. Lewis based the rate of poaching decline on the decrease in the number of fresh carcasses of rhino and elephant found in the project area. Critics indict this methodology on several grounds. The incentives and skill of the village scout/NPWS patrols' counting may produce low counts, poachers could have hidden carcasses, and the use of the fresh carcass technique does not take into account baseline populations or possible animal migration.

45. The project, like many development projects, gave access to decision-making powers and material benefits to the chief and his followers. The project had no provision to include nonelites in decision-making structures.

46. NPWS originally selected units on the criterion that their safari concession fees would cover the costs of ADMADE programs. Thus, some units' boundaries coincided with areas already marked as hunting blocks. However, most units followed established GMA borders, apparently to reduce possible administrative confusion. See NPWS/LDP, *Wildlands and Human Needs Newsletter*, p. 3. However, neither the ability of areas to support safari hunting nor their potential for effective wildlife management correlates with GMA boundaries.

47. Mwenya, Kaweche, and Lewis, *ADMADE: Policy*, p. 6.

48. Interview with D. Lewis, Nyamaluma Camp, Zambia, 28 June 1991.

49. Mwenya, Kaweche, and Lewis, *ADMADE: Policy*, p. 6.

50. Interview with D. Lewis; see also NPWS/LDP, *Wildlands and Human Needs Newsletter*, p. 4.

51. Mwenya, Kaweche, and Lewis, *ADMADE: Policy*, pp. 6–7. The full terms of reference for the WMA were the following:

   • monitor both legal and illegal off-takes of wildlife resources;
   • initiate projects for improved wildlife management;
   • approve allocation of sustained-yield quotas of wildlife as recommended by NPWS for various forms of use: safari hunting, export and restocking, culling, resident hunting, etc.;
   • liaise with the Director, NPWS, on the issuance of hunting licenses;
   • ensure that 40 percent of the revenue generated from the exploitation of wildlife resources is committed to the management costs of wildlife resources within the unit;
   • ensure that 35 percent of the revenue earned is used by local village communities from whose area such revenues were generated;
   • prepare a work plan for the unit's wildlife management program and local community improvement on an annual basis;
   • enforce the National Parks and Wildlife Act, Cap. 316, and other relevant Acts through the office of that unit's unit leader;
   • furnish the Director of NPWS records of its meetings;
   • encourage applied management research and solicit outside expertise where needed;
   • act as a planning body for formulating new wildlife policies and appropriate management activities;
   • implement policy concerning wildlife management for its unit; and
   • manage self-help schemes by appointed communities.

52. Mwenya, Kaweche, and Lewis, "Administrative Management," p. 13.

53. NPWS/LDP, *Wildlands and Human Needs Newsletter*, 6 (August 1990), p. 2.

54. NPWS/LDP, *Wildlands and Human Needs Newsletter*, 9 (September 1991), p. 1.

55. WWF gave ADMADE $124,000 for the purchase of two vehicles and the construction of unit headquarters for two GMAs. Additional funding was also provided by USAID and a U.S. citizen who had befriended Dale Lewis. See NPWS/LDP, *Zambian Wildlands and Human Needs Newsletter*, 1 (May 1988), p. 4.

56. Ibid. In 1988, revenue from the fourteen ADMADE units was U.S. $391,250. Safari–hunting concession fees accounted for well over 90 percent of the total.

57. Republic of Zambia, "Project Grant Agreement between the Republic of Zambia and the United States of America for Natural Resources Management," 1990, annex I, p. 3 (mimeo.).
58. Although the grant allowed for a project officer from the WWF to supervise ADMADE, NPWS had a say in the individual selected.
59. Ibid., p. 4.
60. Ibid., p. 5.
61. USAID gave $1.1 million to ADMADE through WWF and $1.8 million to ADMADE for capital expenditure. USAID kept $100,000 for future evaluation expenses and discretionary funds. The final agreement was not signed until 16 January 1990. Interview with Jim Harmon, USAID Zambia, Lusaka, 15 February 1991.
62. USAID, "Project Grant Agreement," p. 2.
63. In fact, the Zambian government agreed to make these changes *before* the disbursement of any USAID funds. See USAID, "Project Grant Agreement," p. 3.
64. Ibid., p. 4.
65. The National Commission for Development Planning (NCDP) is the Zambian agency responsible for overseeing all interministerial development projects in the country.
66. Larsen, a Norwegian wildlife biologist, did not possess primary expertise in either Africa or development projects; his most well-known work concerned polar bears. To overcome his lack of knowledge, Larsen relied a great deal on the knowledge and opinions of the European conservationist community in Zambia. Lungu, although employed as a NPWS biologist, had always felt excluded from the department's inner circle of decision makers. Lungu was ambitious, knew the Zambian political environment well, and had experience working with international conservation organizations. Interviews with Mike Faddy, Save the Rhino Trust, Lusaka, 21 March 1991; Monica Ngoma, former senior economist, Land and Natural Resource Unit, National Commission for Development Planning, Lusaka, 10 October 1991; and Fidelis Lungu, former codirector LIRDP, Chipata, Zambia, 28 May 1991.
67. Another NORAD consultant, Trond Vedeld, helped Larsen and Lungu from 13 June to 10 July 1985. ADMADE's Dale Lewis claims that Larsen rewrote the terms of reference to further his own vision of the Lupande area project. Interview with D. Lewis, Nyamaluma Camp, Zambia, 22 July 1991.
68. Although LIRDP sought to manage the full range of natural resources, wildlife clearly remained the means and the ends of most of LIRDP's proposed activities. Wildlife tourism and hunting would generate the majority of LIRDP's funds, and policies to strengthen wildlife management dominated LIRDP's planned activities. Thor Larsen, Fidelis B. Lungu, and Trond Vedeld, "Preparation Report on the Luangwa Integrated Resource Development Project (LIRDP)" Chipata, September 1985 (photocopy).

   Some NCDP and NORAD officials believed LIRDP's focus on wildlife reflected the professional background of the Larsen and Lungu and cynically remarked that some of the project's activities, such as the women's program, "were merely window-dressing designed to get the sponsorship of foreign donors for a big wildlife project."
69. Interview with Arne Lonning, NORAD, Lusaka, 10 September 1991. This was Larsen's first experience with a development project. Further, had Larsen and Lungu reviewed current development literature – which normally appears in NORAD project proposals – they would have realized that experts were beginning to reject IRDPs in favor of supporting key institutions at the local level and locally sustainable projects.
70. Interview with Richard Bell, codirector LIRDP, Chipata, Zambia, 28 May 1991.

71. Revealingly, most of Larsen and Lungu's discussion of NPWS in their "Preparation Report" occurs only in the context of which staff and resources the department should bequeath to the new LIRDP program.
72. Larsen and Lungu advocated an approach similar to Zimbabwe's experiments with community participation in wildlife management but acknowledged that the Zimbabwean approach "can probably not be transferred directly to Zambia, for various reasons including the differences in legislation." See their "Preparation Report," p. 85.
73. Despite LIRDP's goal of self-sufficiency, and its desire to expropriate all wildlife-related revenues in the project area, the consultants estimated that the project would still require $25 million in external funds over the first five years before it became self-sufficient. See Larsen and Lungu, "Preparation Report," p. 67. In comparison, the Ministry of Health's expenditures for the entire country totaled about $23 million in 1986.
74. At this time, Larsen and Lungu suggested that the committee's membership be "open to all organizations (Government Ministries, District Councils, Chiefs, etc.) which might be affected by the Project or have a legitimate interest in it." See their "Preparation Report," p. 61. Aside from chiefs, rural residents were not mentioned.
75. Larsen and Lungu proposed seven organizational subunits under the codirectors' authority (extension/development, operation and logistics, antipoaching, information/education, women's program, research/management, and cooperatives) but thought it best to allow the future codirectors to design the activities and structures of these subunits in more detail. Ibid., pp. 64–65.
76. Richard Bell and Fidelis Lungu tell a less political tale about Larsen and Lungu's meeting with Kaunda. They assert that during the president's annual visit to the presidential lodge in the Luangwa Valley, Kaunda had heard of the report being prepared by Larsen and Lungu and had "demanded" that they journey to his lodge to present their findings. Their ensuing discussion supposedly moved Kaunda deeply; he declared LIRDP to be the "answer to my prayers" and insisted on being the chair of the Steering Committee. Interviews with Bell and Lungu, Chipata, Zambia, 28 May 1991.

    Kaunda had good reasons to be enthusiastic about Bell and Lungu's proposals. Through LIRDP, Kaunda could direct a great deal of resources into an area that had long been a UNIP stronghold and that was the home of his wife's family. As a result of LIRDP, Mambwe would eventually receive full district status, which would increase its political importance and government services. Finally, LIRDP offered Kaunda a way to respond to the international press, which had been highly critical of Zambia's conservation efforts.
77. Interview with Gilson Kaweche, deputy director – NPWS, Chilanga, Zambia, 10 October 1991. Kaweche avers that NCDP questioned the procedures that LIRDP followed.
78. Ibid. NCDP Permanent Secretary Alamakuni told Chief Wildlife Research Officer Gilson Kaweche that the positions should have been advertised.
79. On 7 May 1986, President Kaunda formally initiated LIRDP in a letter to the Ministry of Finance that outlined the principal features of the program, including LIRDP's control of the South Luangwa National Park and Lupande Game Management Areas, responsibility for all programs concerning natural resource study and use in the project area, right to a revolving fund mechanism, and management by two codirectors. See R. H. V. Bell and F. B. Lungu, "The Luangwa Integrated Resource Development Project, Progress of Phase I and Proposals for Phase II," August 1986, viii–ix (mimeo.).
80. The ministries were Finance; National Commission for Development Planning, Lands and Natural Resources; Tourism; Agriculture and Water Manage-

ment; Decentralization; Cabinet Office and Personnel Division; and Cooperatives.

81. Interviews with Bell and Lungu, Chipata, Zambia, 28 May 1991.
82. Bell and Lungu, "LIRDP, Progress of Phase I and Proposals for Phase II," p. 11.
    See also "The Luangwa Integrated Resource Development Project, The Phase
    Two Programme," LIRDP Project document no. 4 (November 1987), p. 14.
83. President Kaunda also chaired the NCDP.
84. Bell realized that decentralized programs often failed for lack of independent
    sources of revenue and cited the poor success of Zambia's decentralization plans
    in the early 1980s as proof (Decentralisation Act of 1980, Act No. 15 of 1980).
    He claims the decentralization effort floundered because although responsible
    for implementing policies and delivering services to the district level, district
    councils were not given any powers to raise revenues. See Bell and Lungu, "The
    Luangwa Integrated Resource Development Project, A Presentation to the Na-
    tional Assembly," December 1990, p. 2 (mimeo.).
85. LIRDP, "Phase 2 Programme," p. 56.
86. Bell and Lungu's final proposal slated subcommittees for agriculture, women's
    programs, forestry, fisheries, works and supply, water development, and wildlife
    management. The chairman of each technical subcommittee would be the high-
    est ranking departmental officer of the province.
87. LIRDP, "Phase 2 Programme," p. 16.
88. Many of these same permanent secretaries would recommend the dismantling
    of LIRDP's institutions after Kaunda's electoral loss in 1991.
89. Interview with M. Ngoma, Lusaka, Zambia, 10 October 1991.
90. See the Republic of Zambia, "Agreement between the Government of the King-
    dom and the Government of the Republic of Zambia Regarding the Integrated
    Resource Development of the Luangwa Valley in Zambia," October 1988
    (mimeo.). This "Agreement" refers to the LIRDP "Phase 2 Programme" as the
    referent document.
91. Ibid., p. 4.
92. Paul Andre DeGeorges, "ADMADE: An Evaluation Today and the Future Pol-
    icy Issues and Direction," 1 July 1992, p. 28 (mimeo.).
93. Interview with B. Nair, Ministry of Finance – Internal Accounts, Lusaka, Zam-
    bia, 1 April 1991.
94. USAID/Zambia, "Project Paper Supplement," pp. 29–30. Local communities
    received only about 10 percent of the Fund's income. Peter Alpert and Paul
    Andre DeGeorges, "Midterm Evaluation of the Zambia Natural Resources
    Management Project," 1 July 1992, p. 11 (mimeo.).
95. DeGeorges, "ADMADE," p. 29. See also USAID/Zambia, "Project Paper Sup-
    plement (Social Analysis)," p. 7.
96. Interview with Michael Wright, Nature Conservancy, Washington, D.C., 2
    September 1993.
97. DeGeorges, "ADMADE," p. 29.
98. A. N. Mwenya, D. M. Lewis, and G. B. Kaweche, *ADMADE: Policy, Back-
    ground & Future* (Lusaka, Zambia: National Parks and Wildlife Service, 1990),
    p. 13.
99. USAID/Zambia, "Project Paper Supplement," pp. 3–4.
100. H. K. Mwima, "Wildlife Conservation Revolving Fund Annual Report 1991,"
    report submitted to the National Parks and Wildlife Services, 1992; quoted
    from Alpert and DeGeorges, "Midterm Evaluation," p. 9.
101. USAID/Zambia, "Project Paper Supplement," pp. 3–4.
102. Alpert and DeGeorges, "Midterm Evaluation," p. 15.
103. USAID/Zambia, "Project Paper Supplement (Technical Analysis)," pp. 13–16.
    See also DeGeorges, "ADMADE," p. 59.

104. USAID/Zambia, "Project Paper Supplement (Technical Analysis)," p. 13.
105. Alpert and DeGeorges, "Midterm Evaluation," pp. 1 and 13.
106. Ibid., p. 15.
107. USAID/Zambia, "Project Paper Supplement," p. 29.
108. Ibid. "Project Paper Supplement (Technical Analysis)," p. 12.
109. Ibid.
110. Alpert and DeGeorges, "ADMADE," p. 11.
111. The lack of an appropriate organizational setup was cited by an audit conducted by an independent accounting firm. See International Union for Conservation of Nature and Natural Resources (IUCN) – World Conservation Union, *Third Review Mission, Luangwa Integrated Resource Development Project* (Gland, Switzerland: World Conservation Union, August 1991), p. 38.
112. The Steering Committee had met only once by April 1992. See H. Hedlund, M. Jones, and D. Lewis, "A Feasibility Study to Advise on the Institutional Structure of the Luangwa Integrated Resource Development Project," Report to the Senior Permanent Secretary, National Commission for Development Planning (GRZ), and the Resident Representative, NORAD, Lusaka, April 1992, p. 33.
    LIRDP's Steering Committee did not have a clearly defined legal status. The Third Review Mission thought such a situation made it too "open to the charge that it exists purely for political purposes since it is not the executive board of LIRDP." See IUCN, *Third Review Mission*, p. 38. NORAD responded to this criticism by instructing the LIRDP's Executive Committee to outline the Steering Committee's role. See LIRDP, "Agreed Minutes of the Third Annual Meeting for the Luangwa Integrated Resource Development Project," 13 February 1991, p. 13 (mimeo.).
113. The Executive Committee had met once by August 1990. See The World Conservation Union (IUCN), *Second Review Mission, Luangwa Integrated Resource Development Project* (Gland, Switzerland: World Conservation Union, August 1990), p. 25; also LIRDP, "Third Annual Meeting," p. 13.
114. IUCN, *Third Review Mission*, p. 38.
115. Ibid., p. 31.
116. Ibid., p. 41.
117. Committee meetings themselves were held infrequently. See IUCN, *Second Review Mission*, p. 26.
118. IUCN, *Third Review Mission*, pp. 44–45.
119. See IUCN, *First Review Mission*, p. 33; *Second Review Mission*, p. 2; *Third Review Mission*, pp. 42–45.
120. Interview with Arne Lonning, NORAD, Lusaka, Zambia, 10 September 1991.
121. J. H. Madubansi, E. Jhala, E. Chidumayo, A. Sakala, and G. Kaweche, "Draft Report of the Technical Committee on Proposed Legislative Control and Management of Wildlife Resources in the Luangwa Integrated Resources Development Project Area," n.d., p. 23 (mimeo.). This exception to the Exchange Control Act was unique in the country.
122. *Zambia Daily Mail*, 16 January 1995, p. 2.
123. Interview with J. H. Madubansi, senior planner, National Commission for Development Planning, Lusaka, 10 September 1991.
124. NORAD was consistently unhappy with the depth and frequency of the codirectors' financial reporting; for example, in a stinging reminder about their power of financial oversight, the delegation pointed out that the bilateral agreement stipulated LIRDP's obligation to provide to NORAD audited accounts of their yearly expenditures and budgets for the upcoming year. See LIRDP, "Second Annual Meeting," p. 2. NORAD pressed the LIRDP codirectors for more timely and accurate documentation at every subsequent annual meeting.
125. The codirectors did give NORAD reviews of its accounts.

126. Luangwa Integrated Resource Development Project, *The Phase Two Programme* (Chipata, Zambia: LIRDP, November 1987), p. 25. The codirectors also defined their own expenditure priorities, sometimes in direct conflict with NORAD's preferences. The Norwegian delegation to the Third Annual Meeting expressed concern that its provision of funds had created high-volume activities that make LIRDP operations dependent on donor-supplied foreign exchange and suggested the program limit its expansion and focus on income-generating activities. See LIRDP, "Third Annual Meeting," p. 10. At the Fourth Annual Meeting, the Norwegian delegation again expressed displeasure at the expansion of LIRDP operations as outlined in the 1992 work plans. See LIRDP, "Fourth Annual Meeting," p. 2.

127. Hedlund, Jones, and Lewis, "Feasibility Study," p. 33.

128. The codirectors made this effort in response to the Steering Committee's recommendation that they "investigate and make recommendations on possible legislation that would strengthen and streamline the project and further extend the application of the same approach to land use in other parts of Zambia." See Madubansi et al., "Draft Report," p. 1.

129. Ibid., p. 12.

130. The issue of government officer secondment also worried the LIRDP codirectors, who wanted government staff to be seconded to the program, not just "attached." Without secondment the codirectors feared a loss of control and threat to their program. See IUCN, *First Review Mission*, pp. 33–34. The review team found evidence that the codirectors' attitude led to ambivalence of other government agencies about lending their staff to LIRDP.

131. LIRDP, *Annual Report 1990* (Chipata: LIRDP, 5 September 1991), pp. 1–3. The codirectors felt that NPWS staff, as well as that from all government departments that worked in the LIRDP area, should be formally seconded to the program. The codirectors believed that without full secondment, personnel were caught between two supervisors. They stated that they had "most problems with NPWS staff" and complained about their lack of control over their activities. See IUCN, *First Review Mission*, p. 33.

132. The resolutions of the first meeting of the Steering Committee are partially reported in Madubansi et al., "Draft Report," p. 1; see also Fidelis B. Lungu and Richard H. V. Bell, *Luangwa Integrated Resource Development Project, A Presentation to the National Assembly* (Chipata, Zambia: LIRDP, December 1990), app. 1.

133. NORAD claimed to have no position on the statutory instrument debate. See LIRDP, "Third Annual Meeting," p. 14. But Michael Wright asserts that NORAD had suggested that LIRDP seek such authority over their program area (interview with Wright, Nature Conservancy, Washington, D.C., 2 September 1993). NORAD/Oslo also apparently accepted LIRDP's attempts to avoid or bypass any GRZ institutions with which it had difficulty cooperating. See NORAD/NATURE, "Comments on the Report from the First IUCN Review Mission," p. 3, quoted in IUCN, *Second Review Mission*, p. 17.

134. In fact, given the president's assurances, the Norwegian delegation to the Second Annual Meeting for LIRDP held in September were surprised and concerned that the matter was still outstanding. See LIRDP, "Second Annual Meeting," p. 4.

135. LIRDP, *Annual Report 1990*, p. 2.

136. See sec. 37–42 of Government of the Republic of Zambia, *The National Parks and Wildlife Act 1991*, National Assembly Bulletin, no. 9 (Lusaka: Government Printers, 5 July 1991), pp. 45–46.

137. It is instructive to compare sec. 37–40 of the 1991 act with sec. 18–19 of the 1972 Wildlife Act; the acts use identical language when referring to the powers

of the director of National Parks and Wildlife Service. The sections that define and empower the IRDCs in the 1991 act are inserted before the section that empowers the director and clearly indicate the IRDCs preeminence. As stated in the 1991 act, however, the IRDCs' actual powers do not lend themselves to a clear interpretation. First, section 38 provides the IRDC authority over *all* natural resources in their respective national parks and game management areas. This clause both fails to define the extent of natural resource, and appears out of place in an act concerned only with wildlife. Section 38 would also appear to be in direct conflict with the mandates of other ministries concerned with natural resources; it also refers to the management of "human resources" without defining them or what constitutes their management.

138. This status was based on the Sri Lankan Mahaweli Authority. See LIRDP, *Proposals for the Phase II Programme* (Chipata: LIRDP, June 1987), p. 20; also LIRDP, *Phase Two Programme*, p. 25.

139. Madubansi et al., "Draft Report," p. 22.

140. This list would include inter alia the Forests Act, National Parks and Wildlife Act, Fisheries Act, Water Act, and Natural Resources Conservation Act. Legislation would also have to be drawn up to redefine the powers of district and provincial administrative bodies.

141. LIRDP, "Background Paper on the Institutional Proposal for the National Integrated Resource Development Programme" 5 October 1991 (mimeo.).

142. IUCN, *Third Review Mission*, p. 51. Lungu claims that NORAD strongly supported the idea that LIRDP be replicated throughout Zambia and was ready to support the expansion financially. He asserts that ministers and permanent secretaries, afraid of losing their power to LIRDP, prevented the idea from advancing beyond the planning stages. He especially indicts the senior officers at NPWS. Interview with Fidelis Lungu, Chinzombo Safari Lodge, 3 August 1992.

143. IUCN, *Third Review Mission*, p. 38.

144. Ibid., p. 29.

145. Ibid.

146. See, for example, IUCN, *First Review Mission*, p. 25; *Second Review Mission*, pp. 1–2; *Third Review Mission*, p. 51.

147. The Second Review Mission team asserted that LIRDP intentionally weakened those government institutions with which it interacted; see IUCN, *Second Review Mission*, pp. 1–2, 16–17, and 41. The same topic is mentioned by the next review team; see IUCN, *Third Review Mission*, p. 29; see also the discussion of the effects of Kaunda's support in Hedlund, Jones, and Lewis, "Feasibility Study," pp. 33–34.

148. IUCN, *First Review Mission*, p. 40. The Second Review team had noticed this resentment had grown despite the first mission's criticisms. See IUCN, *Second Review Mission*, p. 2.

149. Ibid., p. 20; IUCN, *First Review Mission*, p. 40.

150. 1994 receipts at $450 million from nonconsumptive use by tourists. Dominic Moran, "Contingent Valuation and Biodiversity: Measuring the User Surplus of Kenyan Protected Areas," *Biodiversity and Conservation* 3(8) (1994): 663–84.

151. The politics of structural choice that surround Leakey's demands have yet to be investigated.

152. Walter Lusigi, "New Approaches to Wildlife Conservation in Kenya," *Ambio* 10(2–3) (1981): 88–92; Jane Perlez, "Only Radical Steps Can Save Wildlife in Kenya, Leakey Says," *The New York Times*, May 23, 1989, sec. C, p. 1.

153. Mark Doyle, "Leakey to End Great Crusade," *The Guardian*, 15 January 1994.

154. "Driven Out of Africa," *Daily Mail*, 23 January 1994.

155. Ntimama had gained political prominence under Moi by calling for the "ethnic cleansing" of Kikuyu from Masai areas. Along with Moi and his Kalenjin followers, Ntimama was involved in fomenting ethnic unrest against the Kikuyu. As the self-proclaimed "King of the Masai," Ntimama, in attacking Leakey, also helped his standing among Masai, who have endured long battles with the Kenyan government over access to game parks.
156. "Driven Out of Africa."
157. James C. Murombedzi, *Decentralization or Recentralization? Implementing CAMPFIRE in the Omay Communal Lands of the Nyaminyami District*, Centre for Applied Social Science, Working Paper 2 (Harare: University of Zimbabwe, May 1992), p. 47.
158. Ibid., p. 46.
159. Leslie A. King, *Inter-Organisational Dynamics in Natural Resources Management: A Study of CAMPFIRE Implementation in Zimbabwe*, Centre for Applied Social Science, Occasional Paper Series NRM (Harare: University of Zimbabwe, 1994), p. 11.
160. See the extensive list of work in Anne Dix, *CAMPFIRE: Communal Areas Management Programme for Indigenous Resources, An Annotated Bibliography, 1985–1996* (Harare: University of Zimbabwe, Centre for Applied Social Science, June 1996).
161. The foundational document is Rowan B. Martin, *CAMPFIRE: Communal Areas Management Programme for Indigenous Resources*, rev. version (Harare: Department of National Parks and Wildlife Management, Branch of Terrestrial Ecology, 1986). For a more detailed history of CAMPFIRE's origins see J. H. Peterson, "CAMPFIRE: A Zimbabwean Approach to Sustainable Development and Community Empowerment through Wildlife Utilization," manuscript (Harare, Zimbabwe: Centre for Applied Social Science, 1991).
162. Martin, "CAMPFIRE," p. 17.
163. It seems that most observers of CAMPFIRE miss the irony behind its designers' initial desire for a single national-level parastatal to implement a program of decentralization.
164. King, *Inter-Organisational Dynamics*, p. 10. Only after the Department successfully recruited the NGOs did CAMPFIRE have the staff necessary to spread to other districts. Peterson, "CAMPFIRE: A Zimbabwean Approach," p. 71.
165. Peterson, "CAMPFIRE: A Zimbabwean Approach," p. 26.
166. Ibid., p. 29.
167. One Zimbabwe dollar = 0.44 U.S. dollar in 1989. Thus, the totals in U.S. dollars are approximately $120,000 and $20,700, respectively.
168. Nearly all of the reports and analyses of CAMPFIRE have been written by individuals associated with the program. Notable critics include Richard Hasler, *Agriculture, Foraging and Wildlife Resource Use in Africa* (London and New York: Kegan Paul, 1996); Kevin A. Hill, "Interest Groups and the Politics of the Environment: Wildlife Conservation Policy, the State, and Organized Interests in Zimbabwe" (Ph.D. dissertation, University of Florida, 1993); and James C. Murombedzi, *Decentralization or Recentralization?*
169. Murombedzi, *Decentralization or Recentralization?*, p. 15.
170. Ibid., p. 10. See also Peterson, "CAMPFIRE: A Zimbabwean Approach," p. 73; A. H. J. Helmsing, *Transforming Rural Local Government: Zimbabwe's Post-independence Experience*, Department of Rural and Urban Planning Occasional Paper, no. 19 (Harare: University of Zimbabwe, 1989). District councils raise their own revenue through means such as taxes on beer, sales of alcoholic beverages, school fees, lease rents, and business licenses.
171. Peterson, "CAMPFIRE: A Zimbabwean Approach," p. 83.
172. Ibid., p. 33. See also Gordon Edwin Matzke and Nontokozo Nabane, "Out-

comes of a Community Controlled Wildlife Program in a Zambezi Valley Community," *Human Ecology* 24(1) (1996): 80.

173. Peterson, "CAMPFIRE: A Zimbabwean Approach," p. 71. See also *Policy for Wildlife* (Harare: Ministry of Natural Resources and Tourism, 1989).

174. Graham Child, *Wildlife and People: The Zimbabwean Success* (Harare: Wisdom Foundation, 1995), table 7, p. 172. The Department's target for the district council's "service charge" is 15 percent, so there still exists some slippage between what the Department wants and what the district councils are doing.

175. Moe, "The Politics of Structural Choice," pp. 116–35.

176. In fact, within the enormous literature produced by program supporters or observers few mention Mugabe at all, whereas other ministers and parliamentarians who were suspicious of the white community's conservation plans are mentioned. CAMPFIRE fit well with President Mugabe's general policy preferences. He had declared his support of the program's foundations when he told parliament that "with regard to wildlife management, it is my government's intention to extend this responsibility to the communal people through the management of indigenous resource." See Peterson, "CAMPFIRE: A Zimbabwean Approach," p. 76.

177. Interview with Dale Lewis, ADMADE technical adviser, Nyamaluma Camp, Zambia, 28 June 1991.

178. See, for example, the photograph of President Kaunda in Mwenya, Kaweche, and Lewis, *ADMADE: Policy, Background & Future*, p. 12.

179. See, for example, Harold Seidman and Robert Gilmour, *Politics, Position, and Power: From the Positive to the Regulatory State*, 4th ed. (Cambridge: Oxford University Press, 1986); and Frederick C. Mosher, *Democracy and the Public Service*, 3d ed. (Cambridge: Oxford University Press, 1982). Terry Moe points out that these authors, understanding the influence of politics on bureaucratic structure, still hope for public agencies to serve some "national interest." See Moe, "Politics of Bureaucratic Structure," pp. 267–68.

5. THE CONSEQUENCES OF INSTITUTIONAL DESIGN: THE IMPACT OF "COMMUNITY-BASED" WILDLIFE MANAGEMENT PROGRAMS AT THE LOCAL LEVEL

1. The observations in this section come from the sources cited in the rest of the chapter, as well as field notes and observations. Of course, the rural areas of Zambia can vary enormously. This section attempts to provide only a general overview.

2. Doris Jansen, *Trade, Exchange Rate and Agricultural Pricing Policies in Zambia* (Washington, D.C.: World Bank, 1988), pp. 30–33.

3. Eugenia West, "The Politics of Hope" (Ph.D. dissertation, Yale University, 1989), pp. 54–55.

4. Stuart Marks, *The Imperial Lion: Human Dimensions of Wildlife Management in Central Africa* (Boulder: Westview Press, 1984), p. 52.

5. Not all rural areas have an abundance of wildlife. Years of hunting and expansion of settlement have left regions without most species. As a general rule, wildlife increases the farther an area is from an urban center.

6. This fact has long been acknowledged by Zambia's wildlife departments in their annual reports, although they continue to focus their energies on the conservation of the larger species. Chief Chitungulu reserved special ire for the bush pigs and monkeys that destroy local crops. He claimed that in his area, big animals did not harm many local fields, but "we are only in trouble with these small monkeys eating some maize and we have these wild pigs. They are clever and they trouble

us a lot." Interview with Chief Chitungulu, Chitungulu Village, Luangwa Valley, 3 August 1991.

7. Rural residents may fear the crocodile more than any other single animal. Crocodiles are silent, quick, strong, and difficult to see. Because many villagers depend on the water from rivers, they face the possibility of an encounter with a crocodile on a daily basis. Some communities build fences near the areas where they collect water and wash clothes, but these often are weak or fall into disrepair. Consequently, crocodiles drag many villagers, especially children, into the river to be drowned, and then eaten. Few scenes are more tragic than that of a village learning that one of its children has been killed by a wild animal.

8. Surveys that actually investigate game meat consumption are rare. But even if such an effort were mounted, no incentive exists for a rural resident to give accurate information.

9. Robert and Christine Prescott-Allen, *What's Wildlife Worth?* (London: International Institute for Environmental Development, 1982), p. 15.

10. Stuart Marks, *Large Mammals and a Brave People: Subsistence Hunters in Zambia* (Seattle: University of Washington Press, 1976), p. 204. Other studies of the Zambian diet estimate lower consumption of game meat. See Thayer Scudder, *The Ecology of the Gwembe Tonga* (Manchester: Rhodes – Livingstone Institute of Northern Rhodesia Manchester University Press, 1962); B. P. Thomson, *Two Studies in African Nutrition*, Rhodes – Livingstone Paper no. 24 (Lusaka, 1954); and G. Kay, *Chief Kabala's Village*, Rhodes – Livingstone Paper no. 35 (Lusaka, 1964).

11. Marks, *Imperial Lion*, pp. 87–102. This practice varies with the importance of kinship groups in rural society. As rural areas have been increasingly penetrated by outsiders – and thus outside markets – the control over hunting once possessed by kinship groups has rapidly eroded.

12. Interview with Edwin Matokwani, NPWS wildlife ranger, Nyamaluma Camp, 21 July 1991.

13. Patrols usually fail to surprise rural hunters. When a hunter detects a patrol, he will usually hide his weapon, himself, and any kill he might be carrying. If caught, he will deny that the gun or meat is his.

14. The following account from the field notes of Stuart Marks illustrates how some locals thwart arrests:

> Village scouts were suspicious of Chibeza, who they thought was killing animals without a license. They asked a woman, Chibeza's neighbor, to serve as an informer and to report to them whenever she saw Chibeza with game meat. One day, when she saw him returning home with meat from an impala, she told the scouts. The scouts entered his home and found the fresh impala kill together with dried warthog meat in a white basin. The scouts took the white basin and confronted Chibeza, who at the time was drinking beer at the scouts' own camp. Chibeza acknowledged that he had brought the meat to his home, but asserted that the impala had been killed by his father who possessed the required license. Chibeza further claimed the warthog meat had been given to him by his son, who had killed the animal on a hunting foray with the scouts' sons several days earlier. He said his son also possessed the requisite license. Despite his statements, the scouts arrested Chibeza, handcuffed him, and took his gun. Chibeza's father, a respected elder who had retired from work in the copper mines, showed the scouts his properly endorsed license for the impala, offered to reveal its kill site, and was prepared to testify in court in support of his son's story. Scouts, figuring they would lose the case if the father testified, released Chibeza after six days in custody. They also repaired his muzzle-

loading gun after Chibeza noted evidence of their tampering with it. The female informant began to tell the scouts that she feared that either Chibeza or his relatives would kill her. After all, three days after Chibeza's arrest, a bush fire destroyed her house; residents strongly suspected Chibeza's family had set the "natural" fire. Although informally implicated in the arson, Chibeza told other villagers that he bore no grudges against his female neighbor. Chibeza soon married another wife, a cross-cousin, and moved to live in a village much farther from the scouts' camp.

15. Marks, *Imperial Lion*, p. 102. These observations are based on hundreds of conversations with rural residents, scouts, professional hunters, chiefs, politicians, and government personnel.

16. Of course, scouts experience a variety of conditions: Different camps encounter varying levels of wild animals, illegal hunters, infrastructure, access to urban centers, supervision from senior officers as one moves from the Sioma National Park near Zambia's southwest border with Angola, to Sumbu National Park in the north on Lake Tangyanika, to North and South Luangwa National Parks in the east at the bottom of the Luangwa Valley. This section extracts the most common experiences of scouts from discussions with individuals who had worked all over the country.

17. Almost all wildlife scouts are men, although the NPWS has recently turned its attention to hiring more women.

18. During the period covered by this study, scouts only needed a form 2 education. As of 1993, the minimum level was increased to form 5. (Personal communication with Mike Faddy, Save the Rhino Trust, 29 October 1993, Lusaka, Zambia.) Although this is a civil service job, those intending to be scouts apply directly to NPWS headquarters at Chilanga, not the Public Service Commission.

19. European conservationists and professional hunters often indicate that the preference for scouts for urban jobs results in less patrolling. These mostly European observers maintain that Europeans did a better job of wildlife management in the days before the "Zambianization" of the civil service because they enjoyed the rugged nature of their occupation, and therefore wanted to be in the field.

20. Scouts posted nearer to district or central headquarters are more likely to get their pay and food allotments on time, receive new uniforms and boots, and have easier access to stores, schools, and clinics.

21. Dale Lewis, "Profile of a Hunting Area: Mainstay of Zambia's Safari Hunting Industry," n.d. [1994], p. 5 (mimeo.). This average is probably high, given that (1) ADMADE monies had allowed the department to enlarge the number of scouts in the field and (2) NPWS posts additional scouts to areas important to professional hunters because their Wildlife Conservation Revolving Fund depends heavily on revenues derived from the safari–hunting business.

22. Chief Chitungulu, who had been a wildlife scout for nearly twenty-nine years, once requested a post near his sick uncle. His uncle also wrote to the director of NPWS to support the transfer, and the department relocated Chitungulu to the desired post. Interview with Chief Chitungulu, Lundazi, Zambia, 3 August 1991.

23. Lewis, "Profile," p. 5. I claim this is the "best" situation because Lewis describes this condition for scouts working in a relatively well funded and supplied part of the ADMADE program.

24. NPWS has difficulty affording new weapons and ammunition. It is also difficult for donors to supply these goods, for obvious political reasons.

One example of the state of NPWS firearms comes from a casual conversation I had while walking with a scout in the Luangwa Valley. He showed me his rifle. Its barrel had been secured to the gun's stock with adhesive tape, and the weapon was thirty years old. Apparently undaunted by its condition, the scout insisted that it was still a good weapon and that he had become a very accurate marksman with it.

25. Scouts frequently use this lack of ammunition to justify their lack of patrolling and their failure to shoot animals that raid local gardens.

26. Scouts perform this function rarely because it forces them to expend effort and ammunition, as well as exposing them to danger. Residents have few effective means to protest this inactivity. In a survey I conducted in the Luangwa Valley of 133 rural residents from nine villages, only 39 percent agreed with the statement "Scouts are always ready to drive animals away from our crops."

27. Scouts also admit they arrest more locals because it is usually less dangerous than patrolling for outside poachers.

28. Lewis, "Profile," p. 5.

29. The scouts I traveled with possessed an informed fear of wild animals. Once, while we were camping in a scout compound, a small herd of elephants decided to feast on the few mango trees they had not already destroyed that season. One wandered over to the hut that four scouts and I shared. As the elephant probed the thatch above us, the scouts who had weapons put them to their shoulders; I heard the click of safeties being thumbed off. Our inquisitive elephant and her friends finally retreated, leaving all of us a bit shaken. The scouts spent the rest of the night regaling me with numerous stories about how family members, friends, and fellow scouts had less luck in their confrontations with wildlife. Several scouts die each year from encounters with wild animals. See NPWS, *Annual Reports* (Lusaka: Government Printer, various years).

30. Outsiders do not have the social networks that could help to have a criminal charge dropped or a sentence reduced. Outsiders are also more likely to be "commercial poachers."

31. The debate over "danger allowances," a small amount once paid to scouts for every day on patrol, illustrates how scouts generally dislike patrols. When the Public Service Commission scrapped this allowance in 1980, the number of patrols greatly declined. Interview with Dr. Siwana, Acting chief warden – NPWS, Chilanga, Zambia, 17 September 1991.

32. Chief Chitungulu, who had had extensive experience as a wildlife scout before assuming his area's chieftaincy, asserted that the shortage of good weapons was a primary reason scouts feared engagements with poachers. "They (scouts) have got .3006, the 12 bore and .300 rifles of which they cannot compete with someone who is having an AK47." Interview with Chief Chitungulu, Lundazi, Zambia, 3 August 1991.

33. Chief Mwanya reports that women accuse scouts of raping them when huts are searched. He believes one solution might be for NPWS to hire more female scouts, to accompany their male colleagues on search missions. Interview with Chief Mwanya, Mwanya Village, Luangwa Valley, 24 July 1994.

34. Stuart Marks, personal communication, 15 July 1994. In a survey I conducted in five chieftaincies in the Luangwa Valley, respondents split nearly equally on their opinion of whether or not people approved of ADMADE's village scouts: forty-eight percent agreed and 52 percent disagreed with the statement "Most people disapprove of village scouts." This result is remarkable if one understands that local residents will rarely voice displeasure about any government employee to a stranger – especially a European survey taker, who, in their minds, is likely to be working for the government. The result is also remarkable because it demonstrates that, despite NPWS officers' claims, ADMADE scouts are no better liked than other scouts – and frequently are more despised.

35. It is very difficult to sack a scout. A senior officer described the "uphill battle" in this way: "If a scout is caught poaching, which is highly unlikely, the department can take him to court. If he is found guilty, the department writes to the Perma-

nent Secretary of Tourism to terminate his employment. If he is found innocent, but the department still believes he is guilty, he can write to the Permanent Secretary who in turn must get the approval for dismissal from the Public Service Commission, the government body that regulates Zambia's Civil Service. Such activities can take two years. Because of these difficulties, only cases that the department considers extreme are pursued."

36. This section derives from my interviews with chiefs, observations of chiefs' behavior, and discussions with, inter alia, Ilse Mwanza, Institute for African Studies, University of Zambia (IAS-UNZA); Dr. Oliver Saasa, IAS-UNZA; Dr. Mwelwa Musambachime, Department of History, UNZA; Bradford Strickland and Stuart Marks, University of North Carolina at Chapel Hill.

37. See, for example, Marks, *Imperial Lion*; David Western, "Amboseli National Park: Human Values and the Conservation of a Savanna Ecosystem," in J. A. McNeely and K. R. Miller, eds., *National Parks, Conservation and Development: The Role of Protected Areas in Sustaining Society: Proceedings of the World Congress on National Parks (Bali, Indonesia)* (Washington, D.C.: Smithsonian Institution Press, 1984), pp. 93–100. Recent analyses include David Anderson and Richard Grove, "The Scramble for Eden: Past, Present and Future in African Conservation," in Anderson and Grove, eds., *Conservation in Africa: People, Policies and Practice* (Cambridge: Cambridge University Press, 1987), pp. 1–12; W. K. Lindsay, "Integrating Parks and Pastoralists: Some Lessons from Amboseli," in Anderson and Grove, eds., *Conservation in Africa*; Marshall W. Murphree, "Communities and Institutions for Resource Management," paper presented to the National Conference on Environment and Development, Maputo, Mozambique, 7–11 October 1991, pp. 149–69; and Agnes Kiss, ed., *Living with Wildlife: Wildlife Resource Management with Local Participation in Africa*, World Bank Technical Paper no. 130 (Washington, D.C.: World Bank, 1990).

38. See Richard Bell, "Conservation with a Human Face: Conflict and Reconciliation in African Land Use Planning," in Anderson and Grove, eds., *Conservation in Africa*, pp. 79–102. For LIRDP generally, see Lungu and Bell, *A Presentation to the National Assembly*, pp. 1–2; Luangwa Integrated Resource Development Project, *The Phase 2 Programme*, foreword by President Kaunda (Chipata, Zambia: LIRDP, November 1987). For ADMADE, see A. N. Mwenya, G. B. Kaweche, and D. M. Lewis, *Administrative Management Design for Game Management Areas (ADMADE)* (Chilanga, Zambia: National Parks and Wildlife Service, January 1988), pp. 1–2 and passim.; A. N. Mwenya, D. M. Lewis, and G. B. Kaweche, *ADMADE: Policy, Background & Future* (Lusaka, Zambia: National Parks and Wildlife Service, 1990), pp. 1–13; National Parks and Wildlife Services, *Proceedings of the First ADMADE Planning Workshop* (Lusaka, Zambia: National Parks and Wildlife Services, December 1988), pp. 1–7.

39. I present a one-shot, rather than a repeated, game. I defend this choice on two grounds. First, rural residents of developing countries generally have short time horizons. Second, because rural residents experience numerous policy changes and reversals, they know that they may be playing a new game tomorrow. See, for example, Samuel L. Popkin, *The Rational Peasant: The Political Economy of Rural Society in Vietnam* (Berkeley: University of California Press, 1979).

40. For the fundamentals of noncooperative game theory, an excellent introduction can be found in David M. Kreps, *A Course in Microeconomic Theory* (Princeton: Princeton University Press, 1990), pp. 355–451.

41. The ranking of choices by scouts and rural residents is based on observations of their behavior; interviews with hunters, scouts, NPWS officers, and conservationists; and interviews with Stuart Marks and analysis of his works. See Stuart Marks, *Large Mammals* (Seattle: University of Washington Press, 1976), and idem, *Imperial Lion*. These observations have been extended recently by more

intensive interviews with hunters in Zambia's Luangwa Valley (Marks, field notes).

42. Elephant, rhino, and hippo provide more meat than other species, and their ivories or horns could be sold for considerable cash on the black market. The larger meat yields, together with the sale of trophies, were the main reasons hunters preferred to pursue the larger species.

43. Such strong incentives encouraged aged or disabled gun owners to lend their guns to relatives to provide meat, consumer goods, and crop protection for others.

44. Kreps, *Microeconomic Theory*, pp. 398–99.

45. Not enforcing the law means overlooking illegal practices.

46. The death of the bigger animals attracts a host of vultures and other scavengers (whose feasting can last for days) and leaves considerable skeletal material. Unlike the smaller animals, larger species have dark colors and great size that make them easy to count by wildlife managers calculating numbers of animals, dead or alive, by air.

47. The game in Table 1 is dominance solvable. The scout will choose not to enforce; the hunter will always choose to hunt large game. These strategies intersect at the Not Enforce/Hunt Large Game outcome.

48. For example, Bell and Lungu claim that the alienation of locals from the legal use of their natural resources under colonial-style policy "removed incentives toward sustainable resource use and encouraged the rural population to participate in the illegal, unsustainable exploitation of their resources, a traffic that has cost Zambia hundreds of millions of dollars; the solution lies in the institutional and legislative change that will transfer control of resource use back to local communities; this transfer of control will give back to local communities the economic power to generate and sustain their own development; and . . . the incentives to manage their resources wisely." See Fidelis B. Lungu and Richard H. V. Bell, *Luangwa Integrated Resource Development Project: A Presentation to the National Assembly* (Chipata, Zambia: LIRDP, December 1990), p. 1.

49. A "cull" is a wildlife management euphemism for a legal, selective kill of wild animals, usually carried out by department staff.

50. See Mwenya, Lewis, and Kaweche, *ADMADE: Policy, Background & Future*, pp. 1–10; Luangwa Integrated Resource Development Project, *Phase 2 Programme*, pp. 129–50.

51. This game is also dominance solvable: The scout always prefers to enforce, and the resident always prefers not to hunt. The intersection of these two strategies is the outcome Not Hunt/Enforce.

52. United States Agency for International Development/Zambia, "Project Paper Supplement for the Natural Resources Management Project (Technical Analysis)," 1993, p. 25 (mimeo.). Also interview with Dale Lewis, ADMADE technical adviser, Nyamaluma Camp, Zambia, 28 June 1991.

53. Lewis, "Profile," p. 3. This statement does not correspond well with what is known about chiefs in Zambian history. See Appendix A for a short review of this history.

54. Lewis, "Profile," p. 3; see also Mwenya, Lewis, and Kaweche, *ADMADE: Policy, Background & Future*, p. 1.

55. Interview with D. Lewis, Nyamaluma Camp, Zambia, 28 June 1991.

56. Ibid. Lewis made numerous trips to discuss ADMADE with chiefs in the Luangwa Valley.

57. See Roger Cohn, "The People's War on Poaching" *Audubon* (March/April 1994), p. 78.

58. Mwenya, Lewis, and Kaweche, *ADMADE: Policy, Background & Future*, p. 13. The Kaputa area chief asked that his chiefdom become a GMA and included

within ADMADE. The Chireza chief wanted the ADMADE part of his area extended. See USAID/Zambia, "Project Paper Supplement (Technical Analysis)," p. 9. Lewis and Alpert state that "communities" living in three different areas have requested the government to classify their areas to be GMAs so that they can participate in the ADMADE program. These "communities" are probably the chiefs listed. See Lewis and Alpert, "International Safari Hunting," p. 7.

59. Ibid. See also Cohn, "People's War on Poaching," pp. 70–84. Revealingly, chiefs and wildlife scouts are the source of the article's positive comments about AD-MADE – the two groups who gained the most from the program.

60. Dale Lewis and Peter Alpert, "International Safari Hunting: A Green Bullet for African Wildlife?" May 1994, p. 4 (mimeo.). ADMADE community development officers noted the "insufficient democratization" in the selection of the Sub-Authority members and in the choice of community development projects. Paul Andre DeGeorges, "ADMADE: An Evaluation Today and the Future Policy Issues and Direction," 1 July 1992, pp. 41–42 (mimeo.). Although some chiefs selected WMSA members on the basis of criteria other than parentage, such as social standing or education, individuals still owed their position on the WMSA to the chief. Consultants noticed that in a few cases members were selected by "consensus." See Peter Alpert and Paul Andre DeGeorges, "Midterm Evaluation of the Zambia Natural Resources Management Project," 1 July 1992, p. 13. Chiefs also used their power as the WMSA chair to hold few meetings, thus eliminating any kind of open decision-making process. See DeGeorges, "AD-MADE," p. 42.

61. Rehabilitation of chiefs' residences and the roads that led to them was among the first proposals submitted to the WMAs. See Alpert and DeGeorges, "Midterm Evaluation," p. 13.

62. USAID/Zambia, "Project Paper Supplement (Social Analysis)," p. 6.

63. Ibid.

64. Idem, "Project Paper Supplement (Technical Analysis)," p. 25.

65. Idem, "Project Paper Supplement (Social Analysis)," p. 3.

66. Mwenya, Lewis, and Kaweche, *ADMADE: Policy, Background and Future*, p. 12.

67. USAID/Zambia, "Project Paper Supplement (Technical Analysis)," p. 26. Also Alpert and DeGeorges, "Midterm Evaluation," p. 13.

68. Alpert and DeGeorges, "Midterm Evaluation," p. 8.

69. Interview with Dale Lewis, Raleigh, North Carolina, 17 February 1992. Chief Chikwa subdivided his land among local hunters "like the old days." The hunters used snares so that they would not be heard by the scouts. See also C. C. Nkonga, "Lumimba Wildlife Management Authority Progress Report," in National Parks and Wildlife Services, *Proceedings of the First ADMADE Planning Workshop* (Lusaka: National Parts and Wildlife Services, 1988).

70. Lungu and Bell, *Presentation to the National Assembly*, p. 4.

71. LIRDP's project area included the uninhabited South Luangwa National Park and the inhabited South Lupande Game Management Area. The project covered fourteen thousand square kilometers.

72. Lungu and Bell, *Presentation to the National Assembly*, p. 2.

73. Ibid.

74. See World Conservation Union (IUCN), *Second Review Mission, Luangwa Integrated Resource Development Project* (Gland, Switzerland: World Conservation Union, August 1990), p. 22. The precise terms of reference for the Local Leaders' Sub-Committee were never made clear. In general, all of LIRDP's subcommittees provide technical advice in their subject areas to the Advisory Committee, develop work plans for their resources, oversee the implementation of those plans, and monitor their progress. The Advisory Committee retained control over

the expenditure ceiling for all subcommittees. See LIRDP, *Phase 2 Programme*, p. 22.

75. Consultants asserted that local leaders felt removed from the process of agenda setting by LIRDP project management. See World Conservation Union, *Second Review Mission*, pp. 21–22. Project management vehemently denies this charge. See Luangwa Integrated Resource Development Project, "Errors of Fact in Review Mission Reports, Selected Examples," January 1991, p. 3 (mimeo.).

76. LIRDP put these funds into separate bank accounts with the chief, an adviser, the ward chairman, and the ward vice-chairman as signatories to the account.

77. World Conservation Union, *Second Review Mission*, p. 22.

78. See World Conservation Union, *First Review Mission, Luangwa Integrated Resource Development Project* (Gland, Switzerland: World Conservation Union, October 1989), p. 36; idem, *Second Review Mission*, pp. 21–23.

79. International Union for Conservation of Nature and Natural Resources (IUCN) – World Conservation Union, *Third Review Mission, Luangwa Integrated Resource Development Project* (Gland, Switzerland: World Conservation Union, August 1991), p. 29.

80. Ibid. In 1991 only one of the six areas spent its entire allotment; one area used none of its allotment.

81. Ibid, 30. Senior Chieftainess Nsefu received 2,500 Zambian kwacha, other chiefs ZK2,000, and ward chairmen ZK1,500. At this time, the real exchange rate was approximately ZK250 to $1.00 U.S.

82. USAID/Zambia, "Project Paper Supplement (Social Analysis)," p. 5. Village scouts made approximately U.S. $320 per annum in 1993. Lewis, "International Safari Hunting," p. 6.

83. Ibid., pp. 5–6. This refers to the nine original ADMADE GMAs funded by USAID/WWF from 1989 to 1992.

84. Mwenya, Lewis, and Kaweche, *ADMADE: Policy, Background & Future*, pp. 1–2 and passim. Luangwa Integrated Resource Development Project, *Phase 2 Programme*, p. 5.

85. Mwenya, Lewis, and Kaweche, *ADMADE: Policy, Background & Future*, pp. 14–15; Luangwa Integrated Resource Development Project, *Phase 2 Programme*, p. viii.

86. See the tables in DeGeorges, "ADMADE," 29a and 29b. NPWS admits having received around $4 million in direct and indirect support to ADMADE from 1990 to 1994. NPWS also received approximately $4 million in other revenues to the Wildlife Conservation Revolving Fund over the same period. In 1991, NPWS reports distributing $53,000 in development projects. If 1991 is taken to be an average year, then the department has distributed approximately $212,000 of the nearly $8 million it has taken in over those four years. See Dale Lewis and Peter Alpert, "International Safari Hunting: A Green Bullet for African Wildlife?" n.d., pp. 5–6 (mimeo.).

87. USAID/Zambia, "Project Paper Supplement (Social Analysis)," p. 6.

88. Ibid; see the tables on pp. 5–6.

89. DeGeorges, "ADMADE," p. 30; USAID/Zambia, "Project Paper Supplement (Social Analysis)," p. 6; see also B. S. Kalomo, "Fulaza WMU Unit Leaders Report," in NPWS *Proceedings*. Lewis and Alpert agree that the amounts provided to the communities have "been small," but they claim that the funds and projects have stimulated "self-reliance" and "appreciative goodwill." See Lewis and Alpert, "International Safari Hunting," p. 6.

90. World Conservation Union, *Third Review Mission*, p. 29.

91. USAID/Zambia, "Project Paper Supplement (Social Analysis)," pp. 5–6.

92. DeGeorges, "ADMADE," p. 48; World Conservation Union (IUCN), *First Review Mission*, p. 68. Additionally, Lewis and Alpert admit the "revenues from

culling have been minor (e.g., $400–$500 in 1991 in two GMAs)." Lewis and Alpert, "International Safari Hunting," p. 6.

93. USAID/Zambia, "Project Paper Supplement (Social Analysis)," p. 9; DeGeorges, "ADMADE," pp. 28–29.

94. USAID/Zambia, "Project Paper Supplement (Social Analysis)," p. 10. Some chiefs did use the backing of district governors to threaten squatters who encroached on potentially valuable wildlife lands.

95. Ibid.

96. USAID/Zambia, "Project Paper Supplement (Technical Analysis)," p. 27.

97. USAID/Zambia, "Project Paper Supplement," p. 6.

98. Alpert and DeGeorges, "Midterm Evaluation," p. 6; see also Mwenya, Lewis, and Kaweche, *ADMADE: Policy, Background & Future*, p. 13.

99. Dale Lewis had expected that the villagers I had surveyed would be more positive in their assessment of village scouts than regular scouts, because village scouts were locals and were charged with establishing cooperative ties with their community. The results demonstrated that village scouts were, in fact, more disliked than regular NPWS troops in many cases. Village scouts pursued their enforcement duties with more zeal and lived closer to villages. In Chief Chitungulu's area, an ADMADE scout's parents and sister were burned in their hut, simply because the scout was suspected of responsibility for the arrest of someone's relative. See C. C. Nkonga, "Lumimba WMA Progress Report," in *Proceedings*.

100. DeGeorges, "ADMADE," pp. 61–62.

101. USAID/Zambia, "Project Paper Supplement (Technical Analysis)," p. 16. Also, my unpublished surveys in five chiefdoms in the Luangwa Valley, conducted June–July 1991.

102. This game is also solved by using the concept of dominance. The scout has the dominant strategy of Enforce. Knowing this, the resident chooses his best option given that the Scout will enforce the law. The resident chooses to Hunt Small Game.

103. Such a decrease in arrests could also result from a change in hunting tactics, making it more difficult for scouts to detect poaching.

104. The Munyamadzi GMA is one of Zambia's prime safari sites and a large revenue earner for ADMADE.

105. Two factors account for the decrease in off takes during this drought. First, men received jobs from the government delivering food aid to the area, which reduced the time they spent hunting. Second, the drought altered the normal patterns of animal movement. Local hunters spent more time in the field trying to find game, thus reducing their overall off takes.

106. Mwenya, Lewis, and Kaweche, *ADMADE: Policy, Background & Future*, p. 13.

107. Munyamadzi, like other areas, has suffered from a succession of weak AD-MADE unit leaders, the program's chief executive officers at the Sub-Authority level. The first four appointees to this post were dismissed in as many years for corruption, loss of funds, public drunkenness, abuse of local residents, and failure to implement the program. Such difficulties likely influenced the comparatively few arrests made during the initial years of ADMADE. During 1991–1992, arrests increased – in part as a result of the expiration of an amnesty for possession of unregistered firearms instituted by the chief. Interview with Stuart Marks, Durham, North Carolina, 10 June 1994.

108. Interview with Crispin Siachibuye, chief prosecutor NPWS, Chilanga, Zambia, 12 November 1991.

109. Ibid. Also, interview with Gilson Kaweche, deputy director – NPWS, Chilanga, Zambia, 10 October 1991. Lewis and Alpert claim that the number of weapons

and illegal hunters seized has "increased notably." Lewis and Alpert, "International Safari Hunting," p. 7.

110. Arrests would also not decline if rural residents were uninformed about the ADMADE program. Given locals' generally rapid response to economic incentives (e.g., agriculture), it is unlikely that lack of information is the cause of the sustained level of arrests made by the Wildlife Department.

111. Interview with Crispin Siachibuye. See also DeGeorges, "ADMADE," p. 70.

112. DeGeorges, "ADMADE," p. 54.

113. Interview with Stuart Marks, Durham, North Carolina, 10 June 1994.

114. DeGeorges, "ADMADE," p. 70.

115. LIRDP probably delivered more benefits to the project area's inhabitants because it was better funded and covered a smaller region.

116. Cash is a scarce resource in African rural areas generally. Participation in or use of projects that require cash payment is a sure way of reducing the number of people willing to take part.

117. The very first LIRDP review mission warned the program against trying to change locals' resource use with widely distributed community level projects (although the report does not discuss the theoretical implications of offering public goods to reward individual behavior). See World Conservation Union, *First Review Mission*, p. 87.

118. J. M. Buchanan, *The Demand and Supply of Public Goods* (Chicago: Rand McNally, 1968). If the supply of these goods is decreased by crowding, then they could be characterized as common-pool resources. The salient feature here is that both public goods and common-pool resources are nonexcludable. See Elinor Ostrom, Roy Gardner, and James Walker, *Rules, Games, and Common-Pool Resources* (Ann Arbor: University of Michigan Press, 1994).

119. Of course, the models presented are simplifications of the reality of complex community-level interactions; scouts and residents confront a larger array of choices than the ones presented here. One important choice excluded by the games is collusion, a phenomenon endemic to the scout/resident relationship. Confronted with the social problems resulting from arresting a local (e.g., exclusion from community life) and faced with the uncertainties of government support (some ADMADE scouts waited months for their pay and rations), scouts may work with local hunters to secure meat. Residents caught in the act of hunting will frequently bribe their way out of arrest. Scouts and residents can each gain from a strategy of collaboration rather than conflict.

120. The information from this section comes from L. Talbot and P. Olindo, "The Maasai Mara and Amboseli Reserves," in Agnes Kiss, ed., *Living with Wildlife: Wildlife Resource Management with Local Participation in Africa* (Washington, D.C.: World Bank, 1990), pp. 67–74; and David Western, "Ecosystem Conservation and Rural Development: The Case of Amboseli," in David Western and R. Michael Wright, eds., *Natural Connections: Perspectives in Community-Based Conservation* (Washington, D.C.: Island Press, 1994), pp. 15–52.

121. Talbot and Olindo, "Maasai Mara," p. 69.

122. Western, "Ecosystem Conservation," p. 17.

123. David Western attributed a drastic decline of lion populations in the Amboseli area to poisoning by the Maasai. See Jane Perlez, "An African Park in Peril," *The New York Times*, 19 May 1991.

124. For descriptions of daily interactions with wildlife in rural Zimbabwe, see especially Richard Hasler, *Agriculture, Foraging and Wildlife Resource Use in Africa* (London: Kegan Paul, 1996).

125. J. H. Peterson, "CAMPFIRE: A Zimbabwean Approach to Sustainable Development and Community Empowerment through Wildlife Utilization" (Zimbabwe: Centre for Applied Social Science, 1991), p. 73 (manuscript).

126. Ibid., pp. 199–121.
127. James C. Murombedzi, *Decentralization or Recentralization? Implementing CAMPFIRE in the Omay Communal Lands of the Nyaminyami District*, Working Paper No. 2 (Harare: Centre for Applied Social Science, May 1992), p. 36.
128. Ibid.
129. Ibid.
130. Leslie A. King, *Inter-Organisational Dynamics in Natural Resources Management: A Study of CAMPFIRE Implementation in Zimbabwe*, Occasional Paper Series – NRM (Harare: Centre for Applied Social Science, 1994), p. 30.
131. Ibid., p. 33. See also Murombedzi, *Decentralization or Recentralization?*, p. 44.
132. Murombedzi, *Decentralization or Recentralization?*, p. 44.
133. Peterson, "CAMPFIRE: A Zimbabwean Approach," pp. 43–44.
134. J. H. Peterson, 1991, *A Proto-CAMPFIRE Initiative in Mahenye Ward, Chipinge District: Development of a Wildlife Utilization Programme in Response to Community Needs*, Occasional Paper Series – NRM (Harare: Centre for Applied Social Science, 1992), p. 15.
135. Africa Resources Trust and the CAMPFIRE Association, *Zimbabwe's CAMPFIRE: Empowering Rural Communities for Conservation and Development* (Harare: The Trust/the Association, 1996), p. 4.
136. Murombedzi, *Decentralization or Recentralization?*, p. 44.
137. Ibid., p. 16; see also King, *Inter-Organisational Dynamics*, p. 28. Some locals view CAMPFIRE areas just as they do national parks. See Vupenyu Dzingirai, *Take Back Your CAMPFIRE: A Study of Local Level Perceptions to Electric Fencing in the Framework of Binga's CAMPFIRE Program*, Centre for Applied Social Sciences Occasional Paper Series – NRM (Harare: University of Zimbabwe 1995).
138. Peterson, *CAMPFIRE: A Zimbabwean Approach*, p. 78; Murombedzi, *Decentralization or Recentralization?*, p. 37; King, *Inter-Organisational Dynamics*, p. 21.
139. Lewis and Alpert assert that "the evidence that [the money from] safari hunting has benefited wildlife conservation is mostly indirect. The establishment of Wildlife Management Units clearly had improved capacity to enforce hunting regulations by NPWS and monitor resource management problems." See Lewis and Alpert, "International Safari Hunting," pp. 6–7.
140. Marshall Murphree calls our attention to the disingenuous use of labels to disguise conventional wildlife policy: " 'Participation' and 'involvement' turn out to mean the co-optation of local elites and leadership for exogenously-derived programmes; 'decentralization' turns out to mean simply the addition of another obstructive administrative layer to the bureaucratic hierarchy which governs wildlife management." See Marshall W. Murphree, *Community Conservation and Wildlife Management outside Protected Areas: Southern African Experiences and Perspectives: Implications for Policy Formation: A Report to the African Wildlife Foundation* (22 August 1990), p. 8.
141. David Throup, *The Economic and Social Origins of the Mau Mau* (Athens: Ohio University Press, 1987). See also Vail, *The Creation of Tribalism*; Kathryn Firmin-Sellers, "Custom and Capitalism: The Evolution of Property Rights in the Gold Coast, 1927–1957" (Ph.D. dissertation, Duke University, 1993).
142. See, for example, James C. Scott, *The Moral Economy of the Peasant* (New Haven, Conn.: Yale University Press, 1976); a closely related analysis of the "economy of affection" can be found in Goran Hyden, *Beyond Ujamaa: Underdevelopment and an Uncaptured Peasantry* (Berkeley: University of California Press, 1980).
143. Many scholars refute the assumptions of the moral economy school and, instead, focus on the incentive-driven actions of individuals. Popkin critiques Scott's "moral economy" in Popkin, *Rational Peasant*, pp. 1–28.

144. Discussions of the difficulty of protest for the poor and powerless abound. Important contributions to this literature are Frances Fox Piven and Richard Cloward, *Poor People's Movement* (New York: Vintage Books, 1977); and Mayer N. Zald and John D. McCarthy, *Social Movements in an Organizational Society* (New Brunswick and Oxford: Transaction Books, 1987).

145. Such a tactic resonates with the resistance activities of peasants worldwide. See James C. Scott, *Weapons of the Weak: Everyday Form of Peasant Resistance* (New Haven: Yale University Press, 1986).

146. The most powerful chief was probably the *lewanika* (king) of Barotseland (now Western Province). The lewanikas controlled a significant area of land and administered it through a vast system of subchiefs and headman. The strong political structures in Barotseland allowed the Lozis to sign a separate treaty with the British, preserving a certain amount of Lozi independence from colonial rule. This independence ended in 1969, when Kaunda terminated any last vestiges of self-government. See, for example, Max Gluckman, *Essay on Lozi Land and Royal Property*, Rhodes–Livingstone Institute Papers no. 10 (Manchester: Manchester University Press, 1968); L. H. Gann, *The Birth of a Plural Society* (Manchester: Manchester University Press, 1958); Gwyn Prins, *The Hidden Hippopotamus: Reappraisal in an African History: The Early Colonial Experience in Western Zambia* (London: Cambridge University Press, 1980).

147. Tonga society did not include chiefs before the arrival of the British. However, after the British designated chiefs, they quickly flexed their new European-backed muscle. See Gann, *Birth of a Plural Society*, p. 230.

148. Marks, *Large Mammals and a Brave People*, p. 33. See also Mwelwa Musambachime, "Development and Growth of the Fishing Industry in Mweru, Luapula 1920–1964" (Ph.D. Dissertation, University of Wisconsin-Madison 1981), p. 206; Gann, *Birth of a Plural Society*, p. 292; Nawa Nawa, "The Role of Traditional Authority in the Conservation of Natural Resources in the Western Province of Zambia, 1878–1989" (M.A. thesis, University of Zambia, 1990).

149. Nawa, "Role of Traditional Authority," pp. 5–32.

150. Ibid. Nawa demonstrates that the Litunga's rules regarding wildlife use allowed him to monopolize certain resources. The rules also enriched him, because he controlled the region's access to the ivory market. The Litunga's ability to dominate wildlife use was a result of his regulation of guns and ammunition, a relatively small population in his region, locals' lack of access to markets for game meat and ivory, and his extensive system of subchiefs and headmen who enforced his edicts. The Litunga rewarded these deputies' efforts to monitor and enforce the rules with their own access to wildlife. Importantly, Nawa suggests that the continuous hunting parties of the Litunga and his subchiefs were responsible for the drastic decline of hippopotami, an animal reserved for the monarch, in the Western Province. Rather than conserve these animals, the Litunga's control allowed him and his followers a monopoly on hunting them. Their innumerable forays led to such a collapse of hippo populations in the late 1930s that the British asked the Litunga to ban hippo hunting for five years. Eventually, outside markets for animal products and firearms undermined the Litunga's control over most other animal species.

151. Henry S. Meebelo, *Reaction to Colonialism: A Prelude to the Politics of Independence in Northern Zambia, 1893–1939* (Manchester: Manchester University Press, 1971), p. 186.

152. Richard Hall, *Zambia 1890–1964: The Colonial Period* (London: Longman, 1976), pp. 43–50.

153. Marks, *Imperial Lion*, pp. 105–110. BSAC administrators knew that they did

not have the staff necessary to enforce their hunting regulations, which were ignored by most Africans and Europeans.

154. Hall, *Zambia*, p. 52.
155. Marks, *Large Mammals*, p. 33.
156. Meebelo, *Reaction*, p. 205.
157. Marks, *Imperial Lion*, p. 29. See also Marks, *Large Mammals*, p. 77.
158. Gann, *A History*, p. 229.
159. Meebelo, *Reaction*, p. 205.
160. Ibid., pp. 186–228.
161. Samuel N. Chipungu, *The State, Technology and Peasant Differentiation in Zambia: A Case Study of the Southern Province, 1930–1986* (Lusaka: Historical Association of Zambia, 1988), p. 92.
162. Ibid., pp. 205–7. In an effort to control chiefs' more egregious acts of excessive punishment and financial impropriety and to strengthen indirect rule, the colonial government passed additional ordinances in 1936. One effect of the new laws was the establishment of Native treasuries. Without adequate sources of revenue, many chiefs did not actively pursue their official duties. British administrators thought they could reduce this apathy by allowing each Native Authority to raise and keep income from court fees, fines, and taxes on bicycles, dogs, arms, and game licenses. The colonial government received 10 percent of this tax income and required the Authority to account for the sources and expenditure of the monies. According to their British principals, chiefs with "good instincts" were those that served the colonial government's interests by efficiently collecting taxes, maintaining law and order, mobilizing unpaid labor for soil conservation projects, and participating in and encouraging agricultural development. To improve indirect rule further after World War II, the British eliminated some minor chieftaincies, merged others, and appointed councilors to help chiefs with administrative tasks. See Chipungu, *The State*, pp. 91–94; Gann, *A History*, p. 292.
163. Marks, *Imperial Lion*, p. 29. See also Gann, *A History*, p. 379.
164. Hall, *Zambia*, p. 55.
165. The colonial government hired game control officers in the 1930s and established a Game Department in 1940, realizing that "in a country where vast rural areas carry small populations, the wild life in one shape or another is a main economic force as much as is the soil or water supply." See Northern Rhodesia Game and Tsetse Control Department, *Progress Report to 31st December, 1943* (Lusaka: Government Printer, n.d.), pp. 1–2.
166. Hall, *Zambia*, pp. 143–44. This was despite UNIP and the ANC's promises to reserve significant authority for chiefs after independence.
167. Republic of Zambia, *Chiefs: Chapter 479 of the Laws of Zambia* (Lusaka: Government Printer, 1965), pp. 1–5.
168. The measure that reorganized local government machinery was the 1965 Local Government Act. See Michael Bratton, *The Local Politics of Rural Development: Peasant and Party-State in Zambia* (Hanover, N.H.: University Press of New England, 1980), p. 33. UNIP's later (1980) attempt to decentralize and streamline government by amalgamating party and government structures at the district level allowed chiefs to occupy at most only one of twelve seats on the District Council. See Republic of Zambia, National Institute of Public Administration, "Decentralisation: A Guide to Integrated Local Administration," 1981 (mimeo.).
169. Bratton, *Local Politics*, p. 76.
170. Marks, *Large Mammals*, p. 33.

6. EXPLORING THE POLITICAL ECONOMY OF AFRICAN WILDLIFE POLICY

1. See, for example, Susan Shirk, *The Political Logic of Economic Reform in China* (Berkeley: University of California Press, 1993); Jerry F. Hough, "Understanding Gorbachev: The Importance of Politics," *Soviet Economy* 7 (1991): 89–109.
2. The use of general categories as explanations for political behavior seems to be reemerging in the study of African political transitions. See, for example, Michael Bratton and Nicholas van de Walle, "Neopatrimonial Regimes and Political Transitions," *World Politics* 46 (1994): 453–89.
3. Important contributions include David Anderson and Richard Grove, eds., *Conservation in Africa: People, Policies and Practice* (Cambridge: Cambridge University Press, 1987); E. I. Steinhart, "Hunters, Poachers and Gamekeepers: Towards a Social History of Hunting in Colonial Kenya," *Journal of African History* 30 (1989): 247–64; John M. MacKenzie, *The Empire of Nature* (Manchester: Manchester University Press, 1988).
4. E. O. A. Asibey, "Wildlife as a Source of Protein South of the Sahara," *Biological Conservation* 6 (1974): 32–39; F. A. Addo, E. O. A. Asibey, K. Quist, and M. B. Dyson, *The Economic Contribution of Women and Protected Areas: Ghana and the Bushmeat Trade* (Accra: Republic of Ghana/Washington, D.C.: World Bank, 1992); S. Anstey, "Wildlife Utilisation in Liberia" (Gland: WWF International, 1991) (mimeo).
5. This is especially true for Kenya, Zimbabwe, and South Africa.
6. Henri Koch, *Magie et Chasse dans la Foret Camerounaise* (Paris: Berger-Levrault, 1968); Stuart A. Marks, *Large Mammals and a Brave People: Subsistence Hunters in Zambia* (Seattle: University of Washington Press, 1976); Marks, *The Imperial Lion: The Human Dimensions of Wildlife Management in Central Africa* (Boulder: Westview Press, 1984).
7. Anderson and Grove, *Conservation in Africa*; Jonathan McShane and Thomas Adams, *The Myth of Wild Africa* (New York: Norton, 1992).
8. Valentine U. James, ed., *Environmental and Economic Dilemmas of Developing Countries: Africa in the Twenty-First Century* (Westport, Conn.: Praeger, 1994).
9. Applying Hirschman's scheme, we would find that for most of the Zambians living in the rural areas, loyalty to the government's wildlife policy made little sense, voicing opposition allowed for some influence over the policy debate, but the most effective strategy by far was to exit, that is, to hunt and trade wildlife illegally. See Albert O. Hirschman, *Exit, Voice, and Loyalty: Response to Decline in Firms, Organizations, and States* (Cambridge, Mass.: Harvard University Press, 1970).

Bibliography

BOOKS AND ARTICLES

Abel, Nick, and Piers Blaikie. "Elephants, People Parks and Development: The Case of the Luangwa Valley, Zambia." *Environmental Management* 10 (1986): 735–751.

Adams, Jonathan S., and Thomas O. McShane. *The Myth of Wild Africa: Conservation without Illusion.* London and New York: Norton, 1992.

Adamson, David. *Defending the World.* London: I. B. Tauris & Co., 1990.

Addo, F. A. et al. *The Economic Contribution of Women and Protected Areas: Ghana and the Bushmeat Trade.* Accra: Republic of Ghana/Washington: The World Bank, 1992.

Alchian, Armen. "Uncertainty, Evolution and Economic Theory." *Journal of Political Economy* 58 (1950): 211–221.

Alchian, Armen, and Harold Demsetz. "Production, Information Costs and Economic Organization." In *The Economic Nature of the Firm*, ed. Louis Putterman, 111–134. New York: Cambridge University Press, 1986.

Aldrich, John H., and Forrest D. Nelson. *Linear Probability, Logit and Probit Models.* Beverly Hills, Calif.: Sage, 1984.

Alpers, E. A. *The East African Slave Trade.* Nairobi: East African Publishing House, 1967. *Ivory and Slaves: Changing Patterns of International Trade in East Central Africa to the Later Nineteenth Century.* Berkeley: University of California Press, 1975.

Alpert, Peter, and Paul Andre DeGeorges. "Midterm Evaluation of the Zambia Natural Resources Management Project." 1992. Mimeo.

Amsden, Alice. "The State and Taiwan's Economic Development." In *Toward a Political Economy of Development*, ed. Robert H. Bates. Berkeley and Los Angeles: University of California Press, 1988.

Anderson, David, and Richard Grove, eds. *Conservation in Africa: People, Policies and Practice.* Cambridge: Cambridge University Press, 1987.
"The Scramble for Eden: Past, Present and Future in African Conservation." In *Conservation in Africa: People, Policies and Practice*, 1–12. Cambridge: Cambridge University Press, 1987.

Anstey, S. "Wildlife Utilisation in Liberia." Gland: WWF International, 1991. Mimeo.

Appleby, Paul H. *Policy and Administration.* Tuscaloosa: University of Alabama Press, 1949.

Bibliography

Apter, David E., and Carl G. Rosberg, eds. "Changing African Perspectives." In *Political Development and the New Realism in Sub-Saharan Africa.* Charlottesville and London: University Press of Virginia, 1994.

Ascher, William, and Robert Healy. *Natural Resource Policymaking in Developing Countries.* Durham and London: Duke University Press, 1990.

Asibey, E. O. A. "Wildlife as a Source of Protein South of the Sahara." *Biological Conservation* 6 (1974): 32–39.

Azarya, Victor. "Reordering State-Society Relations: Incorporation and Disengagement." In *The Precarious Balance: State and Society in Africa,* eds. Donald Rothchild and Naomi Chazan. Boulder, Colo.: Westview Press, 1988.

Barbier, Edward et al. *Elephants, Economics and Ivory.* London: Earthscan Publications, 1990.

Bardach, Eugene. *The Implementation Game.* Cambridge, Mass.: MIT Press, 1977.

Barkan, Joel D., ed. *Politics and Public Policy in Kenya and Tanzania.* New York: Praeger, 1984.

———. "The Electoral Process and Peasant-State Relations in Kenya." In *Elections in Independent Africa,* ed. Fred M. Hayward, 213–237. Boulder, Colo.: Westview Press, 1987.

———. "The Rise and Fall of a Governance Realm in Kenya." In *Governance and Politics in Africa,* eds. Goran Hyden and Michael Bratton, 167–192. Boulder and London: Lynne Rienner, 1992.

Barnes, J. A. "The Fort Jameson Ngoni." In *Seven Tribes of British Central Africa,* eds. Elizabeth Colson and Name Gluckman, 194–252. Manchester: Manchester University Press, 1961.

Barzel, Yoram. "An Economic Analysis of Slavery." *Journal of Law and Economics* 20 (1977): 87–110.

———. "Measurement Cost and the Organization of Markets." *Journal of Law and Economics* 25 (1985): 27–48.

———. *Economic Analysis of Property Rights.* Cambridge: Cambridge University Press, 1989.

Bates, Robert H. *Rural Responses to Industrialization.* New Haven and London: Yale University Press, 1976.

———. *Essays on the Political Economy of Rural Africa.* Cambridge: Cambridge University Press, 1983.

———. "Contra Contractarianism: Some Reflections on the New Institutionalism." *Politics and Society* 16 (1988): 387–401.

———. *Beyond the Miracle of the Market: The Political Economy of Agrarian Development in Kenya.* Cambridge: Cambridge University Press, 1989.

———. "Macropolitical Economy in the Field of Development." In *Perspectives on Positive Political Economy,* eds. James E. Alt and Kenneth A. Shepsle, 31–54. Cambridge: Cambridge University Press, 1990.

———. "Institutions as Investments." Durham, N.C.: Duke University Program in Political Economy Working Papers, 1990.

———. "Social Dilemmas and Rational Individuals: An Essay on the New Institutionalism." Durham, N.C.: Duke University Program in Political Economy Working Papers, 1992.

Bates, Robert H., and Paul Collier. "The Politics and Economics of Policy Reform in Zambia." In *Political and Economic Interactions in Economic Policy Reform,* eds. Robert H. Bates and Anne O. Krueger. Cambridge, Mass.: Blackwell, 1993.

Bibliography

Baumol, William J., and Wallace E. Oates. *The Theory of Environmental Policy*. Cambridge: Cambridge University Press, 1988.

Baylies, Carolyn. "The State and Class Formation in Zambia." Ph.D. dissertation, University of Madison–Wisconsin, 1978.

Baylies, Carolyn, and Morris Szeftel. "Elections in a One-Party State." In *The Dynamics of the One-Party State*, eds. Cherry Gertzel, Carolyn Baylies, and Morris Szeftel, 29–57. Manchester: Manchester University Press, 1984.

Becker, Gary S. "A Theory of the Allocation of Time." *Economic Journal* 75 (September 1965): 494–517.

A Treatise on the Family. Cambridge, Mass.: Harvard University Press, 1985.

Beinart, William, and Peter Coates. *Environment and History: The Taming of Nature in the USA and South Africa*. London: Routledge, 1995.

Bell, Richard H. V. "Conservation with a Human Face: Conflict and Resolution in African Land Use Planning." In *Conservation in Africa: People, Policies and Practice*, eds. David Anderson and Richard Grove, 79–102. Cambridge: Cambridge University Press, 1987.

Bell, Richard H. V., and E. McShane-Caluzi, eds. *Conservation and Wildlife Management in Africa*. Washington: U.S. Peace Corps, 1984.

Benson, C. W. et al. *The Birds of Zambia*. London: Collins, 1971.

Bigalke, R. C. "Mammals." In *Biogeography and Ecology of Southern Africa*, ed. M. J. A. Werger. The Hague: Junk by Publishers, 1978.

Bjornlund, Eric, Larry Garber, and Clark Gibson. *The October 31, 1991 National Elections in Zambia*. Washington: National Democratic Institute for International Affairs, 1992.

Bonner, Raymond. *At the Hand of Man: Peril and Hope for Africa's Wildlife*. New York: Knopf, 1993.

Bratton, Michael. "Beyond the State: Civil and Associational Life in Africa." *World Politics* (April 1989): 407–430.

"Zambia Starts Over." *Journal of Democracy* 3 (1992): 81–94.

Bratton, Michael, and Nicholas van de Walle. "Neopatrimonial Regimes and Political Transitions." *World Politics* 46 (1994): 453–489.

Buchanan, J. M. *The Demand and Supply of Public Goods*. Chicago: Rand McNally, 1968.

Buchanan, J. M., Robert D. Tollison, and Gordon Tullock, eds. *Toward a Theory of a Rent-Seeking Society*. College Station: Texas A&M Press, 1980.

Burdette, Marcia M. "The Dynamics of Nationalization between Multinational Companies and Peripheral States: Negotiations between AMAX, Inc., and the Anglo-American Corporation of South Africa, Ltd., and the Government of the Republic of Zambia." Ph.D. dissertation, Columbia University, 1979.

Zambia: Between Two Worlds. Boulder, Colo.: Westview Press, 1988.

Caldwell, Lynton Keith. *Environment: A Challenge to Modern Society*. Garden City, N.Y.: Doubleday, 1971.

International Environmental Policy: Emergence and Dimensions. Durham and London: Duke University Press, 1990.

Calvert, Randall. "Coordination and Power: The Foundation of Leadership among Rational Legislators." Chicago: American Political Science Association Annual Meeting, 1991. Mimeo.

Calvert, Randall, Mark Moran, and Barry Weingast. "Congressional Influence over Policy Making." In *Congress: Structure and Policy*, eds. Mathew

Bibliography

McCubbins and Terry Sullivan. Cambridge: Cambridge University Press, 1987.

Carruthers, Jane. *The Kruger National Park: A Social and Political History.* Pietermaritzburg: University of Natal Press, 1995.

Carter, Gwendolyn, ed. *African One-Party States.* Ithaca, N.Y.: Cornell University Press, 1962.

Caughly, G., and J. Goddard. "Abundance and Distribution of Elephants in the Luangwa Valley, Zambia." *East African Wildlife Journal* 13 (1975): 39–48.

Chabal, Patrick, ed. *Political Domination in Africa.* Cambridge: Cambridge University Press, 1986.

Chazan, Naomi, and Donald Rothchild, eds. *The Precarious Balance: State and Society in Africa.* Boulder, Colo.: Westview Press, 1988.

Cheung, Steven N. S. "A Theory of Price Control." *Journal of Law and Economics* 12 (1974): 23–45.

"The Contractual Nature of the Firm." *Journal of Law and Economics* 17 (1983): 53–71.

Chikulo, Bornwell. "The 1978 Zambian Elections." In *The Evolving Structure of Zambian Society: Proceedings of a seminar held in the Centre of African Studies, University of Edinburgh, 30th and 31st May, 1980.* Edinburgh: Centre of African Studies, University of Edinburgh, 1980.

"The Impact of Elections in Zambia's One Party Second Republic." *Africa Today* 35 (1988): 37–49.

Child, Graham. *Wildlife and People: The Zimbabwean Success.* Harare: Wisdom Foundation, 1995.

Chipungu, Samuel N. *The State Technology and Peasant Differentiation in Zambia: A Case Study of the Southern Province, 1930–1986.* Lusaka, Zambia: Historical Association of Zambia, 1988.

Chubb, John E. "The Political Economy of Federalism." *American Political Science Review* 79 (1985): 994–1015.

Clark, J. Desmond, and Steven A. Brandt. *From Hunters to Farmers: The Cause and Consequences of Food Production in Africa.* Berkeley: University of California Press, 1984.

Coase, Ronald H. "The Economic Nature of the Firm." *Econometrica* 4 (November 1937): 386–405.

"The Problem of Social Cost." *Journal of Law and Economics* 3 (1960): 1–44.

Cocheba, Donald J., and William A. Langford. "Wildlife Valuation: The Collective Good Aspect of Hunting." *Land Economics* 54(4) (November 1978): 490–504.

Colson, Elizabeth. "The Plateau Tonga of Northern Rhodesia." In *Seven Tribes of British Central Africa*, eds. Elizabeth Colson and Max Gluckman, 94–162. Manchester: Manchester University Press, 1961.

The Social Organization of the Gwembe Tonga. Manchester: Manchester University Press, 1960.

Colson, Elizabeth, and Max Gluckman, eds. *Seven Tribes of British Central Africa.* Manchester: Manchester University Press, 1961.

Cowie, M. *Walk with Lions.* New York: Macmillan, 1961.

Darling, Frasier. *Wildlife in an African Territory: A Study Made for the Game and Tsetse Control Department of Northern Rhodesia.* London: Oxford University Press, 1960.

Davies, Clarence J. *The Politics of Pollution.* New York: Pegasus, 1970.

Bibliography

Davies, Hywel, ed. *Zambia in Maps*. London: University of London Press, 1971.

DeGeorges, Paul Andre. "ADMADE: An Evaluation Today and the Future Policy Issues and Direction." 1992. Mimeo.

Derman, B. "Environmental NGOs, Dispossession, and the State: The Ideology and Praxis of African Nature and Development." *Human Ecology*, 23(2) (1995): 199–215.

Dix, Anne. *CAMPFIRE: Communal Areas Management Programme for Indigenous Resources, An Annotated Bibliography, 1985–1996*. University of Zimbabwe: Centre for Applied Social Science, June 1996.

Dizard, Jan. *Going Wild: Hunting Animal Rights, and the Contested Meaning of Nature*. Amherst: University of Massachusetts Press, 1994.

Douglas-Hamilton, Iain and Oria. *Battle for the Elephants*. New York: Viking, 1992.

Doyle, Mark. "Leakey to End Great Crusade." *The Guardian*, 15 January 1994.

Drinkwater, M. *The State and Agrarian Change in Zimbabwe's Communal Areas*. London: Macmillan, 1991.

Eggertsson, Thrainn. *Economic Behavior and Institutions*. Cambridge: Cambridge University Press, 1990.

Eisner, Marc A., and Kenneth J. Meier. "Presidential Control versus Bureaucratic Power: Explaining the Reagan Revolution in Antitrust." *American Journal of Political Science* 34 (1990): 269–287.

Elster, Jon. *Explaining Technical Change*. Cambridge: Cambridge University Press, 1983.

Epstein, David, and Sharyn O'Halloran. "Administrative Procedures, Information, and Agency." *American Journal of Political Science* 38 (1994): 697–722.

Evans-Pritchard, E. E. *The Nuer*. London: Oxford University Press, 1947.

Evans, Peter B., Dietrich Rueschemeyer, and Theda Skocpol, eds. *Bringing the State Back In*. Cambridge: Cambridge University Press, 1985.

Falconer, J. *Non-Timber Forest Products in Southern Ghana*. Overseas Development Administration Forestry Series, No. 2. London: Natural Resources Institute, 1992.

Fama, Eugene F., and Michael C. Jensen. "Agency Problems and Residual Claims." *Journal of Law and Economics* 26 (June 1983): 327–349.

"Separation of Ownership and Control." *Journal of Financial Economics* 14 (1985): 101–119.

Firmin-Sellers, Kathryn. "Custom and Capitalism: The Evolution of Property Rights in the Gold Coast, 1927–1957." Ph.D. dissertation, Duke University, 1993.

Ford, John. *The Role of Trypanosomiasis in African Ecology*. London: Oxford University Press, 1971.

Foss, Phillip O. *Politics and Ecology*. Belmont, Calif.: Duxbury Press, 1972.

Gann, L. H. *A History of Northern Rhodesia: Early Days to 1953*. London: Chatto and Windus, 1964.

"Malawii, Zambia, and Zimbabwe." In *Politics and Government in African State, 1960–1985*, eds. Peter Duignan and Robert H. Jackson, 162–201. London: Croom Helm, 1986.

Gertzel, Cherry. *The Politics of Independent Kenya, 1963–1968*. Evanston, Ill.: Northwestern University Press, 1970.

"Dissent and Authority in the Zambian One-Party State." In *The Dynamics*

Bibliography

of the One-Party State, eds. Cherry Gertzel, Carolyn Baylies, and Morris Szeftel, 79–118. Manchester: Manchester University Press, 1984.

Gilbert, Fred, and Donald Dodds. *The Philosophy and Practice of Wildlife Management*. Florida: Krieger Publishing, 1987.

Gluckman, Max. "The Lozi of Barotseland in North-Western Rhodesia." In *Seven Tribes of British Central Africa*, eds. Elizabeth Colson and Max Gluckman, 1–93. Manchester: Manchester University Press, 1961.

Gould, D. J. "The Administration of Underdevelopment." In *Zaire: The Political Economy of Underdevelopment*, ed. Guy Gran, 87–107. New York: Praeger, 1979.

Gray, Gary. *Wildlife and People: The Human Dimensions of Wildlife Ecology*. Urbana and Chicago: University of Illinois Press, 1993.

Greve, Michael S., and Fred L. Smith, Jr., eds. *Environmental Politics: Public Costs, Private Benefits*. New York: Praeger, 1992.

Grindle, Merilee. *Bureaucrats, Politicians, and Peasants in Mexico: A Case Study in Public Policy*. Berkeley: University of California Press, 1977.

Grove, Richard. "Early Themes in African Conservation: The Cape in the Nineteenth Century." In *Conservation in Africa: People, Policies and Practice*, eds. David Anderson and Richard Grove, 21–39. Cambridge: Cambridge University Press, 1987.

Green Imperialism, Colonial Expansion, Tropical Island Edens, and the Origins of Environmentalism, 1600–1860. New York: Cambridge University Press, 1995.

Hall, Peter A., and Rosemary Taylor. "Political Science and the Four New Institutionalisms." Toronto: American Political Science Association Annual Meeting, 1994. Mimeo.

Hanks, J. *Mammals of Zambia*. Government of Zambia: National Tourist Bureau, 1972.

Hardin, Garrett. "The Tragedy of the Commons." *Science* 162 (December 1968): 1243–1248.

Hardin, Russell. "Difficulties in the Notion of Economic Rationality." *Social Science Information* 19 (1984): 453–467.

Hasler, Richard. "Cultural Perceptions and Conflicting Rights to Wildlife in the Zambezi Valley." In *Elephants and Whales: Resources for Whom?*, eds. Milton Freeman and Urs Kreuter. Basel, Switzerland: Gordon and Breach Science Publishers, 1994.

Agriculture, Foraging and Wildlife Resource Use in Africa. London: Kegan Paul, 1996.

Hayek, Friedrich A. "Economics and Knowledge." *Economica* (February 1937): 33–54.

"The Use of Knowledge in Society." *American Economic Review* (September 1945): 519–530.

Hays, Samuel P. *Beauty, Health and Permanence: Environmental Policy in the United States, 1955–1985*. Cambridge: Cambridge University Press, 1987.

Heady, Ferrel. *Public Administration: A Comparative Perspective*. New York: Dekker, 1984.

Henning, Daniel. *Environmental Policy and Administration*. Elsevier, N.Y.: American Press, 1974.

Herbst, Jeffrey. *State Politics in Zimbabwe*. Berkeley: University of California Press, 1990.

Heymans, J. C., and J. S. Maurice. *Introduction a l'Exploitation de la Faune*

Bibliography

come Resource Alimentaire en Republique du Zaire. Forum Universitaire. 2 (1973): 6–12.

Hiltzik, Michael A. "Public Backs Noted Paleontologist Leakey." *The Los Angeles Times*, May 8, 1989.

Hirschman, Albert O. *Exit, Voice, and Loyalty: Response to Decline in Firms, Organizations, and States.* Cambridge, Mass.: Harvard University Press, 1970.

Hill, Kevin A. "Interest Groups and the Politics of the Environment: Wildlife Conservation Policy, the State, and Organized Interests in Zimbabwe." Ph.D. dissertation, University of Florida, 1993.

Hobbes, Thomas. *Leviathan: or the Matter, Forme and Power of a Commonwealth, Ecclesiastical and Civil.* New York: Collier, 1962.

Hodgson, Geoffrey M. "Institutional Economics: Surveying the Old and New." *Metroeconomica* 44 (1993): 1–28.

Holmstrom, Bengt. "Moral Hazard in Teams." *Bell Journal of Economics* 13 (1982): 324–340.

Homewood, K. M., and W. A. Rogers. *Maasailand Ecology.* Cambridge: Cambridge University Press, 1991.

Horn, Murray J. "The Political Economy of Public Administration." Ph.D. dissertation, Harvard University, 1988.

Horn, Murray J., and Kenneth A. Shepsle. "Commentary on: Administrative Arrangements and the Political Control of Agencies." *Journal of Law, Economics and Organization* 8 (1992): 53–67.

Hornsby, Charles. "The Social Structure of the National Assembly in Kenya, 1963–83." *Journal of Modern African Studies* 27(2) (1989), pp. 275–296.

Hyden, Goran. *Beyond Ujamaa: Underdevelopment and an Uncaptured Peasantry.* Berkeley: University of California Press, 1980.

Jackson, Robert H., and Carl G. Rosberg. *Personal Rule in Black Africa: Prince, Autocrat, Prophet, Tyrant.* Berkeley and Los Angeles: University of California Press, 1982.

"The States of East Africa: Tanzania, Uganda, and Kenya." In *Politics and Government in African States*, eds. Peter Duignan and Robert H. Jackson. Stanford, Calif.: Hoover Institution Press, 1986.

"The Political Economy of African Personal Rule." In *Political Development and the New Realism in Sub-Saharan Africa*, eds. David E. Apter and Carl G. Rosberg. Charlottesville and London: University Press of Virginia, 1994.

James, Valentine U., ed. *Environmental and Economic Dilemmas of Developing Countries: Africa in the Twenty-first Century.* Westport, Conn.: Praeger, 1994.

Jansen, Doris. *Trade, Exchange Rate and Agricultural Pricing Policies in Zambia.* Washington: The World Bank, 1988.

Jensen, Michael C. "Separation of Ownership and Control." *Journal of Financial Economics* 14 (1985): 101–119.

Jensen, Michael C., and William H. Meckling. "Theory of the Firm: Managerial Behavior, Agency Costs and Capital Structure." *Journal of Financial Economics* 3 (October 1976): 305–360.

"The Theory of the Firm: Managerial Behavior, Agency Costs and Ownership Structure." In *The Economic Nature of the Firm*, ed. Louis Putterman, 209–249. New York: Cambridge University Press, 1986.

Jewell, P., and S. Holt, eds. *Problems in Management of Locally Abundant Wild Animals.* New York: Academic Press, 1981.

Bibliography

Johnson, Ronald N., and Gary D. Libecap. "Agency Growth, Salaries, and the Protected Bureaucrat." *Economic Inquiry* 27 (1989): 53–67.

Joseph, Richard A. *Democracy and Prebendal Politics in Nigeria: The Rise and Fall of the Second Republic.* Cambridge: Cambridge University Press, 1987.

Kalt, Joseph. "Where's the Glue? Institutional Bases of American Indian Economic Development." Cambridge, Mass.: John F. Kennedy School of Government Working papers, 1991. Mimeo.

Kamieniecki, Sheldon, ed. *Environmental Politics in the International Arena: Movements, Parties, Organizations, and Policy.* Albany: State University of New York Press, 1993.

Kariuki, James. " 'Paramoia': Anatomy of a Dictatorship in Kenya." *Journal of Contemporary African Studies,* 14(1) (1996), pp. 70–86.

Katzenstein, Peter. *Small States and World Markets.* Ithaca, N.Y.: Cornell University Press, 1985.

Kay, G. "Chief Kabala's Village." Lusaka: Rhodes-Livingstone Paper no. 35, 1964.

Keller, Edmund J. "The State in Contemporary Africa: A Critical Assessment of Theory and Practice." In *Comparative Political Dynamics: Global Research Perspectives,* eds. Dankwart A. Rustow and Kenneth P. Erickson. New York: HarperCollins, 1991.

Key, V. O. *Southern Politics in State and Nation.* New York: Knopf, 1949.

King, Leslie A. "Inter-Organisational Dynamics in Natural Resources Management: A Study of CAMPFIRE Implementation in Zimbabwe." Centre for Applied Social Science, Occasional Paper Series NRM, University of Zimbabwe, 1994.

Kisangani, Emizet. "Social Divisions and the Massacre of Elephants in Zaire." In *Elephants and Whales: Resources for Whom?,* eds. Milton Freeman and Urs Kreuter, 73–84. Basel, Switzerland: Gordon and Breach Science Publishers, 1994.

Kiser, Larry L., and Elinor Ostrom. "The Three Worlds of Action: A Metatheoretical Synthesis of Institutional Approaches." In *Strategies of Political Inquiry,* ed. Elinor Ostrom, 179–222. Beverly Hills, Calif.: Sage Publications, 1982.

Knight, Frank H. *Risk, Uncertainty and Profit.* Boston: Houghton Mifflin, 1921.

Knight, Jack. *Institutions and Social Conflict.* Cambridge: Cambridge University Press, 1992.

Knight, Jack, and Itai Sened. *Explaining Social Institutions.* Ann Arbor: University of Michigan Press, 1995.

Koch, Henri. *Magie et Chasse dans la Foret Camerounaise.* Paris: Berger-Levrault, 1968.

Kreps, David M. *A Course in Microeconomic Theory.* Princeton, N.J.: Princeton University Press, 1990.

Kreps, David, and R. Wilson. "Reputation and Imperfect Information." *Journal of Economic Theory* 27 (1982): 253–279.

Kreuter, Urs P., and Randy P. Simmons. "Who Owns the Elephant? The Political Economy of Saving the African Elephant." In *Wildlife in the Marketplace,* eds. Terry L. Anderson and Peter J. Hill. Lanham, Md.: Rowman and Littlefield, 1995.

Krueger, Anne O. "The Political Economy of Rent-Seeking." *American Economic Review* 3 (1974): 291–303.

Lambrecht, Franz L. "Aspects of the Evolution and Exology of Tsetse Flies and Trypanosomiasis in Prehistorc African Environments." In *Papers in African*

Bibliography

Prehistory, eds. J. D. Fage and R. A. Oliver, 75–98. Cambridge: Cambridge University Press, 1970.

Lan, D. *Guns and Rain: Guerrilla and Spirit Mediums in Zimbabwe*. Berkeley and Los Angeles: University of California Press, 1985.

Laycock, George. *Diligent Destroyers*. Garden City, N.Y.: Doubleday, 1970.

Leader-Williams, N., and S. D. Albon. "Allocation of Resources for Conservation." *Nature* 336 (1988): 533–535.

Lemarchand, Rene. "The State, the Parallel Economy, and the Changing Structure of Patronage Systems." In *The Precarious Balance: State and Society in Africa*, eds. Donald Rothchild and Naomi Chazan, 149–170. Boulder, Colo.: Westview Press, 1988.

Leonard, David K. *Reaching the Peasant Farmer: Organization Theory and Practice in Kenya*. Chicago: Chicago University Press, 1977.

Levi, Margaret. *Of Rule and Revenue*. Berkeley: University of California Press, 1988.

"A Logic of Institutional Change." In *The Limits of Rationality*, eds. Karen Schweers Cook and M. Levi, 402–418. Chicago and London: University of Chicago Press, 1990.

"Death, Taxes and Bureaucrats." Baltimore: University of Maryland, 1994. Mimeo.

Lewis, Dale. "Profile of a Hunting Area: Mainstay of Zambia's Safari Hunting Industry." 1994. Mimeo.

Lewis, Dale, and Nick Carter, eds. *Voices from Africa*. Washington: World Wildlife Fund, 1993.

Lewis, Dale, and Peter Alpert. "International Safari Hunting: A Green Bullet for African Wildlife?" 1994. Mimeo.

Lewis, David. *Convention*. Cambridge, Mass.: Harvard University Press, 1969.

Libecap, Gary D. *Contracting for Property Rights*. Cambridge: Cambridge University Press, 1989.

Luce, R. D., and Howard Raiffa. *Games and Decisions*. New York: Wiley, 1957.

Lupia, Arthur, and Mathew McCubbins. "Learning from Oversight: Fire Alarms and Police Patrols Reconstructed." *Journal of Law, Economics, and Organization* 10(1) (1994): 96–125.

Lusigi, Walter. "New Approaches to Wildlife Conservation in Kenya." *Ambio* 10(2–3) (1981).

Macey, Jonathan R. "Organizational Design and Political Control of Administrative Agencies." *Journal of Law, Economics and Organization* 8 (1992): 93–110.

MacKelvey, John. *Man Against Tsetse: Struggle for Africa*. Ithaca, N.Y.: Cornell University Press, 1973.

MacKenzie, John M. "Chivalry, Social Darwinism and Ritualised Killing: The Hunting Ethos in Central Africa up to 1914." In *Conservation in Africa: People, Policies and Practice*, eds. David Anderson and Richard Grove, 41–61. Cambridge: Cambridge University Press. 1987.

The Empire of Nature: Hunting, Conservation and British Imperialism. Manchester: Manchester University Press, 1988.

"Experts and Ameteurs Tsetse, Nagana and Sleeping Sickness in East and Central Africa." In *Imperialism and the Natural World*, ed. John M. MacKenzie, 187–212. Manchester: Manchester University Press, 1990.

Mangun, W. R. *American Fish and Wildlife Policy: The Human Dimension*. Carbondale: Southern Illinois Press, 1992.

Bibliography

Marks, Stuart A. *Large Mammals and a Brave People: Subsistence Hunters in Zambia.* Seattle: University of Washington Press, 1976.

The Imperial Lion: The Human Dimensions of Wildlife Management in Central Africa. Boulder, Colo.: Westview Press, 1984.

Martin, D., and B. Johnson. *The Struggle for Zimbabwe: The Chimurenga War.* London: P. Faber and Faber, 1981.

Martin, Rowan. *Communal Areas Management Program for Indigenous Resources (CAMPFIRE).* Harare: Department of National Parks and Wildlife Management, 1986.

Mashaw, Jerry. "Explaining Administrative Process: Normative, Positive, and Critical Stories of Legal Development." *Journal of Law, Economics, and Organization* 6 (1990): 267–298.

Masona, Tafirenyika. "Colonial Game Policy: A Study of the Origin and Administration of Game Policy in Southern Rhodesia—1890–1945." M.A. thesis. University of Zimbabwe, 1987.

Matowanyika, J. Z. Z. "Cast Out of Eden: Peasants Versus Wildlife Policy in Savanna Africa." *Alternatives* 16 (1) (1989): 30–35.

Matzke, Gordon Edwin, and Nontokozo Nabane. "Outcomes of a Community Controlled Wildlife Program in a Zambezi Valley Community." *Human Ecology* 24(1) (1996): 65–85.

Mayers, J. "Getting Back to Bushmeat." *BBC Wildlife* (January 1991): 16.

McCormick, John. *Reclaiming Paradise.* Bloomington: Indiana University Press, 1989.

McCraken, John. "Colonialism, Capitalism and the Ecological Crisis in Malawi: A Reassessment." In *Conservation in Africa,* eds. David Anderson and Richard Grove. Cambridge: Cambridge University Press, 1987.

McCubbins, Mathew D., and Talbot Page. "A Theory of Congressional Delegation." In *Congress: Structure and Policy,* eds. Mathew D. McCubbins and Terry Sullivan, 409–425. Cambridge: Cambridge University Press, 1987.

McCubbins, Mathew D., and Thomas Schwartz. "Congressional Oversight Overlooked: Police Patrols Versus Fire Alarms." *American Journal of Political Science* 28 (1984): 165–179.

McCubbins, Mathew D., and Terry Sullivan, eds. *Congress: Structure and Policy.* Cambridge: Cambridge University Press, 1987.

McCubbins, Mathew D., Roger G. Noll, and Barry R. Weingast. "Administrative Procedures as Instruments of Political Control." *Journal of Law, Economics and Organization* 3 (1987): 243–277.

"Structure and Process, Politics and Policy: Administrative Arrangements and the Political Control of Agencies." *Virginia Law Review* 75 (1989): 431–482.

McKelvey, Richard D. "Intransitivities in Multidimensional Voting Models and Implications for Agenda Control." *Journal of Economic Theory* 12 (1976): 472–482.

McNeely, Jeffrey, and David Pitt, eds. *Culture and Conservation: The Human Dimension in Wildlife Planning.* London: Croon Helm, 1985.

McShane, Jonathan, and Thomas Adams. *The Myth of Wild Africa.* New York: Norton, 1992.

Medard, Jean-François. "The Underdeveloped State in Tropical Africa: Political Clientelism or Neopatrimonialism." In *Private Patronage and Public Power: Political Clientelism in the Modern State,* ed. Christopher Clapham. London: Francis Pinter, 1982.

Bibliography

Meyns, Peter. "The Road to One-Party Rule in Zambia and Zimbabwe." In *Democracy and the One-Party State in Africa*, eds. Peter Meyns and Dani Wadada Nabudere, 179–202. Hamburg: Institut fur Afrika-Kunde, 1989.

Meyns, Peter, and Dani Wadada Nabudere, eds. *Democracy and the One-Party State in Africa*. Hamburg: Institut fur Afrika-Kunde, 1989.

Mijere, Nsolo. "The State and Development: A Study of the Dominance of the Political Class in Zambia." *Africa Today* 35(2) (1988): 21–36.

Miers, Suzanne, and Igor Kopytoff, eds. *Slavery in Africa: Historical and Anthropological Perspectives*. Madison: University of Wisconsin Press, 1977.

Miller, Gary. *Managerial Dilemmas: The Political Economy of Hierarchy*. New York: Cambridge University Press, 1992.

Miller, Gary, and Kathleen Cook. "Leveling and Leadership in States and Firms." Baltimore: University of Maryland, 1994. Mimeo.

Miller, Gary, and Terry M. Moe. "Bureaucrats, Legislators, and Size of Governments." *American Political Science Review* 77 (1983): 297–323.

Milner-Gulland, E. J., and Nigel Leader-Williams. "Illegal Exploitation of Wildlife." In *Economics for the Wilds: Wildlife, Wildlands, Diversity and Development*, eds. Timothy M. Swanson and Edward B. Barbier. London: Earthscan, 1992.

Miracle, Marvin P. *Maize in Tropical Africa*. Madison: University of Wisconsin Press, 1966.

Mitchell, J. C. "The Yao of Southern Nyasaland." In *Seven Tribes of British Central Africa*, eds. Elizabeth Colson and Max Gluckman, 292–353. Manchester: Manchester University Press, 1961.

Mitchell, B. L., and W. F. H. Ansell. *Wildlife of Kafue and Luangwa: A Tourist Field Guide*, 1965.

Moe, Terry M. "The New Economics of Organization." *American Journal of Political Science* 28 (1984): 739–777.

———. "Control and Feedback in Economic Regulation." *American Political Science Review* 79 (1985): 1094–1116.

———. "The Politics of Bureaucratic Structure." In *Can the Government Govern?*, eds. John E. Chubb and Paul E. Peterson, 116–153. Washington: The Brookings Institution, 1989.

———. "Political Institutions: The Neglected Side of the Story." *Journal of Law, Economics, and Organization* 6 (1990a): 213–266.

———. "The Politics of Structural Choice: Toward a Theory of Public Bureaucracy." In *Organizational Theory from Chester Bernard to the Present*, ed. Oliver Williamson, 116–153. Oxford: Oxford University Press, 1990b.

Moe, Terry M. "Regulatory Performance and Presidential Administration." *American Journal of Political Science* 26 (1992): 197–224.

Molteno, Robert. "Cleavage and Conflict in Zambian Politics: A Study in Sectionalism." In *Politics in Zambia*, ed. William Tordoff. Manchester: Manchester University Press, 1974.

Molteno, Robert, and Ian Scott. "The 1968 General Election and the Political System." In *Politics in Zambia*, ed. William Tordoff, 155–196. Manchester: Manchester University Press, 1971.

Moran, Dominic. "Contingent Valuation and Biodiversity: Measuring the User Surplus of Kenyan Protected Areas." *Biodiversity Conservation* 3(8) (1994).

Mosher, Frederick C. *Democracy and the Public Service*. 3rd ed. Oxford: Oxford University Press, 1982.

Muir, Kay, Jan Bojo, and Robert Cunliffe. "Economic Policy, Wildlife, and Land

Use in Zimbabwe." In *The Economics of Wildlife: Case Studies from Ghana, Kenya, Namibia, and Zimbabwe*, ed. Jan Bojo, 117–137. Washington: The World Bank, 1966.

Murindagomo, Felix. "Zimbabwe: WINDFALL and CAMPFIRE." In *Living with Wildlife: Wildlife Resource Management and Local Participation in Africa*, ed. Agnes Kiss, 123–140. World Bank Technical Paper no. 130. Washington: The World Bank.

Murombedzi, James C. "Decentralization or Recentralization? Implementing CAMPFIRE in the Omay Communal Lands of the Nyaminyami District." Harare, Zimbabwe: Centre for Applied Social Sciences Working Papers, 1992. Mimeo.

Murphree, Marshall W. "Community Conservation and Wildlife Management Outside Protected Areas Southern African Experiences and Perspectives: Implications for Policy Formation." Washington: African Wildlife Foundation, 1990. Mimeo.

Musambachime, Mwelwa C. "Colonialism and the Environment in Zambia, 1890–1964." In *Guardians in Their Time: Experiences of Zambians Under Colonial Rule, 1890–1964*, ed. Samuel N. Chipungu, 8–29. London: Macmillan, 1992.

Nagel, Stuart S., ed. *Environmental Politics*. New York: Praeger, 1974.

National Mirror (15 July 1991).

Nawa Nawa. "The Role of Traditional Authority in the Conservation of Natural Resources in the Western Province of Zambia, 1878–1989." M.A. thesis, UNZA, 1990.

Niskanen, William. *Bureaucracy and Representative Government*. Chicago: Aldine-Atherton, 1971.

Norman, R., and G. L. Owen-Smith, eds. *Management of Large Mammals in African Conservation Areas*. Pretoria: Haum Educational Publishers, 1983.

North, Douglass C. *Structure and Change in Economic History*. New York: Norton, 1971.

Institutions, Institutional Change and Economic Performance. Cambridge: Cambridge University Press, 1990.

North, Douglass, and Paul Thomas. *The Rise of the Western World*. Cambridge: Cambridge University Press, 1973.

North, Douglass C., and Barry R. Weingast. "Constitutions and Credible Commitments: The Evolution of Institutions of Public Choice in 17th Century England." *Journal of Economic History* 49 (1989): 803–832.

Nyong'o, Peter Anyang'. "State and Society in Kenya: The Disintegration of the Nationalist Coalitions and the Rise of Presidential Authoritarianism, 1963–78." *African Affairs* 88(351)(1989): 229–251.

Ofcansky, Thomas. "A History of Game Preservation in British East Africa, 1895–1963." Ph.D. dissertation, West Virginia University, 1981.

Ollawa, P. E. *Participatory Democracy in Zambia*. Elms Court, Great Britain: Arthur H. Stockwell, 1979.

Olson, Mancur. *The Logic of Collective Action*. Cambridge, Mass.: Harvard University Press, 1965.

Ordeshook, Peter C. *Game Theory and Political Theory*. Cambridge: Cambridge University Press, 1986.

Ostrom, Elinor. *Governing the Commons: The Evolution of Institutions for Collective Action*. Cambridge: Cambridge University Press, 1990.

Bibliography

Ostrom, Elinor, Roy Gardner, and James Walker. *Rules, Games and Common-Pool Resources*. Ann Arbor: University of Michigan Press, 1994.

Owen-Smith, A., and R. Norman, eds. *Management of Large Mammals in African Conservation Areas*. Pretoria: Haum Educational Publishers, 1983.

Palmer, Robin, and Neil Parsons, eds. *The Roots of Rural Poverty in Central and Southern Africa*. Berkeley: University of California Press, 1977.

Pareto, Vilfredo. *Sociological Writings*, trans. by Derrick Mirfin, ed. S. E. Finer. New York: Praeger, 1966.

Perlez, Jane. "Only Radical Steps Can Save Wildlife in Kenya, Leakey Says." *The New York Times*, May 23, 1989.

Peterson, John H., Jr. "CAMPFIRE: A Zimbabwean Approach to Sustainable Development and Community Empowerment Through Wildlife Utilization." Zimbabwe: Centre for Applied Social Science, 1991.

"A Proto-CAMPFIRE Initiative in Mahenye Ward, Chipinge District." Occasional Paper no. 3/1992. Harare: Centre for Applied Social Sciences, University of Zimbabwe, 1992.

"Sustainable Wildlife Use for Community Development." In *Elephants and Whales: Resources for Whom?*, eds. Milton M. Freeman and Urs P. Kreuter, 99–111. Basel, Switzerland: Gordon and Breach Science Publishers, 1994.

Pierce, John C., Mary Ann E. Steger, Brent S. Steel, and Nicholas P. Lovrich. *Citizens, Political Communication, and Interest Groups*. Westport, Conn.: Praeger, 1992.

Piven, Frances Fox, and Richard Cloward. *Poor People's Movements*. New York: Vintage, 1977.

Popkin, Samuel L. *The Rational Peasant: The Political Economy of Rural Society in Vietnam*. Berkeley: University of California Press, 1979.

Porter, Gareth, and Janet Welsh Brown. *Global Environmental Politics*. Boulder, Colo.: Westview Press, 1991.

Posner, Richard A. "A Theory of Primitive Society with Special Reference to Law." *Journal of Law and Economics* 23 (1980): 1–53.

Prescott-Allen, Robert, and Christine Prescott-Allen. *What's Wildlife Worth?* London: IIED, 1982.

Putterman, Louis. "The Economic Nature of the Firm: Overview." In *The Economic Nature of the Firm: A Reader*, ed. Putterman, 1–29. Cambridge: Cambridge University Press, 1986.

Ranger, T. *Peasant Consciousness and Guerrilla War in Zimbabwe*. Harare: Zimbabwe Publishing House, 1985.

Rasmussen, Thomas. "The Popular Basis of Anti-Colonial Protest." In *Politics in Zambia*, ed. William Tordoff, 40–61. Manchester: Manchester University Press, 1974.

Repetto, Robert, and Malcolm Gillis, eds. *Public Policy and the Misuse of Forest Resources*. Cambridge: Cambridge University Press, 1988.

Richards, Audry I. "The Bemba of North-Eastern Rhodesia." In *Seven Tribes of British Central Africa*, eds. Elizabeth Colson and Max Gluckman, 164–193. Manchester: Manchester University Press, 1961.

Ridgeway, James. *The Politics of Ecology*. New York: Dutton, 1970.

Riker, William H. *Liberalism Against Populism*. San Francisco: W. H. Freeman, 1983.

Robinson, John, and Kent Redford. "Community-based Approaches to Wildlife Conservation in Neotropical Forests." In *Natural Connections*, eds. David Western and R. Michael Wright. Washington: Island Press, 1994.

Bibliography

Robinson, S. "Saving the Rhino: Zambia's Fight Against Big-time Poaching." *Black Lechwe* 1 (1981): 7–9.

Root, Hilton L. "Tying the King's Hands: Credible Commitments and Royal Fiscal Policy During the Old Regime." *Rationality and Society* 1 (October 1989): 240–258.

Rosenbaum, Walter A. "The Bureaucracy and Environmental Policy." In *Environmental Politics and Policy*, ed. James P. Lester, 206–241. Durham, N.C.: Duke University Press, 1995.

Rothchild, Donald, and Naomi Chazan, eds. *The Precarious Balance*. Boulder and London: Westview Press, 1980.

Roussopoulos, Dimitrios I. *Political Ecology: Beyond Environmentalism*. Montreal and New York: Black Rose Press, 1993.

Sabatier, Paul A., John Loomis, and Catherine McCarthy. "Hierarchical Controls, Professional Norms, Local Constituencies, and Budget Maximization: An Analysis of the US Forest Service Planning Decisions." *American Journal of Political Science* 39 (1995): 204–242.

Sandbrook, Richard. *The Politics of Africa's Economic Stagnation*. Cambridge: Cambridge University Press, 1985.

Scarritt, James A. "The Analysis of Social Class, Political Participation and Public Policy in Zambia." *Africa Today* 30 (1983): 5–22.

Schnaiberg, Allan, Nicholas Watts, and Klaus Zimmermann. *Distributional Conflicts in Environmental Resource Policy*. New York: St. Martin's Press, 1986.

Schneider, Harold K. "Traditional African Economies." In *Africa*, 2nd ed., eds. Phyllis Martin and Patrick O'Meara, 181–198. Bloomington: Indiana University Press, 1986.

Scholz, John T., and Feng Hang Wei. "Regulatory Enforcement in a Federalist System." *American Political Science Review* 80 (1986): 1249–1270.

Scott, James C. *The Moral Economy of the Peasant*. New Haven: Yale University Press, 1976.

Weapons of the Weak: Everyday Forms of Peasant Resistance. New Haven: Yale University Press, 1986.

Scudder, Thayer. *The Ecology of the Gwembe Tonga*. Manchester: Published on Behalf of the Rhodes-Livingstone Institute of Northern Rhodesia by Manchester University Press, 1962.

"Gathering among African Woodland Savannag Cultivators." University of Zambia, Institute for African Studies, Zambian Papers No. 5. 1971.

Seidman, Harold, and Robert Gilmour. *Politics, Position, and Power: From the Positive to the Regulatory State*. 4th ed. Cambridge: Oxford University Press, 1986.

Shepsle, Kenneth A. "Institutional Arrangements and Equilibrium in Multidimensional Voting Models." *American Journal of Political Science* 23 (1979): 27–59.

"Institutional Equilibrium and Equilibrium Institutions." In *Political Science: The Science of Politics*, ed. Herbert Weisberg. New York: Agathon Press, 1986.

"Bureaucratic Drift, Coalitional Drift and Time Consistency: A Comment on Macey." *Journal of Law, Economics and Organization* 8 (1992): 1101–1108.

Shepsle, Kenneth A., and Barry R. Weingast. "Institutional Foundations of Committee Power." *American Political Science Review* 81 (1987): 85–104.

Bibliography

Simon, Noel. *Between the Sunlight and the Thunder.* Boston: Houghton Mifflin, 1963.

Skalnes, Tor. *The Politics of Economic Reform in Zimbabwe: Continuity and Change in Development.* New York: St. Martin's Press, 1995.

Spulber, Daniel, and David Besanko. "Delegation, Commitment, and the Regulatory Mandate." *Journal of Law, Economics and Organization* 8 (1992): 126–154.

Steinhart, E. I. "Hunters, Poachers and Gamekeepers: Towards a Social History of Hunting in Colonial Kenya." *Journal of African History* 30 (1989): 247–264.

Stigler, George J. "The Economics of Information." *Journal of Political Economy* (June 1961): 213–215.

Stoneman, Colin, and Lionel Cliffe. *Zimbabwe: Politics, Economics and Society.* London and New York: Pinter Publishers, 1989.

Stroup, Richard, and John A. Baden. *Natural Resources: Bureaucratic Myths and Environmental Management.* Cambridge, Mass.: Ballinger Publishing, Harper & Row, 1983.

Sugden, Robert. *The Economics of Rights, Cooperation and Welfare.* London: Basil Blackwell, 1986.

Switzer, Jacqueline V. *Environmental Politics: Domestic and Global Dimensions.* New York: St. Martin's Press, 1994.

Sylvester, Christine. *Zimbabwe: The Terrain of Contradictory Development.* Boulder and San Francisco: Westview, 1991.

Taylor, Michael. *Anarchy and Cooperation.* London: Wiley, 1976.

The Possibility of Cooperation. Cambridge: Cambridge University Press, 1987.

Taylor, Russell D. "Elephant Management in the Nyaminyami District, Zimbabwe: Turning a Liability into an Asset." In *Elephants and Whales: Resources for Whom?*, eds. Milton Freeman and Urs Kreuter, 113–27. Basel, Switzerland: Gordon and Breach Science Publishers, 1994.

Thelen, Kathleen, and Sven Steinmo. "Historical Institutionialism in Comparative Politics." In *Structuring Politics: Historical Institutionalism in Comparative Analysis*, eds. Sven Steinmo, Kathleen Thelen, and Frank Longstreth. Cambridge: Cambridge University Press, 1992.

Thomas, Stephen J. "Seeking Equity in Common Property: Wildlife in Zimbabwe." In *Elephants and Whales: Resources for Whom?*, eds. Milton Freeman and Urs Kreuter, 129–42. Basel, Switzerland: Gordon and Breach Science Publishers, 1994.

Thomson, B. P. *Two Studies in African Nutrition.* Lusaka: Rhodes-Livingstone Institute, 1954.

Throup, David. *The Economic and Social Origins of the Mau Mau.* Athens: Ohio University Press, 1987.

Timberlake, Lloyd. *Africa in Crisis.* Philadelphia: New Society Publishers, 1986.

Times of Zambia (28 November 1986; 7 February 1989; 8 January 1991; 22 May 1991).

Tisdell, Clement. *Economics of Environmental Conservation.* New York: Elsevier, 1991.

Tordoff, William. "Residual Legislatures in African One-Party States." *Journal of Commonwealth and Comparative Studies* 15 (November 1977): 235–249.

Tordoff, William, and Robert Molteno. "Introduction." In *Politics in Zambia,*

Bibliography

ed. William Tordoff, 1–39. Manchester: Manchester University Press, 1974.

"Government and Administration." In *Politics in Zambia*, ed. William Tordoff, 242–287. Manchester: Manchester University Press, 1974.

"Parliament." In *Politics in Zambia*, ed. William Tordoff, 197–241. Manchester: Manchester University Press, 1974.

Tordoff, William, and Ian Scott. "Political Parties: Structure and Policies." In *Politics in Zambia*, ed. William Tordoff, 107–154. Manchester: Manchester University Press, 1974.

Tsebelis, George. *Nested Games: Rational Choice in Comparative Politics.* Berkeley: University of California Press, 1990.

United National Independence Party. *1967 Constitution.* Lusaka: UNIP, 1967. Mimeo.

United National Independence Party. *UNIP Manual of Rules and Regulations Governing the 1973 General Elections.* Lusaka: UNIP Central Committee, n.d. Mimeo.

United Nations International Labor Office (ILO). *Zambia: Basic Needs in an Economy Under Pressure.* Addis Ababa: United Printers, 1981.

Vail, Leroy. "Ecology and History: The Example of Eastern Africa." *Journal of Southern African Studies* 3 (1977): 129–155.

Vail, Leroy, ed. *The Creation of Tribalism in Southern Africa.* Berkeley: University of California Press, 1989.

von Richter, W. "Report to the Government of Botswana on a Survey of the Wild Animal Hide and Skin Industry." UNDP/FAO No. TA2637. Mimeograph. 1969.

Wallis, Malcolm. "District Planning and Local Government in Kenya." *Public Administration and Development* 10 (1990), 437–452.

Walvin, James. *Black Ivory: A History of British Slavery.* London: Fontana Press, 1992.

Weingast, Barry R. "The Congressional-Bureaucratic System: A Principal-Agent Perspective." *Public Choice* 44 (1984): 147–192.

"A Rational Choice Perspective on the Role of Ideas: Shared Belief Systems and State Sovereignty in International Cooperation." *Politics and Society* 23(4) (1995): 449–64.

"The Economic Role of Political Institutions." 1992. Mimeo.

Weingast, Barry R., and Mark Moran. "Bureaucratic Discretion or Congressional Control: Regulatory Policymaking by the Federal Trade Commission." *Journal of Political Economy* 91 (1983): 765–800.

Weingast, Barry R., and William Marshall. "The Industrial Organization of Congress; or, Why Legislators, Like Firms, Are Not Organized as Markets." *Journal of Political Economy* 96 (1988): 132–163.

West, Eugenia. "The Politics of Hope." Ph.D. dissertation, Yale University, 1989.

Western, David. "Amboseli National Park: Human Values and the Conservation of a Savanna Ecosystem." In *National Parks, Conservation and Development: The Role of Protected Areas in Sustaining Society: Proceedings of the World Congress on National Parks (Bali, Indonesia)*, eds. J. A. McNeely and K. R. Miller. Washington: Smithsonian Institution Press, 1984.

Western, David, and R. Michael Wright. *Natural Connection: Perspectives in Community-based Conservation.* New York: Island Press, 1994.

White, Leonard D. *The Civil Service in the Modern State.* Chicago: University of Chicago Press, 1930.

Bibliography

Widner, Jennifer A. "Single Party States and Agricultural Policies: The Cases of Ivory Coast and Kenya." *Comparative Politics* 26(2) (Jan. 1994): 127–48.

Williamson, Oliver E. *Markets and Hierarchies: Analysis and Antitrust Implications.* New York: Free Press, 1975.

The Economic Institutions of Capitalism: Firms, Markets, Relational Contracting. New York: Free Press, 1985.

Wilson, James Q. *Bureaucracy: What Government Agencies Do and Why They Do It.* New York: Basic Books, 1989.

Wilson, Woodrow. "The Study of Administration." *Political Science Quarterly* 2 (1887): 197–222.

Wood, Dan B. "Federalism and Policy Responsiveness: The Clean Air Case." *Journal of Politics* 53 (1991): 851–859.

"Modeling Federal Implementation as a System." *American Journal of Political Science* 36 (1992): 40–67.

World Wide Fund for Nature. *Campaign Report.* Washington: WWF, April 1991.

Wright, R. Michael. "Alleviating Poverty and Conserving Wildlife in Africa: An 'Inefficient' Model from Africa." *The Nature Conservancy* (n.d.).

Wunsch, James S., and Dele Olowu, eds. *The Failure of the Centralized State.* Boulder, Colo.: Westview Press, 1990.

Yeager, Rodger, and Norman N. Miller. *Wildlife, Wild Death: Land Use and Survival in Eastern Africa.* Albany: State University of New York Press, 1986.

Zald, Mayer N., and John D. McCarthy. *Social Movements in an Organizational Society.* New Brunswick and Oxford: Transaction Books, 1987.

Zambia Daily Mail (16 January 1995).

Zolberg, Aristide. *Creating Political Order: The Party-States of West Africa.* Chicago: Rand McNally, 1966.

GOVERNMENT AND PROJECT DOCUMENTS

Atkins, S. L. "The Socio-Economic Aspects of the Lupande Game Management Area." In *Proceedings of the Lupande Development Workshop*, ed. D. B. Dalal-Clayton. Lusaka: Government Printer, 1984.

Bell, Richard H. V., and Fidelis B. Lungu. "The Luangwa Integrated Resource Development Project, Progress of Phase I and Proposals for Phase II." Chipata, Zambia: LIRDP, 1986. Mimeo.

"The Luangwa Integrated Resource Development Project, A Presentation to the National Assembly." Chipata, Zambia: LIRDP, 1990. Mimeo.

Dalal-Clayton, D. B., ed. *Proceedings of the Lupande Development Workshop.* Lusaka: Government Printer, 1984.

Department of Game and Fisheries. Annual Report. (series). Lusaka: Government Printer, 1959–1968.

Department of Wildlife, Fisheries and National Parks. Annual Report. (series). Lusaka: Government Printer, 1969–1973.

Hedlund, H., M. Jones, and D. Lewis. "A Feasibility Study to Advise on the Institutional Structure of the Luangwa Integrated Resource Development Project. Report to the Senior Permanent Secretary, National Commission for Development Planning (GRZ) and the Resident Representative, NORAD." Lusaka: NORAD, 1992. Mimeo.

International Union for Conservation of Nature and Natural Resources World

Bibliography

Conservation Union. Third Review Mission, Luangwa Integrated Resource Development Project. Gland, Switzerland: The World Conservation Union, 1991. Mimeo.

Kalomo, B. S. "Fulaza WMU Unit Leaders Report." In Proceedings of the First ADMADE Planning Workshop. Lusaka: National Parks and Wildlife Services, 1988. Mimeo.

Kaweche, G. B., F. Munyenyembe, H. Mwima, F. B. Lungu, and R. H. V. Bell. Aerial Census of Elephant in the Luangwa Valley. Chipata, Zambia: LIRDP, 1987. Mimeo.

Larsen, Thor, Fidelis B. Lungu, and Trond Vedeld. "Preparation Report on the Luangwa Integrated Resource Development Project." Chipata, Zambia: LIRDP, 1985. Mimeo.

Luangwa Integrated Resource Development Project, LIRDP. The Phase Two Programme. Chipata, Zambia: LIRDP, 1987. Mimeo.

Proposals for the Phase Two Programme. Chipata, Zambia: LIRDP, 1987. Mimeo.

The Phase Two Programme. Chipata, Zambia: LIRDP, 1987. Mimeo.

Annual Report 1990. Chipata, Zambia: LIRDP, 1991. Mimeo.

"Agreed Minutes of the Third Annual Meeting for the Luangwa Integrated Resource Development Project." Chipata, Zambia: LIRDP, 1991. Mimeo.

"Background Paper on the Institutional Proposal for the National Integrated Resource Development Programme." Chipata, Zambia: LIRDP, 1991. Mimeo.

"Errors of Fact in Review Mission Reports, Selected Examples." Chipata, Zambia: LIRDP, 1991. Mimeo.

Lungu, Fidelis B., and Richard H. V. Bell. LIRDP, A Presentation to the National Assembly. Chipata, Zambia: LIRDP, 1990. Mimeo.

Madubansi, J. H., E. Jhala, E. Chidumayo, A. Sakala, and G. Kaweche. "Draft Report of the Technical Committee on Proposed Legislative Control and Management of Wildlife Resources in the Luangwa Integrated Resources Development Project Area." N.d. Mimeo.

Mwenya, A. N., G. B. Kaweche, and D. M. Lewis. Administrative Design for Game Management Areas (ADMADE). Chilanga, Zambia: National Parks and Wildlife Service, 1988.

ADMADE: Policy, Background & Future. Lusaka, Zambia: National Parks and Wildlife Service, 1990.

National Parks and Wildlife Department. Annual Report for the Year 1971. Lusaka: Government Printer, 1972.

Annual Report. (series). Lusaka: Government Printer, 1974–1986.

National Parks and Wildlife Service. Annual Reports, 1968–1973.

Lupande News and Views No. 1 (September 1985). Mimeo.

Zambian Wildlands and Human Needs Newsletter. (series). Nyamaluma Camp, Zambia, 1988–1991. Mimeo.

Nkonga, C. C. "Lumimba WMA Progress Report." In Proceedings of the First ADMADE Planning Workshop. Lusaka: National Parks and Wildlife Services, 1988. Mimeo.

Northern Rhodesia, Game and Tsetse Control Department. Annual Report. (series). Livingstone: Government Printer, 1944–1957.

Northern Rhodesia. Legislative Council Debates: Second Session of the First Council, May 15th – May 30th, 1925. Livingstone: Government Printer, 1925.

Bibliography

Annual Report on African Affairs: Namwala District. Lusaka: Government Printer, 1957.

Southern Province—Annual Report. Lusaka: Government Printer, 1957.

Annual Report—Southern Province. Lusaka: Government Printer, 1957.

Annual Report of African Affairs: Fort Jameson District. Lusaka: Government Printer, 1960.

Fauna Conservation, Chapter 241 of the Laws. Lusaka: Government Printer, 1964.

Poles, W. E. "A Report on a Tour in the Luangwa (Southern) Game Reserve and the Areas of Native Settlement Closely Adjacent Thereto." Mpika, Northern Rhodesia: Game and Tsetse Control Department, 1947. Mimeo.

Republic of Zambia. *First National Development Plan, 1966–70*. Lusaka: Government Printer, 1966.

Manpower Report: A Report and Statistical Handbook on Manpower, Education, Training and Zambianization, 1965–66. Lusaka: Government Printer, 1967.

Office of Elections. Report on the Results of the 1968 Presidential and Parliamentary Elections. Lusaka: Government Printer, 1968.

Annual Estimates of Revenue and Expenditure. Lusaka: Government Printer, 1969–1984.

Parliamentary Debates of the National Assembly. 1st session (30 October 1968).

Parliamentary Debates of the National Assembly. 2nd session (7 January – 25 March 1970).

Parliamentary Debates of the National Assembly. 3rd session (9 December 1971).

Statutory Instruments Nos. 1–5, 80, 88 of 1971 (amendments to the National Parks and Wildlife Act of 1971).

Report of the National Commission on the Establishment of a One-party Participatory Democracy in Zambia (The Chona Commission). Lusaka: Government Printer, 1972.

Report of the National Commission on the Establishment of a One-Party Participatory Democracy in Zambia: Summary of Recommendations Accepted by Government. Lusaka: Government Printer, 1972.

The Electoral Act of 1973. Lusaka: Government Printer, 1973.

Constitution of Zambia Act. Lusaka: Government Printer, 1973.

Financial Reports. Lusaka: Government Printer, 1975–1980.

Election Special. Lusaka: Government Printer, 1978.

Parliamentary Debates. 4th session, no. 60h (10 August 1982).

Parliamentary Debates. 4th session, no. 61h (13 August 1982).

Parliamentary Debates. 4th session, No. 60 (10 December 1982).

Pilot Household Budget Survey: Some Preliminary Findings. Lusaka: Government Printer, 1986.

"Agreement between the Government of the Kingdom or Norway and the Government of the Republic of Zambia regarding the integrated resource development of the Luangwa Valley in Zambia." 1988. Mimeo.

"Project Grant Agreement between the Republic of Zambia and the United States of America for Natural Resources Management." 1990. Mimeo.

The National Parks and Wildlife Act 1991. Lusaka: Government Printers, 1991.

Bibliography

Anti-Corruption Commission. "Govt./Quasi-Govt. Persons Arrested by SPD for Poaching Related Offenses." 1991. Mimeo.

The World Conservation Union. First Review Mission, Luangwa Integrated Resource Development Project. Gland, Switzerland: The World Conservation Union, 1989.

Second Review Mission, Luangwa Integrated Resource Development Project. Gland, Switzerland: The World Conservation Union, 1990.

United States Agency for International Development. "Project Paper Supplement for the Natural Resources Management Project." Lusaka: USAID, 1993. Mimeo.

United States Agency for International Development, "Environmental Profile of Zambia." 1982 (draft) National Park Service Contract CX-001-0-0003.

Vaughan-Jones, T. G. C. Game and Tsetse Control Department: Progress Report to 31st December, 1943. Lusaka: Government Printer, 1943.

A Short Survey of the Aims and Functions of the Department of Game and Tsetse Control. Lusaka: Government Printer, 1948.

INTERVIEWS

Ashley, Nikki, director, Wildlife Conservation Society of Zambia. Interview by author, 4 April 1991, Lusaka, Zambia.

Astle, W., former officer, Department of Game and Fisheries. Interviews by author, 24 July 1992; 12 August 1992, Lusaka, Zambia.

Bell, Richard, co-director, Luangwa Integrated Rural Development Programme. Interviews by author, 28 May 1991, 15 June 1991, Chipata, Zambia.

Berry, P. S. M., former officer, Department of Game and Fisheries. Interviews by author, 22 June 1991, 2 August 1992, Chinzombo Lodge, Mfuwe, Zambia.

Carr, Norman, former officer, Department of Game and Tsetse Control. Interview by author, 10 August 1991, Kapani Lodge, Mfuwe, Zambia.

Chanda, R., lecturer, University of Zambia. Interview by author, 9 September 1991, Lusaka, Zambia.

Chidumayo, M., lecturer, University of Zambia. Interview by author, 25 March 1991, Lusaka, Zambia.

Chikwa, Chief. Interview by author, 20 July 1991, Chikwa village, Chama, Zambia.

Chinkuli, Kingsley, member of UNIP Central Committee. Interview by author, 11 August 1992, Lusaka, Zambia.

Chitungulu, Chief. Interview by author, 3 August 1991, Chitungulu Village, Lundazi, Zambia.

Chongo, Rabbison, former Minister of Finance. Interviews by author, 7 August 1992; 10 August 1992, Lusaka, Zambia.

Chona, Mainza, former Vice-President of the Republic of Zambia. Interview by author, 8 August 1992, Lusaka, Zambia.

Eggertsson, Thrainn. Interview by author, 20 February 1995, Bloomington, Indiana.

Faddy, Mike, founder, Save the Rhino Trust; president, Professional Hunters Association of Zambia. Interviews by author, 21 March 1991, 29 October 1993, 23 August 1994, Lusaka, Zambia.

Feron, Eric, Resident Representative, International Union for the Conservation of Nature. Interview by author, 12 September 1991, Lusaka, Zambia.

Bibliography

Foster, John, United States Agency for International Development. Interview by author, 20 July 1992, Lusaka, Zambia.

Frost, David, former president, Professional Hunters Association of Zambia. Interview by author, 23 March 1991, Lusaka, Zambia.

Harmon, Jim, United States Agency for International Development. Interview by author, 15 February 1991, Lusaka, Zambia.

Jeffries, Richard, officer, World Wildlife Fund. Interview by author, 29 April 1991, Chilanga, Zambia

Kamwenda, M. C., ADMADE unit leader. Interview by author, 4 August 1991, Chanjuzi, Luangwa Valley, Zambia.

Kaunda, Kenneth, President of the Republic of Zambia. Interview by author, 14 August 1992, Lusaka, Zambia.

Kaunda, Wezi, Member of Parliament, Malambo constituency. Interview by author, 6 August 1992, Lusaka, Zambia.

Kaweche, Gilson, Deputy Director, Zambian National Parks and Wildlife Service. Interviews by author, 10 August 1991; 14 July 1992; 5 August 1992, Chilanga, Zambia.

Kelly, Clive, safari guide, Chinzombo Safari Lodge. Interview by author, 2 August 1992, Mfuwe, Zambia.

Lewis, Dale, ADMADE Technical Advisor. Interviews by author, 28 June 1991; 22 July 1991, Nyamaluma Training Camp, Zambia. Interview by author, 17 February 1992, Raleigh, North Carolina, USA.

Lonning, Arne, Program Officer, Norwegian Agency for International Development. 10 August 1991; 10 September 1991, Lusaka, Zambia.

Lungu, Fidelis, co-director, Luangwa Integrated Resource Development Project. Interviews by author, 28 May 1991, 3 August 1992, Chipata, Zambia.

Madubansi, J. H., Senior Planner, National Commission for Development Planning. Interview by author, 10 September 1991, Lusaka, Zambia.

Makowa, Catherine, headwoman, Sandwe village. Interview by author, 22 August 1991, Sandwe village (Petauke), Zambia.

Marks, Stuart. Interviews by author, 7 April 1993; 10 June 1994, Durham, North Carolina.

Matokwani, Edwin, Wildlife Ranger, Zambian National Parks and Wildlife Service. Interview by author, July 1991, Nyamaluma Training Center, Mfuwe, Zambia.

Miller, Peter, former officer, Wildlife Conservation Society of Zambia; founding member, Game Ranchers Association. Interview by author, 3 March 1991, Lusaka, Zambia.

Mpande, S., headman, Chitungulu village. Interview by author, 3 August 1991, Chitungulu Village, Lundazi, Zambia.

Musambachime, Mwelwa, Department of History, University of Zambia. Interview by author, 2 February 1991, Lusaka, Zambia.

Mwale, C., headman, Chitungulu village. Interview by author, 3 August 1991, Chitungulu Village, Lundazi, Zambia.

Mwale, Clement, investigations officer, Species Protection Department, Anti-Corruption Commission. Interview by author, 3 November 1991, Lusaka, Zambia.

Mwanya, Chief. Interview by author, 24 July 1994, Mwanya Village (Luangwa Valley).

Mwanza, Ilse, Affiliation Officer, Institute for African Studies, University of

Bibliography

Zambia. Interviews by author, 3 February 1991; 7 March 1991; 13 June 1991; 16 September 1991, Lusaka, Zambia.

Mwenya, Akim, director, Zambian National Parks and Wildlife Service. Interviews by author, 14 July 1992; 6 November 1991, Chilanga, Zambia.

Nair, B., director of Internal Accounts, Ministry of Finance. Interview by author, 1 April 1991, Lusaka, Zambia.

Ngoma, Monica, senior economist, Land and Natural Resource Unit, National Commission for Development Planning. Interview by author, 10 October 1991, Lusaka, Zambia.

Ngwisha, John, chief research officer, United National Independence Party. Interview by author, 14 July 1992, Lusaka, Zambia.

Nkhoma, Francis X., former Governor of the Bank of Zambia. Interview by author, 17 July 1992, Lusaka, Zambia.

Patel, Jusef, owner, Busanga Trails. Interview by author, 5 April 1991, Lusaka, Zambia.

Russell, Paul, director, Anti-Corruption Commission. Interviews by author, 7 February 1991; 22 August 1992, Lusaka, Zambia.

Saasa, Oliver, director, Institute for African Studies. Interview by author, 5 February 1991, University of Zambia.

Sandwe, Chief. Interview by author, 12 July 1991, Sandwe village (Petauke), Zambia.

Siachibuye, Crispin, Chief Prosecutor, Zambian National Parks and Wildlife Service. Interview by author, 12 November 1991, Chilanga, Zambia.

Sikala, C., headmaster, Chitungulu village. Interview by author, 3 August 1991, Chitungulu Village, Lundazi, Zambia.

Siwana, S., Chief Warden (acting), Zambian National Parks and Wildlife Service. Interview by author, 17 September 1991, Chilanga, Zambia.

Tembo, Christian, Minister of Tourism. Interview by author, 2 August 1992, Lusaka, Zambia.

Wakanuma, C. C., officer, Ministry of Tourism. Interview by author, 1 October 1991, Lusaka, Zambia.

Index

Administrative Management Design for Game Management Areas (ADMADE), 17, 83, 84, 90–6, 107, 114–15, 119, 158, 159, 162; Coordinating Committee, 95–6; decision-making and revenue sharing structures, 93–5; Directorate, 93, 94–6, 102, 103–4, 115; local level, 119–20, 126, 128, 130, 131–7, 145, 146, 147–50; incentive problems, 142–3

African National Congress (ANC), 29, 30, 31, 32, 34, 35, 50

agriculture, 43–4, 53, 60, 75, 125

Amboseli District Council Game Reserve, 143–5

Banda, W. H., 66, 67

Bell, Richard, 99–101, 102, 104, 105–7

benefits/costs of wildlife/wildlife policies, 4, 5, 22, 76, 89, 128, 130–1; distribution of, 16, 46, 47, 52, 56–8, 61, 92, 104, 115, 142, 148, 163 (see also distributive uses of wildlife policy); exclusion of Africans from, 42, 44, 45; institutions and, 10, 12; in Kenya, 42, 78, 109; in Zimbabwe, 111, 113, 145, 147

British East Africa Company (BEAC), 41

British South Africa Company (BSAC), 24, 25, 27, 41, 151

bureaucratic level/bureaucrats, 2, 7–8, 9, 16–17, 84, 85, 114, 116, 148, 149, 163; institutions designed by, 147–8, 157; and structural choice: Kenya and Zimbabwe, 108–14; wildlife policy at, 159, 162

chiefs, 57, 93–4, 107, 120, 127–8, 135, 136, 148, 163; and ADMADE, 133–4; authority of, 150–2

civil service, 35, 36, 37, 38, 123, 124, 125

colonial governments, 5, 9, 14–15, 43, 121, 128, 133, 148, 150, 152, 154, 161–2; Kenya, 41, 42

colonial wildlife policy, 3, 9, 16, 21, 22, 27, 28–9, 33, 35, 42; retained, 40, 153, 154–5

Communal Areas Management Programme for Indigenous Resources (CAMPFIRE), 111–14

community-based wildlife policy/programs, 3, 7, 17, 83–116, 120, 137, 148, 150; impact of, 119–52; in Kenya and Zimbabwe, 143–7

conservation, 3, 6, 8, 9, 32, 60–1, 148; Europeans and, 41; Kenya, 42–3, 104; opposition to, 75–6, 109; studies of, 163–4; Zimbabwe, 43, 44, 75–6, 110–11

conservation organizations, international, 1, 2, 38, 41, 108, 154; see also international sponsors/support

conservation policy, 2, 6–7, 15, 22, 28, 38, 40, 89–90; opposition to, 61–2; see also wildlife policy(ies)

conservation programs, 4, 114–16, 157, 159

constituency interests/service, 63–4, 65, 69, 71, 72, 76, 77, 162

constitutions, 13, 29, 31, 50–1, 75, 152

copper/copper prices, 35, 49, 50, 52, 53, 55, 57, 121

crop damage, 4, 25, 44, 111, 122, 125

decision making: ADMADE, 102, 103; LIRDP, 98, 105; local level, 122, 131, 136; structures, 93–5, 114, 115

development policy, participatory, 160

development projects, 127–8, 130–1, 133–4, 135–6, 142, 149

distributive uses of wildlife policy, 33–4, 35–40, 47, 61, 62, 119–20, 148

239

Index

and Zimbabwe), 108–14; politics of, 83–116, 159
Sumbu National Park, 59

Tanzania, 63
tourism, 2, 4, 32, 33, 34, 60–1, 62, 66, 106, 130, 132; benefits from, 128; Kenya, 15, 41–2, 43, 72, 74, 78, 108, 144, 145, 156; Zimbabwe, 46
trophies, 27, 37, 58, 96, 122
trypanosomiasis, 4, 25, 44, 122
tsetse fly, 4, 25, 27, 44, 122

United National Independence Party (UNIP), 16, 21, 22, 31, 32, 39, 47, 60, 63–4, 77, 134, 155; Central Committee, 29–30, 31, 51, 52, 57, 63, 99, 100; employment policies, 35–6; General Conference, 29, 51, 52; government, 34–5, 38, 50–1, 53, 55, 58, 60, 62, 72, 152; National Council, 29, 30, 52; and National Parks and Wildlife Bill, 33, 34–5; wildlife policy, 37
United Progressive party (UPP), 50
United States Agency for International Development (USAID), 83, 95, 96, 104, 114
University of Zambia, 98; Centre for Applied Social Sciences, 112
urban residents, 2, 53–4, 57, 60, 64, 66

village scouts, 92, 93, 103, 106, 126–7, 131, 134, 135, 137
villagers: strategic interaction with scouts, 137–41

whites, 75, 76, 109, 154
wildlife, 4–5, 73–4, 161; authority over, devolving to local level, 147–8; control over, 61, 149, 151, 152; dangers from, 122, 124; human interaction with, 41, 44; ministerial powers over, 37–40; ownership of, 5, 33, 113, 148; political importance of, 160–2; products, 16, 23, 49, 52, 54, 58, 74, 78, 112; profiteering in (Kenya), 73; property rights over, 143, 147; revenue from (Zimbabwe), 112, 113; rural residents and, 122; significance of, 1–2, 15; and social sciences, 5–9; value of, 56, 61, 62, 154, 155–6, 161
Wildlife Conservation Society of Zambia (WCSZ), 55, 56, 57, 59, 60, 98
wildlife estate, 90, 94; authority/control over, 35, 84, 88, 92, 97, 102, 103, 107, 112, 113, 116, 145
wildlife industry, 45, 46, 60–1, 76

wildlife laws, 44, 47, 59–60, 64, 76; penalties for violation of, 65–6, 68
wildlife management, 33, 58, 62, 75, 89, 114–15; authority over, 98; institutions of, 128; at local level, 119–20
Wildlife Management Authority(ies) (Zambia), 93–4, 95, 134
Wildlife Management Sub-Authority (WMSA) (Zambia), 93–4, 95, 133, 134, 135, 136
wildlife market, 54, 56, 64–5, 74, 78, 155, 162
wildlife policy(ies), 1–18, 22, 76–9, 115, 148; community-based, 83–116; distributive effects of, 17, 35–40; fight for control of, 47; future directions in study of, 163–4; history of (Zambia), 22–9; human dimensions of, 5–6, 163–4; incentives of "old"/"new," 128–32; and independence politics, 40–6; Kenya, 108–10; opposition to, 49, 64–5; political economy of, 153–64; political institutions and, 83; resistance to, 61–2; response of parliament to (Zambia), 62–5; ruler behavior and, 7; structure of competition over, 32, 58–61; Zimbabwe, 3, 14–15, 16, 75–6, 153–64
wildlife programs, 17; Zambia's Second Republic and, 88–102
wildlife resources: citizens' demand for, 64; control over, 46, 47, 48, 65, 90, 105–6, 136, 143, 147, 157–8; exploitation of, 57–8; management of, 61, 75; political use of, 47; revenues from, 147, 150
Wildlife Conservation Revolving Fund, 91, 92, 96, 102–3, 104
Wina, Sikota, 33
World Wide Fund for Nature (WWF), 112
World Wildlife Fund, 59, 95

Zambia, 12, 17, 23f, 148; Capital Law 316, 66; Central Committee, 58; Central Province, 28; chiefly authority in, 150–2; Civil Service Commission, 55, 126–7; community-based programs, 150; conservation programs, 114–15; Copperbelt Province, 28; Department of Game and Fisheries, 36, 47; Department of Game and Tsetse Control, 26–7; Eastern Province, 28, 99; Exchange Control Act, 105; First and Second National Development Plans, 53; First Republic, 7, 16, 22, 29–32, 47, 49, 63, 76, 154, 155; Game Department, 27, 28, 32, 35, 38, 152; history of wildlife policy in, 22–9; Luapula Province, 28; mean annual rainfall, 25f; Ministry of Finance, 55, 92, 105; Minis-

Made in the USA
Las Vegas, NV
03 July 2021